The Psychology of Writing

**Recent Titles in
Contributions in Psychology**

Personality, Power, and Authority: A View from the Behavioral Sciences
Leonard W. Doob

Interactive Counseling
B. Mark Schoenberg and Charles F. Preston, editors

Assessing Sex Bias in Testing: A Review of the Issues and Evaluations of 74 Psychological and Educational Tests
Paula Selkow

Position and the Nature of Personhood: An Approach to the Understanding of Persons
Larry Cochran

Ecological Beliefs and Behaviors: Assessment and Change
David B. Gray in collaboration with Richard J. Borden and Russell H. Weigel

Sexuality: New Perspectives
Zira DeFries, Richard C. Friedman, and Ruth Corn, editors

Portrait and Story: Dramaturgical Approaches to the Study of Persons
Larry Cochran

The Meaning of Grief: A Dramaturgical Approach to Understanding Emotion
Larry Cochran and Emily Claspell

New Ideas in Therapy: Introduction to an Interdisciplinary Approach
Douglas H. Ruben and Dennis J. Delprato, editors

Human Consciousness and Its Evolution: A Multidimensional View
Richard W. Coan

From AI to Zeitgeist: A Philosophical Guide for the Skeptical Psychologist
N.H. Pronko

Inevitability: Determinism, Fatalism, and Destiny
Leonard W. Doob

The Psychology of Writing

The Affective Experience

Alice Glarden Brand

Foreword by PETER ELBOW

Contributions in Psychology, Number 13

GREENWOOD PRESS
New York • Westport, Connecticut • London

Library of Congress Cataloging-in-Publication Data

Brand, Alice Glarden.
　　The psychology of writing : the affective experience / Alice Glarden Brand : foreword by Peter Elbow.
　　　　p.　cm. – (Contributions in psychology, ISSN 0736-2714 : no. 13)
　　Bibliography: p.
　　Includes index.
　　ISBN 0-313-26382-5 (lib. bdg. : alk. paper)
　　1. Authorship–Psychological aspects. 2. Authors–Psychology. 3. Emotions. 4. English language–Rhetoric–Psychological aspects.　　I. Title. II. Series.
　　PN171.P83B7　　　1989
　　801'.92–dc19　　　88-25090

British Library Cataloguing in Publication Data is available.

Copyright © 1989 by Alice Glarden Brand

All rights reserved. No portion of this book may be reproduced, by any process or technique, without the express written consent of the publisher.

Library of Congress Catalog Card Number: 88-25090
ISBN: 0-313-26382-5
ISSN: 0736-2714

First published in 1989

Greenwood Press, Inc.
88 Post Road West, Westport, Connecticut 06881

Printed in the United States of America

The paper used in this book complies with the Permanent Paper Standard issued by the National Information Standards Organization (Z39.48–1984).

10 9 8 7 6 5 4 3 2 1

Into every act of knowing
there enters a passionate
contribution of the person
knowing what is being known.
Polanyi, 1958

Contents

	Figures	ix
	Tables	xi
	Foreword by Peter Elbow	xiii
	Preface	xix
1.	Introduction	1
2.	The Emotions of Established Writers	7
3.	English Education, Linguistic Thought, and the Cognitive Model of Writing	19
4.	The Psychology of Emotion	39
5.	Operational Framework for the Inquiry	57
6.	The Research Program	79
7.	STUDY 1: College Writers	93
8.	STUDY 2: Advanced Expository Writers	103
9.	STUDY 3: Professional Writers	125
10.	STUDY 4: English Teachers	149
11.	STUDY 5: Student Poets	173
12.	Conclusion	199
	Appendixes	215
	References	233
	Index	249

Figures

5.1	BESW TWW form	70
5.2	BESW S form	72
9.1	Evidence of Mark's Frustration	144
9.2	Charles' Struggle to "Say Something Significant"	146
10.1	Dave's Version of the Structured/Planning Composing Style	160
10.2	Ron's Composing Style Guided by Subject Matter	161
10.3	Delores' "Limited Structured" Draft Work	162
10.4	Katie's Planning Against the Grain	164
10.5	Dorothy's Personal Style Reflected in her Composing Style	166
11.1	A Seductive Topic Aroused Mac's Frustration yet Interest	192

Tables

5.1	A Structural Analysis of Emotional Meaning	64
5.2	BESW Emotion Items Grouped by A Priori Factors	69
6.1	Rotated Factor Pattern of the Three Forms of the BESW	81
7.1	Mean State Emotions and Differences of the College Writers across Three Writing Sessions	95
7.2	Rank Order of Means for the Individual Emotions of the College Writers across Three Writing Sessions	96
8.1	Mean Differences for the Three Emotion Clusters of the Advanced Expository Writers across Three Trait Observations and Nine Writing Sessions	106
8.2	Rank Order of Means for the Individual Emotions of the Advanced Expository Writers across Nine Writing Sessions	108
8.3	Rank Order of Means for the Individual Emotions of the Advanced Expository Writers across Three Trait Observations	111
9.1	Rank Order of Means for the Individual Emotions of the Professional Writers across One Trait Observation and One Writing Session	129
10.1	Rank Order of Means for the Individual Emotions of the English Teachers across One Trait Observation and One Writing Session	168

11.1 Rank Order of Means for the Individual Emotions of the Student Poets across Seven Writing Sessions — 176

11.2 Rank Order of Means for the Individual Emotions of the Student Poets across Two Trait Observations — 177

Foreword

With all the research and study of the writing process in the last quarter century, it's remarkable how little research and study there's been of emotion or feelings in writing. With all the research methodologies (e.g., introspection, interviews, speak-aloud protocols, textual analysis, the use of TV cameras trained on writers, and so forth), we hear little about feelings. As we look at models of the composing process, and even as we read most protocols of writers writing, we are usually lulled into forgetting what we all know so well: there is a continuous stream of feelings going on at every moment of the writing process. (This is not to mention those prior feelings that got us to sit down to write in the first place—whether pleasure and anticipation or fear or guilt about failing to do what we have been assigned to do.) These feelings cannot but have an enormous effect on everything that writing researchers research: choices about language, discourse, genre, structure, voice, tone—matters of pausing, audience awareness—and all the rest of the acts and decisions that every writer must make in the act of writing.

Why has there been so little disciplined study of feelings in writing? Perhaps the answer is as simple as that people like Flower and Hayes have managed to do such powerful and effective work *without* attending to feelings. It's hard to quarrel with success. And yet Flower herself (talking about "writer-based prose") whets our appetite to know more about feelings when she shows how a "cognitive overload" can sabotage our writing when we are struggling to work out a difficult idea and then we try to think at the same time about how to suit it to our audience: in saying this she leads me, at least, to think about the "affective overload" that can occur when we have strong feelings about our topic, about our readers, and perhaps also about our own abilities as a writer.

Let's consider a comparable neglect in the study of writing—the neglect of *invention*. If we look to Aristotle's *Rhetoric*, we see that he was interested in invention (if not directly in the psychology of invention, at least in the logic of where to look for all the available arguments about an issue). But after the period of classical rhetoric and especially throughout the flowering of rhetoric during the eighteenth and nineteenth centuries, invention was neglected—and it continued to be neglected for much of this century. Throughout this long forgetfulness it's as though people were saying, "It's too hard to talk about where ideas come from—too messy, too internal, too mysterious. We can only talk clearly about what people *do* with their material once they have it: how they arrange it and what kind of language they use and how they adapt themselves to their audience."

But then a decade or two ago we saw a new interest in invention. People like Young, Becker, and Pike (*Rhetoric: Discovery and Change*) said, in effect, "We've got to stop sweeping invention under the rug and start trying to make sense of it." Research on invention began to take off, and this activity seemed to open the door to that resurgence of activity in our profession that came to be called the "process movement" (and which has of course not stopped accelerating even as it changes its character). Indeed it was this focus on invention—activity-in-time lying behind a text-in-space—that helped give currency to the very concept itself of "process" as opposed to "product."

Now invention no longer seems to be on the front burner in composition studies (I'm curious why). Yet having been established, it will surely remain solidly integrated in the field. No one is likely to forget again that any study of the writing process must deal with the crucial question of where writers get their material.

Interestingly, we can see the same neglect of invention in the study of science. For a long time scientists and commentators on science tended to talk about "scientific thinking" as a logical business of induction or deduction. It's as though they too were saying, "We can't talk about the process of how people come up with ideas; that's too dark and mysterious. We can only talk about the process of checking or verifying ideas. That's rational and systematizable." (In truth, only a few people were actually *making* this distinction between the finding and the verifying of ideas. Most of the trouble came from not realizing how different the processes are: coming up with an idea and figuring out whether the idea is right. To make that distinction was in itself a big step toward starting to realize that scientific thinking is not the logical business we might like to see it as.) But then people like George Polya and Jacques Hadamard got interested in the messy processes by which people came up with hunches and teased them out into full blown hypotheses—hypotheses interesting enough to be worth checking in a more logical fashion. (I am drawing here on accounts by people like Peter Medawar and Gerald Holton. Could the interest in invention in our field have been partly spurred by some of this exploration of science? I know that I was drawing on Medawar when I emphasized the difference between the creative/generative process and the critical/verifying process in *Writing Without Teachers*—written at MIT.)

I am pointing to a narrative parallel, then: neglect of invention and neglect of feelings. But I suspect the two stories are more deeply linked. That is, one of the important reasons why people are tempted to neglect both invention and feelings is that these two domains are both so messy: so hard to plan, to control, and above all to be *rational* about. In short, the neglect of both invention and feelings represent a bias toward order, control, planning, and system. Alice Brand helps us see this large cultural tilt behind the neglect of feelings: that "mental" *means* "cognitive"; and that when "cognition" *is* affected by feelings it means cognition has gone awry.

But people finally got around to training their attention on invention, and it was enormously salutary for composition studies and for the philosophy of science. So too I'm hoping that this new book by Alice Brand might be an important first step in the difficult and complicated process of trying to understand the role of feelings in writing—and that her investigations too might unleash some new and fruitful forces in our profession.

In her book she explains an extensive set of studies of feelings in writing—carried out over many years. But in addition she brings to our field (for the first time I think) an enormous amount of information about the psychology of emotions: history, research, and findings.

She acknowledges that her studies represent only the first stages in what we need and that she uses a single though richly deployed methodology (a complex questionnaire that writers filled out at various points in their writing), whereas of course we must also make use of other methodologies. She emphasizes that the affective domain in writing is huge and complicated. Since her work is *compensatory* (it tries to right an imbalance by focusing entirely on feelings), she also acknowledges that she is not yet able to achieve what must be our goal, namely to study feelings and thinking *together*.

Indeed if one were easily discouraged one might say that Brand brings discouraging news. Her extensive research and discussion show us that we are probably farther away from understanding the role of affect in writing than we might have suspected. She shows how we don't yet even have satisfactory language for these slippery things we comfortably call feelings (while also making a contribution here). One thinks of Augustine's observation that of course we know what time is until we try to talk about it. In addition these pesky entities change quickly according to the context in which they exist. (For example, Brand shows that minimal affect is sometimes experienced as boredom and sometimes as a pleasing calmness; that high anxiety is sometimes experienced as frightening and sometimes as pleasurably exciting.) But Brand is not easily discouraged. Even though she is not putting forth a Grand Theory and even though she leaves us most aware of what we don't know, she is able to suggest many interesting conclusions and hypotheses (which she summarizes in her last chapter). She has made important progress into territory the profession has neglected, and if her research serves to mobilize some portion of the considerable research energies that now exist in our field, the results will be very happy indeed.

I find myself interested in the various roles Brand plays—especially in relation to that pervasive cultural pattern her work calls attention to that shapes how we see the mind: the linked oppositions of thinking versus feeling and hard versus soft. Brand is not just sticking up for what our culture reads as soft (feelings), she does so from a position defined as doubly soft: she is a woman and a published poet. Despite—or because of—this position, she insists on defying these easy oppositions and writing a "hard" book in two senses: she uses a fairly technical, quantitative mode for her research; and the result is not always easy reading. (She also happens to live what I personally see as one of the hardest roles of all, writing program administrator.) Despite the interesting brief mini case studies scattered through most chapters, hers is not a book for people seeking rich and warm poetically nuanced portraits of actual feelings on the hoof.

I cannot resist speculating on an interesting link between "soft" and "hard" in Brand: the role of poet often correlates with the role of fighter—and by means of a link in the affective domain, namely passion. In both her own poetry and in her research Brand is a passionate fighter. The result in her poetry is a quality or stance that doesn't seem out of place. But the result in her research takes a moment to understand: as a fighting pioneer she insists on what might seem like "waging war with the weapons of the enemy"—the cognitive psychologists. But it is important to emphasize that though her war is against the neglect of feelings in research, she has no quarrel at all with the field of cognitive psychology. Indeed she is at pains to point out the intriguing fact that researchers in cognitive psychology have *not* neglected the study of emotions with the unanimity of researchers in composition.* She has mastered a vast professional and

---

*It's true that there has been a steady stream of research on writing apprehension. However this research is often based on the assumption that apprehension is the *problem*. One of Brand's many interesting findings is that apprehension isn't one thing: it takes different forms in different contexts. More important, apprehension is not consistently negative: it often correlates with better writing, and many students and professional writers often experience apprehension as positive.

technical literature in cognitive psychology, and she starts with a summary of the not inconsiderable work about feelings in that field. And she explicitly invites collaboration with writing specialists of the cognitive persuasion.

All of this reinforces what I see as the main message of this important book of research: that even though we now stand in need of a kind of compensatory "affirmative action" focus on feelings in writing, we must not neglect *either* thinking or feeling: that feelings usually create and partly consist of cognitive acts; and that cognition usually comes intertwined with feelings.

PETER ELBOW

There is also Sondra Perl's and Eugene Gendlin's phenomenological exploration of "felt sense" in writing. I think the phenomenological direction will prove promising. Barbara Gleason (presentation at the 1988 Conference on College Composition and Communication) and Louise Wetherbee Phelps (in Tom Waldrep, ed., *Writers on Writing*) have made useful forays in this regard.

Preface

Discourse specialists and educators have long looked at the what of writing—the product. Over the last two decades, they have begun examining the how of writing—the process—and most closely from the cognitive perspective. It is fitting that they now look at the why of writing—writers' emotional processes and motivation.

This book is about people who write. It is a first effort to show that a complete and accurate psychology of writing must include its emotional components. If one believes in the essential unity of thinking and feeling, then not only is it important to view affect and cognition as fused processes, it is misleading to view writing any other way. Studying one without the other simply does not make sense. Then, readers may ask, how can I justify a book that primarily addresses emotion? Am I not promoting the very dualism I question? I do not argue the categorical merits of affective processes. Nor am I inimical to cognitive ones. Nor do I wish to divide people into thinking and feeling parts, though at times this work may appear to. This research tries to do what none other has—to zoom in on human feeling and written language. In order to put Humpty Dumpty back together again, a first step is to understand the nature of *all* its parts.

The accumulation of anecdotes and platitudes about emotion has masked the need to investigate it, while, as Bleich has remarked, the most important motive for writing—having something to say to someone else—is considered too deep or too obvious for serious attention. But things obvious still need to be demonstrated. I wanted to do more than just validate my intuitions. I wanted to transcend them. I was not going to be stricken with "holistic paralysis," the inability to take action because of the complexity of the subject. Nor was I going to be sentimental. This work, however new and small, was going to be systematic.

Seven years ago I became a student of the emotions. I enlisted support from psychologists Bob Plutchik, Hope Conte, Sandra Buechler, and Silvan Tomkins, who kept me supplied with relevant articles and pointed me in useful directions. It soon became clear that I could not promote the interpenetration of affect and cognition without studying cognitive principles. So I studied more.

I was more naive than canny. Despite the rapid evolution of writing research and theory and bandwagon loyalty to things cognitive, when I sought support within composition studies, I believed my work would capture its attention. Response was uneven. Peter Elbow congratulated me and offered his support. Lynn Troyka and Ian Pringle were enthusiastic. Rick Gebhardt accepted an article for *College Composition and Communication*. Donald Graves shuddered at the enormity of the task, wished me luck, and sent me an article. Miles Myers asked if I had a model. Connie Weaver wanted me to build one.

On the other hand, one researcher told me the subject was ho-hum. Another denied our overlapping interests. Others were impatient with the work and didn't want to wait around for findings. Still others were too busy. But even if I wanted to turn back, it was too late.

If critics are looking for imperfections in this work, it will not be difficult. First, colleagues wanted me to start with a model. And rightly so. As Witte put it, it is the sine qua non means of organizing observations, generating basic research questions, and testing and validating theories. After a long while, I abandoned those I had constructed, because too many ideas refused to coalesce. They could not be forced prematurely into a paradigm. Rather, this work begins to compile data around which conceptual scaffolding should eventually fit. I am reminded that when researchers start work, they may not know the full range of relevant constructs. Scientific inquiry often begins by describing phenomena and then proceeds to classify and correlate them. It is only after considerable investigation that researchers formulate with clarity the paradigms underlying the phenomena.

Second, that emotions are not polite and tidy goes without saying, but I cannot resist saying it. Emotional origins are private and intangible. Emotions are difficult to isolate and rarely amenable to verification. Science is not applied easily to something so ephemeral and subtle. But the sheer complexity of inquiries into emotion is not the only reason that such inquiries are without followers. The entire Western world view privileges the cognitive. We are accustomed to disguising, inhibiting, denying our feelings. Owning up to them, with their attendant pejorations is hard enough, much less studying them, the ultimate arrogance.

Perhaps because of this, a third complication arises. Work in the psychology of emotion is in some ways primitive compared to work in cognitive psychology. Cognitively focussed research has benefited from considerable institutional support as well as widespread adoption of its nomenclature and methodologies. Unlike its cognitive counterpart, this research does not examine the flux of affective processes during every instance of writing. This work makes a first inroad into emotional experience by using a traditional self-report at two or three junctures during the composing process. Newer research techniques are available, but I needed to practice the tradition before breaking with it.

I still had to reckon with my own doubts. Suppose the findings showed no significant patterns of emotions related to writing for the subject population as a whole. Although it would be important to establish, for example, that inspired writers become more inspired as they write or that shy people only get angry when they write narratives, the results might indicate that there are no grounds for generalizing among writers. Suppose the findings show that the association of certain emotions and writing does not even depend on a particular subgroup. Or, suppose the results indicate that it doesn't much matter which emotions individuals experience. They are all capable of being recruited in the writing process. I would then be forced to conclude that all emotions are associated with writing because the studies show they all work—a lean harvest indeed.

I maintain that, at the very least, this work can enlighten at the individual level. It should enable writers to become more alert to the particular emotional environment within which their writing takes place—how some emotions blunt the process and how some enhance it, how they compete with or complement one another.

This research may be useful for courses in cognitive psychology, social psychology, English education, rhetorical theory and research, discourse analysis, language acquisition, sociolinguistics, and literary theory. It is also intended for a range of professionals: psychologists, writing specialists, educators, linguists, literary scholars, graduate students, and readers interested in learning more about feelings and writing. It is always a concern not to bore those with considerable background in a subject without at the same time confusing those with less. In some chapters I seem to be talking more to psychologists who may want to know about the New Criticism or cognitive models of writing. In other chapters I seem to be talking more to composition specialists and educators who may want to learn about emotions psychology. Casual readers may wish to read the introductory and concluding chapters first.

Let me outline what readers may expect in the chapters. The overall assertion is presented in Chapter 1. Chapter 2 addresses the emotional experience of established writers where I first legitimated that reality beyond my own. The cognitive psychology of written language presented in Chapter 3 provided me with the theoretical backdrop for looking at its affective counterpart. Chapter 4 offers an historical glimpse of emotions psychology for readers wishing more information on its lineage. But it is not a categorical necessity for understanding the rest of the book. It was difficult to stay within the limits I set for myself particularly in Chapters 3 and 4. I raise but hardly do justice to the related issues of moral orientation, consciousness and the unconscious, and motivation. Chapters 5 and 6 set out the framework for developing an emotion scale for writers and designing the studies. Chapters 7 through 11 report the studies. For readability, some data are placed in the Appendix. Finally, Chapter 12 integrates the major themes of the book and considers their ramifications.

The chapters deal with groups of writers in ways that try to satisfy the canons of good science. But groups are of course made up of individuals. I did not want to be disloyal to them. Nor should readers lose sight of the real people who participated here. To help readers get to know them, Chapters 8 through 11 highlight several respondents at work. These chapters should therefore hold interest for readers more comfortable with case study approaches to the study of emotion or those interested in the actual written material of participants.

Clearly this book begins a long overdue examination of the association between emotion and written language. The set of relationships promises to be so complex that this fledgling work appears embarrassingly simple because it begins at such a basic level. I am aware that the matter is infinitely more complicated than these modest studies suggest. Emotion and writing is a most important coupling that I approach with sensitivity and humility. Even if the findings are less than persuasive, in the final analysis they should be instructive—generating hypotheses to be tested more vigorously in the future and prompting the field to more synthetic thinking.

I want to express my thanks to certain people who helped keep this work alive: John Chibnall, Mae Gordon, Alan Hopfer, Reed Larson, Phoebe Leckie, Patrick McLaughlin, Jack Powell, Prudy Robison, and Amy Adams Squire; to colleagues who allowed their students to participate in the studies: Jane Flinn, Chris Madigan, David Rota, Ken Smith, and Nan Sweet; to Rosemary Misurelli and Curt Harnack of Yaddo who, by providing me with a place to write poetry, empowered me to complete this work; to my staff, Nancy Bayes, Darlette Kampmann, Terry Alaniz, and Barry Wall who kept records straight, encoded the data, repeatedly updated the bibliography, and ran draft after draft of tables and text until they were acceptable; to Peter Elbow who helped me divest the text of a positivism that masked my own feelings about feelings; and to my husband, Ira, who had to live longer with this project than anyone else but me.

1. *Introduction*

Although contemporary psychology generally acknowledges the significance of emotion in human experience, few attempts have been made to understand its role in cognition. Important books on cognition (Anderson, 1976; Ericsson & Simon, 1984; Flammer & Kintsch, 1982) barely mention the subject of affect, emotion, or feeling.

Unlike the strict cognitive psychologists, social psychologists are concerned with emotion. They contend that to consider people as dispassionate, information processing systems is a fearfully inaccurate model of human beings (Averill, 1980a; Bower, 1981). A positivistic psychology has been simply too "cold" to carry the entire burden of human mental activity. What was needed was some way to heat up cognition—a theory that united the cognitively blind but arousing system of emotion with the subtle intellectual apparatus. In an otherwise cold-blooded tradition of cognitive science and flow chart intelligence, the idea of hot cognition (Abelson, 1963) became a major humanizing counterstatement during the mid-1960s and early 1970s.

Essentially, what hot cognition means is cognition colored by feeling. To social psychologists, practically all human experience implicates emotion in some way. The meaning of events is guided by what we feel and the options available to us for its expression. Our language continually projects information about our opinions, preferences, and evaluations. Emotion is the currency by which social intercourse is transacted. Linguistically empty events like body posture and facial expression are guided by affect-laden perceptions. Matters of life and death are not left to the slower-working cognitive system. In 1980 Zajonc observed that people do not get married or divorced, commit murder or suicide, or lay down their lives for freedom based on a detailed cognitive analysis of the pros and cons of their actions. If we stop to consider how much the course of our lives is guided by cognitive processes and how much is guided by emotional ones and how much each influences the other, we must admit that affective phenomena deserve far more attention from cognitivists than they have received.

This is also true of language specialists. The learning and teaching of written discourse has developed a momentum in recent years that is felt by few disciplines. Cognitive psychology has made an additional and unprecedented claim on professional attention. Writing as a cognitive process has been the focus of much recent theoretical and empirical exploration. Cognitive models of composing describe conscious, intellectual acts by which writers determine what they want to accomplish and how they want to accomplish it. These are ambitious and admirable objectives. With support from cognitive science and their own careful research, theorists of this persuasion are exemplars of rigor. They keep the field on its toes. These models are enlightened and sound. However, as Witte (1980) suggests, by making explicit such models, the pure cognitive approach makes apparent the gaps in them. This book endeavors to fill one of those gaps.

The central claim of this book is that, to be complete, a psychology of writing should include an account of emotional experience. The book attempts to narrow the discrepancy between the prevailing theoretical formulations and the subjective experiences of thousands of writers. It tries to show the ubiquity and force of emotion, that emotion may be used to rhetorical advantage. But even if it couldn't, to ignore affective experience would be to severely limit our understanding of the human mind in action.

Although, as Bleich (1976) has noted, feelings have a great deal to do with what one teaches and what one learns, separating the two constructs as a theoretical convenience has become an unfortunate pedagogical fact. Apart from creative writing or the emotional appeals linked to formal argument, classroom practices have ignored emotion. And, except for apprehension and blocking (Daly & Miller, 1975; Rose, 1984b; M. W. Smith, 1984), research examining the role of feeling in writing is virtually nonexistent. Rather, the writing process has been either overrationalized or "overphysicalized." It is viewed as an intellectual act that can be planned, tracked, and predicted. Miller (1983) charts writing back and forth between historical context and grapheme. Mandel (1978) sees writing as a massive coordination of a massive number of motor processes, including the contracting and dilating of muscles in the fingers, hand, arm, neck, shoulder, back, and eye. In her discussion of the interaction of the eye, hand, and brain, Emig (1978) defends the physiology of writing. And what makes the whole process work is a hierarchical network of goals and subgoals (Flower & Hayes, 1981a)—all this without one mention of emotion.

This is curious. The same theorists holding these views turn for support to Polanyi, Piaget, and Langer, none of whom was shy about enunciating the contribution of emotion to intellectual development. Polanyi (1958) argued that knowledge is tacit and personal; Piaget (Inhelder & Piaget, 1958), that affect is the fuel of the cognitive functions; Langer (1967), that the intellect associated with the human mind is a result of the evolution of emotion. Langer particularly tried to show that the entire psychological field—including human conception, responsible action, rationality, and knowledge—is the result of a vast and branching development of feeling.

Using the knowledge of one discipline to extend and deepen the knowledge of another is a traditional if not respected practice. Research on writing has been the beneficiary of knowledge from disciplines as diverse as the physical sciences, the animal psychologies, and mainstream philosophy. We are now learning about writing by applying knowledge from the field of cognitive psychology. It is an appropriate and important merger. But it is easy to lose sight of the impact of emotion on the intellect since, in education and academic psychology alike, cognition has been narrowly interpreted as deliberate and controlled reasoning. Language is cognition incarnate. And, of all discursive activities, writing so exemplifies it.

It is something of a paradox. At the same time that discourse specialists skirt emotion, they propel themselves closer and closer to it. Feeling is strongly implied in the construct of expressive writing described by Britton, Burgess, Martin, McLeod, and Rosen (1975), Kinneavy's (1971) expressive aims, and Macrorie's (1976) personal truth writing. Writing specialists concede that nonlinguistic yet affectively colored mental activities, like intuition and imaging, impinge on writing (Mandel, 1980; Moffett, 1982). Cognitivists note nonlogical, associatively linked representations (Flower, 1988); they talk liberally about evaluation, interpretation, and attitude—all alluding to emotion without saying so. Emotional experience, as embedded in the allied theories of reader-response, has gone serenely undisputed. Composition specialists link writing to moral orientation, a recent equivalent of emotion. Scholars are now applying social and ethnographic principles to written discourse (Bruffee, 1986; Kantor, 1984; Rafoth & Rubin, 1987), coming closest to the study of emotion with this new interdisciplinary exchange.

Writing does not exist in isolation. Daily, as well as developmentally, people respond first to the sensations and demands of their body, then to their person, and last to the people about them (Bleich, 1975). Bodies of knowledge are rapidly forming around the sociology of written discourse. Ethnography and social construction theory answer some questions about the impact of the environment on composing—an idea that cognitivists are just beginning to acknowledge (Heller, 1988). Proponents of these theories state that thought has its source in community. If language is a major source of thought, then written language is also a powerful source of thought, which finds its source in community as well. But it is not just community. It is a language community. It is a knowledge community. What this idea makes room for is interpretation—meaning, according to Bruffee (1984) and Fish (1980), constituted and sustained by sociocultural phenomena. What guides interpretation is accumulated experience, and that is determined by communal life. As is our knowledge, our intuitions and feelings are also a product of this reality (Aronowitz, 1987). Such is the social explanation of reality.

Because of their contextual focus, ethnography and social construction theory are a hairbreadth away from social psychology, where the study of affect has historically fallen and where emotion is a full citizen. Indeed, it is from social contexts that we develop values, attitudes, and opinions—cognitive renderings of affective phenomena. But that line of thinking only specifies the source. Somewhere between taking care of our physical needs and participating in social intercourse, we must still respond to our subjective experience, our feelings.

Research as well as personal experience demonstrates the unique capacity of emotion to enable or disable human activity. Enjoyment energizes, but so does anger. Boredom slows people down. It is associated with thinking slower and decreased attentiveness. But anxiety is also associated with overarousal that may result in disintegrated attention. Anxiety interferes with concentration and reduces what can be held in short-term memory. Anxiety thus cripples, but of course it can also arouse. Affect is often a central component of cognitive processes and seems inescapably related to how we perceive and think. Affective learning is far more pervasive and persistent than cognitive learning and influences performance many years later. Because emotion is implicated in virtually all human behavior, to ignore it when studying written discourse is to reject the very qualities that make us human.

Only by enlisting emotion in composing is the process fully realized. Otherwise there is no human point to it, no urgency or momentum for it. Emotion mobilizes us for writing, accompanies it, sustains us through laborious revisions, helps us find closure, and colors the way we approach writing the next time. It is appropriate to appeal to emotions theory and research in order to obtain a full picture of writers' mental lives when composing.

Epistemologists thus acknowledge the contribution of emotion to language. Psychologists implicate emotion in mental activity. Composition specialist Murray maintains that writing is a rational act in an emotional setting. Personal experience suggests it. Discourse studies appeals to other disciplines to learn about itself. A basic question arises: why then is inquiry into emotion without place in contemporary studies of writing?

A look at three literatures helps us understand our discomfort with the idea of emotional involvement in composing. In Chapter 2 I gather statements from leading authors about the emotional correlates of their writing. Chapter 3 addresses the cognitive process model of writing in terms of emotional experience and then cites some enduring issues that surround thought, language, and emotion. In Chapter 4, I trace the history of emotions psychology on which I draw in order to pursue the empirical research.

2. *The Emotions of Established Writers*

Ambivalence about the role of emotion in writing can be partly explained by looking at twentieth-century literary theory. For a substantial part of this century, the New Criticism dominated literary thinking in America. Introduced by John Crowe Ransom and emanating from work of scholars Cleanth Brooks, Robert Penn Warren, Alan Tate, and Kenneth Burke, the movement enjoyed wide currency. Representing a reaction to romanticism, impressionism, and the expressive theories of the humanities, modernists and New Critics declared themselves guardians of literature for the lay public. Their position held that ordinary individuals could not be trusted to know what to read and what not to. It remained for literary scholars as experts to determine what books people should read, how they should be read, what they meant, even how they should be written.

For students of literature, bare text was declared the proper focus of analysis. Literature was to be examined with exclusive attention to the facts of the work undistorted by any personal encounters with it. Wimsatt and Beardsley (1954) coined a term for such practices. The affective fallacy refers to the confusion between a literary work and its results, between what a work *is* and what it *does* to people. Apparently subjectivity, much less emotional engagement, was proscribed except as it illuminated theme or the structure of the language. Literary explication was to be cleansed of its effects, that is, of emotion.

But far from casting affective language from the canon, scholars recruited it as a way to render a work understandable. It was correct to mine for emotions in biographical research on authors in order to explain a work; or to use the emotions expressed in a work to explain the author; or to read into a work the emotions necessary to explain both—and in so doing conflate attribution with critical interpretation.

Although deeper scrutiny of the New Criticism frequently revealed a more accurate understanding of subjective phenomena, casual readers were apt to find an unfortunate blur between the artistic projections of critics and the psychology that authors themselves brought to the work. One simply slid into the other. Explicating a work through its affective properties gradually came to mean emotions experienced by authors, irrespective of biographical fact. When these were supported by primary sources, fine. When they were not, some scholars took literary license, regardless. Such liberties often had more to do with displaying the scholar's imaginative resources than with revealing writers' emotional profiles. Over the years, as authors and students of literature coming under the influence of the New Criticism gravitated to scholarly careers, they passed along this thinking. They were supposedly so well schooled in this approach that it was hard to distinguish the critic in them from the writer and both from the human being (Carkeet, 1976).

Some scholars took exception to this practice. Rosenblatt's (1938/1976) transactional theory of reading and Shrodes, Van Gundy, and Husband's (1943) bibliotherapeutic perspective clearly challenged textual objectivity and spawned important reversals of that stand. Purves and Beach's (1972) reader-response hierarchy, Bleich's (1975) subjective criticism, Fish's (1980) interpretive communities, and Holland's (1985) application of psychodynamic constructs to literature are recent elaborations of that line of thinking. Fish and Holland so much as say that the whole of meaning resides in the self. And in acknowledging the self they in effect acknowledge feelings—the core of reader response. While Fish is making an impact on literary exegesis, reader-response theory has not made an equivalent impact on writing. While followers of Rosenblatt and Shrodes advocated an intimacy between reader and text, the prevailing sentiment over the decades still severed from participation with literature the emotions of readers, critics, and by extension, writers themselves.

Much work itself was supposedly written in an aesthetically pure, impartial tradition, detached from any emotion. Poetry particularly was expected to be a highly worked and structurally perfected composition, the personal voice unabashedly absent. Even now, long after it has lost its initial momentum, the New Criticism continues to influence the emotions that writers disclose publicly (Cowley, 1958; Plimpton, 1963–1986). Establishment writers seem able to discuss the impalpable qualities of their writing process: their insights, intuitions, and imagination with relative ease. But when it comes to revealing their emotions, some simply do not respond—even when asked directly (Turner, 1977).

After all this, it's a wonder that authors were left with any emotion at all, much less while writing, much less recognizing it and saying so. But, of course, that is precisely what exists. A random and impressionistic review, not of critical material but of writers' diaries, memoirs, autobiographies, and interviews, reveals a complex relationship between writing and feeling. What follows is far from a representative sampling of writers' affective conditions. It is the result of a small labor to confirm the coincidence of emotion and writing while still controlling for critical interpretation. By letting authors speak for themselves, I hope to give some idea of the range of feelings summoned during composing and the language accomplished writers have used to express them.

THE POSITIVE EMOTIONS

When positive emotions have been cited during composing, these have been expressed as joy, heightened awareness, and inspiration. Happiness characterized the writing of Elizabeth Barrett (cited in Moers, 1976). If there were pleasures in literary expression, she enjoyed them. Her "Glimpses into My Own Life and Literary Character," set down in 1820, reflected "naturally cheerful and light" moods, the taking of uncommon "delight" in a life of letters. More than a century later, writing provided Anais Nin (1975) with feelings of "awareness, growth, creativity, and fullness overflowing." She found the emotional source for some of her composing "From joy! From enjoyment. I write when I am in love with something—a scene, a character, a book, a country. . . . For me, to write is to love again—to love twice." Joanna Field's (cited in Moffat & Painter, 1974) sense of well-being resulted from a sensitivity that her writing sharpened: "By keeping a diary of what made me happy I had discovered that happiness came when I was most widely aware." John Updike (cited in Plimpton, 1986) once said that "the minute [I put] an unhappiness down on paper, it metamorphoses into a lump of sugar!" This category of emotion would include William Kennedy's (cited in McCaffery & Gregory, 1987) belief that writing "is the supreme game. . . . There's nothing I'd rather do than . . . play at my typewriter. Writing is the most satisfying game of all." John Gunther (1961) had "fun" while writing the *Inside* books. He finished "writing Wyoming with a whoop and without taking five minutes off [started] Colorado."

At its loftiest, positive emotion is experienced as inspiration. That the "impulse to write a novel comes from a momentary unified vision of life" as Angus Wilson (1965) reported, was stated eloquently by biographer J.H. Griffin in 1981:

I make these notes a little at a time, spending long moments between sentences or paragraphs, just experiencing all this, letting it do with me what it will; aware that I am experiencing something so simple, so profound, so fundamental and out of time that the contemplation of it, right now, is the most important thing I can do. . . . It occasionally fills me so completely that I come to jot down a note. The note is the overflow, thin and hasty of the wealth that God pours into these hours before dawn in these woods. (P. 88)

And inspiration was epigrammatically and unpretentiously stated by William Wordsworth (1800/1965): "Poetry is the spontaneous overflow of powerful feelings: it takes its origins from emotion recollected in tranquillity," with which he follows:

The emotion is contemplated till by a species of reaction the tranquillity gradually disappears, and an emotion, similar to that which was produced before the subject of contemplation, is gradually produced, and does itself actually exist in the mind. (P. 266)

THE AROUSING EMOTIONS

Considerably more common in the literature are the emotions of interest and excitement, often singled out as the overarching precondition for composing and, more often than not, associated with positive feelings (Izard, 1977; Tomkins, 1962). In 1971 Jacques Barzun wrote that authors need an urgency, a "true healthful pressure and excitement," a mixture of the aesthetic and the utilitarian. Of course interest and excitement are not necessarily prompted by something pretty. Quoting the *Oxford English Dictionary*'s definition of muckraking as "a depraved interest in what is morally 'unsavoury' or scandalous," journalist Jessica Mitford (1979) investigated "controversy heated up in a most exhilarating fashion." In 1958 William Carlos Williams wrote of his composing: "I was discovering, pressed by some violent mood." Heywood Broun (cited in Berger & Berger, 1957) reported that the Sacco-Vanzetti case "moved [him] to write the first violent newspaper pieces [he] had ever done." The best advice is given by fiction writer Ray Bradbury (1973), who, guided by his own process, urged new writers to be stimulated before anything else:

For the first thing a writer should be is—excited. He should be a thing of fevers and enthusiasm.... What do you want more than anything else in the world? What do you love, or what do you hate? ... If you are writing without zest, without gusto, without love, without fun, you are only half a writer. (Pp. 28–31)

Robert Ludlum (1982) reported a similar elevation of emotion and attention: "I don't start with a story, plot or character or conflict, I start with an idea, with something that outrages me, amuses, interests me." It doesn't matter whether it is the zest of anger or the zest of love. It is the zest that counts.

Interest and excitement also operate independently of positive or negative qualities. Rather, they are perceived as states of physiological and emotional arousal, a fusion of activity and emotional intensity. These feelings are articulated directly or described hyperbolically by authors given to metaphor and seem to distribute themselves with some evenness over several genres. Novelist Saul Bellow (1982) spoke of being "deeply moved" when he writes, [getting] "turned on by it." Laura Chester (cited in Turner, 1977) found herself "charged up" for writing. For May Sarton (cited in Todd, 1983) "a poem is never completely satisfying unless it's in ... a form ... brought to me by intensity of feeling." Poet W.C. Williams (1958) noted about an early collection that it was "written, as always, in a period of great conviction and excitement." Mitford advised budding journalists to choose subjects of high interest, since writers work best "when besotted by and absorbed in the matter at hand. ... The rhythmic pace was the pace of speech, an excited pace because I was excited when I wrote." And in 1907 Samuel Taylor Coleridge wrote: "the property of passion is not to *create*; but to set in increased activity."

Nonfiction and fiction writers alike credit their productivity to what seems to be an extreme form of interest: a resolute willfulness, a single-mindedness, or what Harriet Beecher Stowe (cited in Moers, 1976) called her "deadly determination" to complete *Uncle Tom's Cabin* despite domestic interferences. Bellow called it a "hardness of intention"; Nin, an "unusual stubbornness" and obsessional writing; Carlos Fuentes (cited in Plimpton, 1984) described this relentless interest as obsessive concerns physically experienced; while Loren Eiseley (1975) described it as writing day and night and "[scuttling] about like the half-wild creature I had become." Jack Anderson (1979) recreated his dogged investigation of Joe McCarthy, and Eiseley recorded his "unswerving pursuit" of forgotten scientific papers.

Emotional response takes a relatively cognitive form in what both writers and discourse specialists alike call "the need to make sense of experience"—writing as a stay against confusion. For Margaret Drabble (cited in John-Steiner, 1985) writing is a way to find meaning and order in experience. Said C. Day Lewis (cited in Murray, 1978):

I do not sit down at my desk to put into verse something that is already clear in my mind. If it were clear in my mind, I should have no incentive or need to write about it. ... [We] do not write in order to be understood; we write in order to understand. (P. 101)

When alone with writing, Franz Kafka (cited in Dunaway & Evans, 1957) described the "slight ordering of my interior takes place and I need nothing more, for disorder is the worst thing in small talents." Katherine Mansfield (cited in Moffat & Painter, 1974) disclosed: "I have been thinking this morning until it seems I may get things straightened out if I try to write."

Writing organizes. Writing empowers. Gabriel Garcia Marquez (cited in Plimpton, 1984) linked his success with writing to emotional and physical health. Henry James (cited in Dunaway & Evans, 1957) stated, "When I am really at work, I am happy, I feel strong." Even Kafka, beset by physical and emotional problems, found that at times he was "fearless, powerful, surprising, moved as I otherwise am only when I write." And in a light mood, Virginia Woolf (cited in Dunaway & Evans, 1957) observed: "Occupation is essential. . . . I must cook dinner. Haddock and sausage meat. I think it is true that one gains a certain hold on sausage and haddock by writing them down," Woolf's metaphor for taking hold of life.

THE NEGATIVE EMOTIONS

If positive emotions catalyze writing or accompany it, the negative emotions seem to outrank the positive in both these respects. Anger figured centrally among the responses gathered here. Czeslaw Milosz (cited in Hoffman, 1982), celebrated in part for his World War II poetry, stated that during that period he "was forced by circumstances to write with anger, with indignation." Leading relatively conventional lives, black poets Nikki Giovanni, June Jordan, Sonia Sanchez, Ntozake Shange, and Robin Morgan have associated their writing with rage toward the white community (Strouse, 1981; Todd, 1983). William Gass (cited in Plimpton, 1981) named anger as a stimulus for his work. Nin disclosed at one point that her diary was a vehicle for expressing anger at her brothers. Anger became a powerful motive for journalist Jack Anderson (1979) who "sought to demolish" the image of Joe McCarthy; and for Mitford who investigated fraud in a "black mood of revenge."

Authors are more widely known for their drive to write their way out of another group of negative emotions, the withdrawing, inhibitory ones represented by unhappiness and depression (Lord Byron, George Sand, Franz Kafka, explorer Robert F. Scott, cited in Dunaway & Evans, 1957). First, the sadness of life itself: Willa Cather (cited in Todd, 1983) reported that each of her books was written out of a personal and usually painful experience. In 1960 Simone de Beauvoir wrote in her diary: "The war is back again, in me and around me, together with an anguish that knows no resting place." Poet Hayden Carruth (cited in Turner, 1977) reported writing poetry from a combination of "agitation, depression, and bitterness." Pablo Neruda (cited in John-Steiner, 1985) experienced anguish and sadness. Edna O'Brien (cited in Plimpton, 1986) observed that what gave birth to her novels was almost always "*conflict*. And *loss*—an innate sense of tragedy." The despondency Woolf experienced during her last year of life prompted a global statement: "All writers are unhappy. The picture of the world in books is thus too dark. The wordless are the happy." Stephen Spender (cited in Plimpton, 1984) would agree: "Unhappiness is something one can absolutely count on." In 1980 poet

Donald Hall wrote that "poetry concerns itself with unpleasant subjects: death, deprivation, loneliness, despair, if love, then the death of love." Sophie Tolstoy (cited in Moffat & Painter, 1974) recorded a similar distress:

A diary once again. It makes me sad to go back to the old habits which I gave up when I got married. I used to take to writing whenever I felt depressed, and I am probably doing it now for the same reason. I have been feeling frightened ever since yesterday when he told me he did not believe in my love. (P. 139)

Frustration with the writing process itself heads up another set of negative emotions, with authors like Nadine Gordimer (cited in Plimpton, 1984) eminently able to describe in writing "terrifying" periods when they couldn't write. Thus, George Eliot:

1860. My want of health and strength has prevented me from working much—still worse has made me despair of ever working well again.

1861. Struggling constantly with depresssion. Got into a state of so much wretchedness in attempting to concentrate my thoughts on the construction of my story that I became desperate and suddenly burst my bonds, saying, I will not think of writing.

1862. Have been reading some entries in my notebook of past times in which I recorded my malaise and despair. But it is impossible that I have ever been in so unpromising and despairing state as I now feel. I am extremely spiritless, dead, and hopeless about my writing. The long state of headache has left me in depression and incapacity. (Cited in Ponsonby, 1923, p. 406.)

Writer's block troubled Jean Paul Sartre (1966): "No sooner was I seated than my head filled with fog. I chewed at my nails and frowned." Mitford "hung around miserably," waiting for inspiration, getting "still nothing," drinking coffee until an idea at last struck. Henry James (cited in Dunaway & Evans, 1957) wrote:

If I can only concentrate myself; this is the great lesson of life. I have hours of unspeakable reaction against my smallness of production; my wretched habits of work—or of un-work; my levity, my vagueness of mind, my perpetual failure to focus my attention, to absorb myself, to look things in the face, to invent, to produce, in a word. (P. 480)

During one unproductive period Simone de Beauvoir (1960) wrote: "Misery sits within me like some intimate personal illness, a sequence of insomnia, nightmares, and migraines." Bernard Malamud (cited in Plimpton, 1984) reported writing despite paralyzing anxiety. Both Iris Murdoch and Gail Godwin (cited in John-Steiner, 1985) speak of writing in the continuous shadow of failure.

THE RESTORATIVE PROCESS

For every occasion of writing anxiety there are no doubt equal occasions during which writing has been enlisted to work out problems—both with writers' personal as well as their literary lives. Articulated in classical Greece, catapulted into prominence by Sigmund Freud, and dotted through contemporary psychotherapeutic practice, the salutary effects of words are axiomatic.[1] After the oral mode, the capacity of writing to restore emotional equilibrium and effect healthy change is unparalleled.

While this work says very little about writing as a therapeutic tool, established writers direct our attention to it. Some are motivated to write by the wish to pull out of depression. Tennessee Williams (cited in Plimpton, 1984) observed: "When you are going through a period of unhappiness... you have no refuge but writing." Woolf (cited in Moffat & Painter, 1974) patently stated: "Melancholy diminishes as I write." When her desire to write flagged, Woolf (cited in Dunaway & Evans, 1957) "[sniffed] around" for an antidote—for "writing to be a daily pleasure." For Sarton (cited in Plimpton, 1986) writing often helps her out of depression. Poet W.C. Williams began his autobiography during a depressed period of his life and found it "good therapy.... It got me back to the typewriter in high spirits." For Nin writing was a way to "transmute the sorrows." She would go to her desk, begin "to work and the depression goes away." "My notebook does not help me think," wrote Florida Scott-Maxwell (cited in Moffat & Painter, 1974), "but it eases my crabbed heart." At one time or another writing "saved" Eldridge Cleaver, Muriel Rukeyser, and Lillian Roth, but Sylvia Plath and Anne Sexton only for a while. Writing helped Eiseley overcome unabashed shame and guilt. Recalling his childhood, Eiseley expressed uncommon guilt for making fun of his deaf, "witchlike" mother. Now, "only an unutterable savagery, my savagery at myself, scrawls it once and once only on this page." "And it was finally by writing that I taught myself to talk with others," disclosed the once-shy Nin. Master diarist Max Frisch (cited in Singular, 1981) used writing as "self-therapy"—to keep the "fear of his own ghosts" under control. And Angus Wilson stated that his novels were a way of working through "problematic emotions."

Drawing on the time-honored cathartic qualities of composing, writers have particularly experienced relief and report it with striking unanimity. The diary gave Nin (cited in Moffat & Painter, 1974) vent to her negative self:

The false person I had created for the enjoyment of my friends, the gaiety, the buoyant, the receptive, the healing person, always on call, always ready with sympathy, had to have its existence somewhere. In the diary I could reestablish the balance. Here I could be depressed, angry, disparaging, discouraged. I could let out my demons. (P. 6)

"Writing every book is like a purge; at the end of it one is empty," said Daphne du Maurier (cited in *Writer's Quotation Book*, 1980), "like a dry shell on the beach, waiting for the tide to come in again." Gunther, expressing concern over U.S.-Soviet relations, observed that his writing "ruined a week," but "I felt better when I had delivered myself of it." "Self-realization and the purging of guilt (or the acceptance of it)" came as Angus Wilson relived "traumatic experiences in memory." Scientist W.N.P. Barbellion (cited in Dunaway & Evans, 1957) disclosed: "I intended never to write in my diary again. But the relief it affords could not be refused any longer." Writing provides poet Philip Larkin (cited in Plimpton, 1986) with a "physical release or solution to a complex pressure of needs." And Lord Byron (cited in Ponsonby, 1923) wrote:

This journal is a relief. When I am tired—as I generally am—out comes this and down goes everything. But I can't read it over: and God knows what contradictions it may contain. If I am sincere with myself (but I know one lies more to one's self than to anyone else) every page should confuse, refute and utterly abjure its predecessor. (P. 264)

EMOTIONAL ANTITHESES

I need finally to state what may be the most apt description of writers' affective experiences when composing—not one negative emotion over another or one positive emotion over another. Writers seem to draw strength from emotional antitheses. Whatever the source, writing often seems propelled by a collision, a tug-of-war between positive and negative feelings, an agony and ecstasy, if you will. During composing, Kafka reported a "fearful strain and joy," swinging between "wanting solitude to write and feeling unable to endure life alone." Sophie Tolstoy brought together personal conflict and writing in her diary:

It makes me laugh to read over this diary. It's so full of contradictions, and one would think I was such an unhappy woman. Yet is there a happier woman than I? It would be hard to find a happier or more friendly marriage than ours. Sometimes, when I am alone in the room, I just laugh with joy, and making the sign of the cross, say to myself, "May God let this last many, many years." I always write in my diary when we quarrel. (P. 13)

Poet and critic Hall contends that "there is no great poem in our language which is simply happy. Conflict makes energy."

These paradoxical feelings multiply. In the face of internal pressures, established writers have described in remarkably compatible terms a host of seemingly incompatible feelings: Carlos Fuentes' (cited in Plimpton, 1984) "painful plentitude," Gunther's feelings of being "crushed by pressure, exhilarated, worn out, desperate, and wildly happy," Mitford's sense of being "cast into a sort of euphoric despair." Raymond Carver (cited in Plimpton, 1986) called his fiction writing "fierce pleasure." At the juncture of the positive and negative it seems that "no simple feelings exist," so said Guy de Maupassant (cited in Murray, 1968). "All that [the writer] sees, his joys, his pleasures, his suffering, his despair, all instantaneously become objects of observation." And James Boswell (cited in Dunaway & Evans, 1957) is said to have written from a boundless cacophony of feelings: confusion, tears, glee, delight, erotic desire, and elation, wildly "struck by things."

END NOTES

While I have looked at only a few writers and a few of the emotions they document, I have every reason to believe that were I to spend a lifetime researching writers' emotions, it would be a task without end. If I looked long and hard enough, every emotion would be represented—from arch ecstasy to the depths of despondency, often residing in one person. Or, somewhere there would be a writer whose composing was accompanied by the very emotion I overlooked. My aim here was not to tally each and every feeling ever experienced during writing. To be sure, feelings and texts are not neat one-to-one equivalents. The array of possible combinations is staggering.

Let me say this much: When I read for this section, I tried to select materials in a disinterested fashion. I simply wanted to get as much firsthand data on emotions as I could—positive or negative, recent or remote. In some instances, I was disappointed. Collections that I thought were direct lines to autobiographical information were critical work artfully disguised. Then I found cultural interferences. I could not always separate the emotional sentience of writers from the tenor of the times. The material seemed more a social phenomenon than a personal one. Then I had to put aside issues regarding the psychological source of creativity: emotional instability or dysfunction, emotional health, or some *tertium quid* (Freud, 1908/1959; Koestler, 1976; Kubie, 1958).

I am not naive enough to deny that we find what we want to find. I had my hunches, and some were borne out. The literature suggests that negative emotions move writers to composing, or to expressing their emotions in writing, as easily if not more easily than positive ones. The emotions accompanying writing sometimes seem to behave as a neutral energy source to which writers attach labels. The affective counterpart of cognitive dissonance also fuels writers, perhaps by making them more uncomfortable than when they feel entirely positive or negative.

We know precious little about how rival feelings act—how emotional dissonance may be used to advantage in composing. We know equally little about how positive or negative feelings alone act on writing. We know probably less about feelings as sheer impulse. What there is to learn is that the writing process cannot be taken for granted. Even the simplest composing is a highly complex bodily task. Writing, at its most elemental, requires getting a writing instrument, making sure it's usable, finding a surface to write on, holding the instrument correctly, putting it on the surface, shaping word thoughts in a certain order in one's head at the same time as moving the instrument on this surface in linear patterns that correspond to each linguistic and nonlinguistic thought. All this is performed while the mind is scanning ahead for ideas, thinking back to others, forming the word thoughts that come next, holding back the letter-sound correspondence until each word thought has had its turn to be converted into graphic symbols strung together and drawn in linear patterns on the surface, to be reabsorbed at several points through the eyes, to be understood and accepted, understood but rejected, understood but modified, or not understood at all. And this in no way accounts for the mental operations from which the ideas were formed in the first place and then remembered in the second.

Furthermore, we know how fragile the process is. It may be delayed, interrupted, or abandoned at any time for an endless catalogue of reasons. Pencils break, minds block, thoughts wander, telephones ring, babies cry. People will fight, shout, run, ignore, forget, and are likely to do all sorts of things instead of write. It's my belief that, in general, fewer people write—in the true sense of the word—than composition specialists and educators are willing to believe. We need only talk to college students or nonstudent adults to know that writing is deeply freighted with negative associations and fertile with opportunities to avoid it. Students change majors; people change jobs. Some individuals go to great lengths to use other means of expression and communication.

The constraints on emotion in general are that its particular quality, intensity, and duration are heavily circumscribed by sociocultural factors—organized decency, as Britton once called it. When it comes to writing, the participation of emotion in it is similarly constrained. So, staying with the task may well mean overcoming a great many resistances; working around, through, or past distractions or interruptions; repeatedly clearing a path for the "approach emotions" to prevail and composing to start or continue.

Then there is the matter of the causal mix. To what are emotions a response? Writing would probably be far more repressible (or nonexistent altogether) than it is now were it not for business to transact, money to earn, fame to secure, essay tests to pass, or jobs to get—all perfectly good reasons for writing. Certainly we all know writers who produce deeply moving work from psychological states seemingly barren of emotion—for strict commercial or professional rewards. Behind many masterpieces can be detected either the itch for fame or the desire to make money (West, 1980). Samuel Johnson, John Milton, and Henry David Thoreau were intensely competitive with healthy egos and a healthy respect for prosperity. Other times, writing is a civic or academic necessity. Still other times there are more idiosyncratic motives. But for many who write—particularly those who write under no obvious pressure—there seems to be a certain quality of emotional engagement that brings them to the writing of words and keeps them at nothing else. All this suggests that writing is important enough for some people to keep doing it. To my mind this means that there is something more crucial about the process than its machine-like objectivity.

NOTE

1. For fuller background on the salutary effects of writing, see Brand, *Therapy in Writing* (1980).

3. *English Education, Linguistic Thought, and the Cognitive Model of Writing*

The involvement of emotion in composition studies has not fared much better than it has in literary criticism. American education brought into the twentieth century an emphasis on pure scholarship for the intellectually able. During World War I, the classical cast to writing gave way to assignments geared to utilitarian and informational purposes. Between the two wars, schooling for social efficiency shared currency with the somewhat misunderstood Progressive Education movement, and writing topics reflected those alternatives. A greater sensitivity to emotion was a pedagogical by-product of World War II. The 1940s life adjustment themes encouraged subjective, idiomatic, often guidance-related writing in which emotional involvement was a given (Brand, 1980). By 1956, however, the Council on Basic Education advocated a return to a formal, intellectual approach to language education. The 1957 launching of Sputnik resulted in new demands for intellectual excellence and a strongly academic model for writing instruction. The Project English curricula, the Basic Issues Conference, and the formation of the Ford Fund for the Advancement of Education represented national efforts in that direction.

If personal writing was tacit recognition of the participation of emotion in composition, it appeared with only cyclical faddishness from 1900 on (Brand 1980; Connors, 1987). Training in the four standard discursive modes of development (narration, description, exposition, and argumentation), plus research writing, encouraged students to move beyond themselves as subjects of their discourse. Continual efforts to transcend personal experience meant, in effect, to transcend the affective.

A cognitive thrust in writing curricula has thus prevailed in American classrooms, except for a short time after World War II and during the 1960s. The 1960s reform movement was the second major period during which interest in a strong cognitive education waned. Before this time the teaching of writing had been characterized by recipe and ritual, prescriptive procedures that bore little resemblance to the processes that writers actually underwent. The end product was the target to aim for, and it was evaluated by the mindless application of arbitrary standards. Or good papers were evaluated by the absence of errors in them.

The social climate of the 1960s, the educational reform accompanying it, and the psychological thrust for language learning emerging in Great Britain set the stage for the 1966 Dartmouth Seminar. As did the Progressive Education and wartime "adjustment" curricula, the International Conference on the Teaching and Learning of English temporarily dislodged the parochial, strictly academic model. The Dartmouth Seminar favored an organic, personal growth model for language education.

The first process models of writing to appear coincided with the 1960s reform movement and transformed the end-product orientation into several three-part stage models. Prewriting, writing, and rewriting or drafting, revising, and editing named two early versions of the stage model (Murray, 1968; Rohman & Wlecke, 1964). Prewriting, a kind of rehearsal, identified a critical first phase that was often characterized by the absence of paper and pencil. The attention paid to prewriting spread to another feature that marked the early phases of writing—expressive writing. This term originated in England (Britton et al., 1975) and was popularized in America as free or natural writing by Elbow (1973) and Rico (1983). Because it was relatively uninhibited and unplanned, expressive writing introduced into classroom parlance activities like automatic writing and saturation journalism—a sort of rhetorical winnowing, wherein kernels of ideas are gradually separated from the chaff. This refreshing naturalism took its most fashionable form in the journal. Journals caught on quickly and widely but were not without their problems. They were—and still are—often used indiscriminantly, with little understanding of their conceptual base or limitations.

Disenchanted with the helter-skelter that resulted from automatic or expressive writing, the proponents of the process concept withdrew uncritical endorsement of these practices, not by rejecting them outright but by gravitating to other themes—basic education and cognitive science. By the end of the 1970s, the field succeeded in bringing under control practices associated with the permissive, anything-goes school of writing. The appreciation and use of expressive writing began to stabilize. It was found acceptable and useful when applied to special forms like poetry or in work with reluctant or apprehensive writers. For everyone else, it was considered instrumental, a bridge to cross to more traditional expository discourse.

As is generally acknowledged, the stage models were a necessary intermediate step. They helped organize disciplinary thinking about composing and provided a coarse but useful overview of it. The stage models rendered a more accurate account of the writing process and suggested research and a pedagogy. Composition studies came away with the constructs of revision and the by-word process. However, these models gradually came under fire for representing a lockstep approach to writing—each phase imprisoned in a sterile and unnatural sequence. Furthermore, the stage models did not go far enough. The media blitz about why-Johnny-can't-write and the 1970s Basics Movement fueled interest in alternative approaches to writing instruction. The partnership between writing theory and cognitive psychology, ascending in its own right, crystallized this interest not simply in an enlarged process model but in an elaborate cognitive one.

THE COGNITIVE PROCESS MODEL OF WRITING

Led by Flower and Hayes (1981a, 1981b; see also Flower, Hayes, Carey, Schriver & Stratman, 1986), the cognitive psychology of writing institutionalized itself quickly. It promised to remedy the aimlessness of the expressive approach and the inflexibility of the stage models. It promised to reunite writing and thinking. It consolidated the shift from product to process by distinguishing considerably more acts of the mind that writers continuously go through regardless of the stage a text is in. The controlling principle—recursion—occurs when a writing subprocess loops back at any point in the larger writing process. The cognitive process model attempts to show how writers bring complex and recursive mental acts to bear on the general stages of composing, obtained by the now familiar think-aloud protocol.

Briefly, the think-aloud protocol, developed originally by cognitive scientists, reveals the intellectual activities that individuals engage in while performing a task. In a writing protocol, individuals exteriorize their thoughts as they compose. When the protocol is over, the transcript, together with knowledge about the writing task and the human mind, enables investigators to infer a model of the mental processes by which writers performed the task.

In the next section I summarize the cognitive process model of writing as developed by Flower and Hayes.[1] Then I review its assumptions in light of emotional experience.

The Structure of the Writing Process

According to the Cognitive Process Theory[2] the writing process is divided into three major substructures:

1. Task environment. This subdivision includes everything outside the writers' skin

that influences the performance of the task. It includes class climate, temporal constraints, writers' motivations (more recently renamed exigencies), and the assignment itself. Once writers start writing, the developing text becomes part of the task environment because it influences what is written next.
2. Long-term memory. Here writers store knowledge about the world as well as about how people write. Long-term memory and the task environment form the context within which the most important substructure operates—the process itself.
3. The writing process. Here writers store general writing plans, heuristics for investigating topics, and information about where to find particular subject-matter information. The writing process is divided into the subprocesses of planning, translating, and reviewing. The relationships between these subprocesses are guided by the monitor or executive. The monitor reflects writers' goals and differences in their writing styles. It also controls which subprocesses prevail at any point in the process (pp. 12–25).

Constraints

Constraints are features built into writers' goals and shape the process of reaching them. Acceptable writing performance should exhibit these goals since they influence not only what individuals write but how they go about it. The three types of constraints include: insufficiently integrated knowledge, inadequate written speech, and excessive or unfamiliar rhetorical demands (pp. 34–40).

Because, by and large, human minds process information serially, people have difficulty managing converging constraints or high demands on their attention. Such information overload results in cognitive strain or performance anxiety, which is likely to disrupt performance of the task (Newell & Simon, 1972). Similarly, in order that writing under such conditions may be undertaken and completed successfully, writers must exercise cognitive economy. They may: (1) ignore some constraints temporarily; (2) partition the larger rhetorical problem and concentrate on manageable subproblems; (3) set priorities for them; (4) choose the first acceptable—but not necessarily the best—solution; (5) draw on strategies so automatic that they don't require conscious processing; or (6) plan—the most critical of subprocesses (pp. 43–44).

Plans are subdivided into: (1) plans "to do," which are plans for addressing the rhetorical problem; (2) plans "to say," or content plans; and (3) plans to "compose," or plans on how to go about writing.

Goal Setting

Just as writers build a hierarchy of processes, according to the cognitive process model, they also tend to set a hierarchy of goals. These goals are conscious and generally conform to the priorities established by the monitor. But these too may be modified during writing. Although goals often go unverbalized, the protocols suggest that strong writers form their goals early in the process. Unskilled writers have problems setting goals. They set goals for writing based on rhetorical plans that fail to match their readers' expectations, or that are too abstract, or not abstract enough. Weak writers are also unwilling or unable to modify their goals in midprocess in light of what they may uncover about their topic or their composing process (LeFevre & Dickerson, 1981).

THE COGNITIVE PROCESS MODEL OF REVISING

In 1986 Flower, Hayes, and their colleagues put forward an elaboration of the cognitive model of writing that focused exclusively on revision.[3] The cognitive model of revision rests on two key variables: knowledge and intention. These are defined as the extent of information that writers have about their text and the ability to use that information (pp. 19–20).

The revising process itself originates in the review subprocess of the cognitive model of writing and is made up of two components: evaluation and revision. The review process begins with evaluation. A complex, generative subprocess, evaluation refers to a constructive, goal-driven activity guided by the intentions (for example, goals, constraints, expectations, and criteria) that writers bring to the task. What guides problem representation during evaluation is the ability of writers to build accurate and adequate representations of their texts (separate from their own private representations of meaning), as well as representations of their intentions. The way in which revisors represent their intentions not only activates awareness of certain textual features, but limits and focuses it (pp. 32–36).

Problem representation is composed of two subdivisions. First, problems that are poorly defined are merely *detected*. Second, problems that are clear and fully defined and provide ideas for solving them are regarded as *diagnosed*. Problem representation originates with detection. This requires an awareness of dissonance between text representation and writers' intentions (p. 29). Once a problem is detected, writers choose from four strategies: to delay, search, rewrite, or revise.

The detect/rewrite strategy (pp. 43–47) means abandoning the existing text and starting again. Writers remaining at the detection stage do not depend on new information for the rewriting task. Instead, they leave the review process and return to the more basic subprocesses of planning and translating (which involve redrafting or paraphrasing).

The diagnosis/revise option (pp. 40–51) is made up of three phases: detection, diagnosis, and strategy selection. The true revision process is still initiated by detecting a problem because it precedes diagnosis on the revision path. However, it is diagnosis that actually guides revision. Diagnosis depends on seeing problems in meaningful patterns and operates on both conscious and automatic levels of awareness. It brings relevant past experience to bear on problems, calls up new information, and points to solutions. The actual set of strategies for improving a text is represented by a means-end table. These options include planning, using heuristics, or applying global or explicit "fix-it" techniques. The global revision of expert writers seems to depend on rewriting, diagnosis, goal modification, and evaluation.

LIMITATIONS OF THE COGNITIVE MODEL OF WRITING

The ascendancy of the cognitive model of writing is a tribute to the vitality and value of this line of thought. However, despite the respect afforded the model, its assumptions, methodology, and utility have raised questions. Brodkey (1987) has argued that the cognitive perspective is wanting because it decontextualizes writing—an omission that Flower is taking pains to correct. Wason (1980) claims it ignores the rich motivational dynamics of individuals in the very act of cognizing. Providing emotion with no name or place in a paradigm is tantamount to stating that it does not exist, even though emotion is implicated at many junctures in the model: motivations or exigencies, plan/write boundaries, intention or goal-setting, conflict in subprocess, process interruptions, cognitive strain, levels of acceptability, and evaluation.

Researchers voice concern that some of the excerpted protocols seem too disciplined, empty of affective tone or what Petrosky in 1983 called personal realities. Cooper and Holzman (1983) contend that their introspectors notice virtually nothing other than that which is to the point. It is difficult to know if such verbal reports are a function of data management or a political expediency.

Then there is the matter of the research setting. No matter how much subjects are encouraged, prepared, and willing to share the matter-of-fact steps in their composing, there are usually expectancy effects and demand characteristics, both artifacts of the laboratory situation (Cooper & Holzman, 1983; Faigley & Witte, 1981). Additional condensation of thought and deliberate self-censoring occur because subjects are apt to report socially acceptable statements. Since most people do not talk out loud or even pay attention to their thoughts about writing when engaged in it, further error threatens.

Protocols are indeed limited to what people can and are willing to articulate. Cognitive research allows for the relatively easy taking of data.[4] But not enough seems taken or ultimately used. Reducing data is a particularly knotty problem in writing research, and investigators must generalize from them. But the degree to which the transcripts are summarized is worrisome. Presumably, statements subject to reduction or omission are of little or no value—as defined by the research goals

(Dobrin, 1986). But discourse specialists are, in a sense, asked to take on faith that they are without value altogether. The more telling material may well be what is summarized or overlooked. What would help complete the "process" picture is an account of how much information was lost in data reduction, where it occurred, and what it was. This would undoubtedly include a lot of grunts and groans, but it would also reveal imagistic and free associative thinking and connotative commentary. This is precisely where differences in cognitive style and personality may be observed. This is where emotions happen. Without this information, can we legitimately say that the mental activities underlying writing have been accurately depicted?

The difficulty lies not only with what the model omits, but what it suggests about people. Information processing metaphors promote a mechanistic view of the human being that we inherited from Descartes, abandon periodically, and now return to. Computer systems are poor if not fierce lies about what happens psychologically when we compose. We may sometimes think of ourselves *as if* we are computers. But computers do not grow. They do not learn with practice or understand what they do. Computers do not realize the significance of anything. And computers do not feel (Dreyfus, 1979; Neisser, 1980; Searle, 1984).

In the rush to demonstrate its practicality, the model has been transformed into what is already an embarrassment of instructional approaches. Selzer as well as Cooper and Holzman claims it encourages others to apply the model directly, to teach students to behave as the model says writers behave. It credits strong student writers with strategies that few practiced writers use, implying that good writers may be distinguished from weak writers by demonstrating more loyalty to the model than to themselves (Glatthorn, 1981; Hairston, 1986; LeFevre & Dickerson, 1981). It assumes a motivation at the same time as it assumes an inert dispassion, a vexing contradiction. How poorly that fits my experience with student writers. Does that mean that I do not teach any strong writers? Clearly not. It is easy to identify accomplished writing from students who defy all our good words about process, and ineffective writing from mindlessly obedient believers. What the cognitive model implies is not that there are different composing styles, but that the cognitive approach is better than others. Nothing could be further from the truth.

THE AFFECTIVE BASES OF LINGUISTIC THOUGHT

These difficulties prompt an exploration of larger conceptual issues. Given the academic tradition and the currency of cognitive science, it is easy to understand our overarching respect for the intellectual enterprise. Of the presentational (spatial/form, intuitive, affective) and the discursive (propositional and syntactic) modes of mental activity, the discursive represents and formulates reality through language (Langer, 1957). Discursive phenomena are said to progress from the simple to elaborate, concrete to hypothetical, specific to general, physical to mental, enactive or behavioral to symbolic or abstract, proximal to remote, and base to transcendental. These increasingly complex processes inform contemporary pedagogy (Bruner, 1968; Hillocks, 1982; Moffett, 1968). And they are evident in taxonomies of discourse structure, whether they are based on text, physical science, function, or psychological distance between language producers and audience (Britton et al., 1975; Eckhardt & Stewart, 1979; Moffett, 1968; Young, Becker, & Pike, 1970).

Writing, in particular, is considered the quintessential representation of thought. Like thought, writing may be identified by levels of sophistication. It is assessed through such syntactic features as t-unit length and incidence of subordination, or such rhetorical features as elaboration of argument, versatility of diction level, and critical thinking.

Skilled critical thinkers transcend the printed word and the here and now. They arrange and rearrange. They decide what belongs and what doesn't. They make inferences. They exercise possibilities. They remember. They predict.

The act of writing demands that concepts, generally global or even imagistic in storage, be forced into the linear patterns of writing, patterns organized by the analytical determination of thesis, sub-theses and details. ... The act of analysis ... implements thinking skills: students select parts of their concepts and arrange them logically—side by side or embedded within each other. Students write them clearly in sentences and then gather those together in paragraphs. (Goldberg, 1983, p. 41)

Thinking materializes on paper as outlines, branching sequences of specificity, inductive and deductive reasoning, summaries, and so on. This is right and good but stops too soon.

Philosopher Langer has stated that the notion of giving something a name is the vastest generative idea that ever was conceived (cited in Berthoff, 1981), because from names generalization and concept form—the well-spring of our intellectual life. The act of naming is without exception a first step away from the phenomenological reality of a thing, and is simultaneously an abstraction and a symbol of the first order. Word symbols are vehicles for conceptualizing objects. Gradually, they come to stand for whole systems of things like them. That is how ideas form and make the kind of sense we call thinking. In order to think critically we appeal to those conceptual systems.

But exact words have a way of escaping us, too. Cognitive psychologists maintain that the immediate memory for discourse is limited in capacity and quickly dumps original verbatim wording. Consequently, the precise repetition of any sentence is a rarity. While exact units fade, essential meaning embodied in that label is stored in long-term memory. The same thing happens when we witness an event that we want to remember: We make a verbal description of it, then remember our verbalization. When we recall that event, we recreate it by secondary elaboration. This means that we do not remember the event. We remember its verbal description, using details consistent with our general knowledge and particular verbal recodings or schemas (Miller, 1956; Neisser, 1967). Language is uniquely suited for this kind of recoding. It enables us to "repackage" information into only a few chunks rich in meaning. Just a word or two can represent a whole experience. In other words, recoding provides much more information than the words simply say.[5]

The relationship between recoding and the relevant schemas is important. In order to make the system work, there must be some congruence between the recoding and the schemas already in place. This requires a fit, and a fit requires interpretation (Gilligan & Bower, 1984). Interpretation reorganizes and stores ideas (in this case, in linguistic form), not only in line with our general knowledge, but also, as Neisser (1967) has stated, with our interests, values, and expectations. Interpretation is what happens in the space between a material reality and human perception—the human understanding of incoming sensory information. Interpretation is appreciating the difference between a shack and a palace, apartment, or log cabin. Put another way, when words do not fully account for reality—what Iser (1978) calls their indeterminancy—individuals fill in the blanks.

Even if all words were neutral, personal experience is not. Because personal experience happens and words effortlessly come to mean, every event and idea that occurs is simultaneously an interpretation—we are always filling in the gaps. It is difficult for many of us to accept a fact independent of interpretation. Interpretation provides meaning to be sure. But because language so quickly shades off into slant, interpretation has an affective base.

This is not new. Vygotsky (1962) reckoned with this issue from another direction. Although Piaget's epistemology was based on behavioral, not linguistic, experience, it lay the groundwork for understanding linguistic thought and provided Vygotsky with the basis for a countervailing theory. In contrast to Piaget's notion that egocentric speech withers as thought develops, Vygotsky envisioned two movements for egocentric speech: one direction, outward to social communication; the other, inward to the self. Linguistic thought develops as social speech moves inward. We talk less and less out loud and speak more and more to ourselves. This inner speech becomes dynamic, shifting, unstable. Its syntax becomes increasingly abbreviated, telegraphic. We think more and more in highly condensed phrases or syntactic predicates. Articles and adjectives disappear, pronouns drop off, and predicates shrink to verbs until what is left in our mind is only the single naming word. We have come to appreciate that, fully internalized, the single naming word comes closest to pure meaning.

The thinking we do in pure meaning is saturated with sense. Sense, according to Vygotsky, is the sum of all the psychological events associated with the word. The single naming word is so saturated with sense that many words would be needed to reconstitute it to external speech. Indeed, the task of translating inner speech into effective language is the job of communication. But what we lose in form and sheer quantity of language when thinking, we gain in substance—that is, images and connotation. Pure meaning is so richly endowed with images and connotation that it is saturated with emotion.

LONG-TERM COGNITIVE AND AFFECTIVE MEMORY

Knowledge and long-term memory figure centrally in information processing theory. Schemas—cognitive constructs for organizing prior knowledge—provide reasonable ways of thinking about that knowledge, about how people see reality, and what goes with what. Memory is formed in terms of that knowledge. But knowledge in memory is not emotion-free. Knowledge represented in memory has affective components which may be called long-term affective memory (Harre & Lamb, 1983).

Let me start with some ideas about schemas and memory in general. I have stated that the strict cognitivists rarely involve the emotions when characterizing schemas. However, according to cognitive social psychologists, whether schemas reside in long-term memory, in the working memory associated with consciousness, or in both, they organize not only cognitions but also emotions.[6] Fiske (1981) cites certain features that distinguish the two. While schemas cue relevance and consistency in both cognition and emotion, affective structures alone govern valence, or sign, and intensity, or strength of meaning. In other words, the data of emotion contribute valence and are amplified in ways that facts are not. Rate of response is also a function of emotion. In fact, automatic judgments are considered cued more quickly when a valence exists than when the cognition is "cold."

Nonetheless, social cognitivists have a special way of treating affective information: not as distinct, but as a special class of cognitive data. These data require mediation, which is often called interpretation, sometimes called appraisal or evaluation, other times called meaning analysis, still other times simply a label (which the cognitive mechanism supplies) (Fiske, 1981; Isen & Hastorf, 1982).

There are lively theories concerning the ways in which emotional experience may be stored: as bonded to cognitive structures, as organized but discrete units (affective tags that cue categorically associated material), as isolated fragments, or as part of a separate network (Clark & Isen, 1982; Fiske, 1981; Gilligan & Bower, 1984).[7] Affective experience may be represented in memory not only by the symbolic codes of words but by the imagistic codes of sensation and perception as well as the motor codes of musculature and behavior. Our mouth feels round when we say ball. We have negative feelings about screech because the required motor state is unpleasant. For now, how affective information is stored is immaterial. The fact is that affective data are there. If we go back far enough in childhood, significant variations of emotionally involving events begin to create a memory string that is uniquely human and social. That's when autobiographical memory begins (Huyghe, 1985; see also Langer, 1972). But that is not where it ends.

At any one point in our history an emotional response must be distinctive enough to warrant a specific name or label. But just as we replace ordinary sentences in memory with an interpretation or gist, we also substitute a semantic shorthand for emotional responses. Both processes implicate choice. Even if we allow for what the senses miss or the musculature rejects, the mind takes in billions of microevents. It collects information from everywhere. The activities of attending and perceiving proceed continuously and spontaneously. We use similar processes when scanning our memory. Just as the entire visual field is potentially available at any given moment, so too all of memory, our penultimate knowledge base, is theoretically available. But perceiving an entire visual field or recalling all of memory is humanly impossible. We select portions of it. We forget more things than we remember and operate consciously on still fewer. In other words, we choose. And, as Neisser has noted, such choices are not random.

Informed by the work of A.R. Luria, Jean Piaget, and George Kelly, Emig (1982) confirmed this pivotal idea: The fact that we can choose how to perceive the world and can elect to define what is distinctly human is precisely what *is* human about human life. But cognitive psychology has yet to explain why we choose what we choose and how it happens. We do the same in language. We are largely responsible for what we come to know. We are responsible for what we say. Parallels exist at the word level through every rhetorical mode and discursive form. Writing, too, is an exercise in inclusion and exclusion, a lesson in decision making and choice. It is the basis on which we make those selections that determines cognitive and writing style. And, as I will trace later, such choices link linguistic thought to emotion.

Whenever we make choices about something new in our experience we draw on parallels to something old (Sternberg, cited in Hunt, 1982)—our prior knowledge. We reason analogically. As I mentioned, long-term cognitive and affective memory reflects emotional proclivities and response style. These long-standing, slowly building feelings become the basis for defining our current states in relation to immediate experience (Gilligan & Bower, 1984).[8] In writing, long-term affective memory is composed of all the history of our feelings about writing in general, including feelings about our competence to perform certain writing tasks. The affective "mind-set" guides response to the immediate, idiosyncratic particulars: This three-page essay on *Native Son* at this very 8:07 A.M. in this very English 302 from this very Mr. Merrill smiling at a very tired me.

Let me be clear. Affective memory is highly influenced by cognition. But, by the same token, emotion plays a crucial role in organizing and using memory. Fiske has stated that our memory for what we consider relevant, and our impressions of who caused what show mediating links: to wit, "affectively laden impressions are highly correlated with memory for data perceived as relevant" (p. 253). Likewise, Hidi and Baird, as well as Hildyard (cited in Flammer & Kintsch, 1982) link affective states with interesting and important, or essential material in certain texts. Bleich (1975) aptly observed that people seem to respond to experience by recalling the relevant events in their lives whose common link with the present is a similarity of feeling. This may explain why facts alone do not change feelings. Cognitions initially involved in forming them eventually drop off, and all that remains is the feeling. So, attempts at persuasion that attack the cognitive elements in forming feelings no longer work (Zajonc, cited in Hall, 1986). It is the affective, not the informational, memory that provides the staying power. So effortless and automatically accruing are these feelings that they often survive long after people forget the stimuli. Such is the power of affective memory.

THE AFFECTIVE ASPECTS OF COGNITIVE DISSONANCE

The mind handles new and deeply atypical data differently. Let me first sketch a typical course of mental events for performing a written task in which individuals already have experience (and thus have schemas established for it). In order to engage in writing, individuals make sense of the task by recognizing its critical features. They reach, so to speak, into long-term affective and cognitive memory for previous tasks like it, a standard, or the closest thing to it. In a typical meaning analysis—to use Mandler's term—writers mentally search their cognitive-affective structures and stop searching when a prior structure adequately accommodates the current experience. The task is interpreted. It is appraised. This appraisal—at whatever level of awareness—stimulates physiological changes. These are transformed into feeling states, which are labeled good, bad, frustrating, surprising, or whatever, depending on what in the writing task we believe is causing them. We process information continuously and spontaneously in just this way. We slot emotional and cognitive data into established, noncontroversial mental categories making unnoticed adjustments when necessary.

New data that defy ready classification warrant a more dramatic kind of interpreting—what Bransford (1979) calls cognitive restructuring—

because the data do not fit the existing structures. True, every departure from a standard strengthens the construal of that standard. However, fringe data make individuals conscious of that adjustment because the data disturb what would otherwise be automatic. Creative thinking develops in just this fashion. So too higher-order thinking. According to Berthoff (1981), concepts form in a kind of Brunerian double helix that operate on an equivalent principle—that of antithesis. Piaget's disequilibrium, Polanyi's heuristic tension, and Festinger's cognitive dissonance are cognitive constructs representing similar phenomena.

Antithesis is also colored affectively. Complex intellectual malaise gives rise to such namable emotions as anticipation, anxiety, or uneasiness, which spontaneously prompt efforts at reconciliation. The mind continually seeks to repair disparities in the phenomenological as well as the discursive world. Our search for balance is the constantly elusive goal toward which mental activities tend (Goldberg, 1983). As we take ownership of new knowledge, we temporarily sacrifice peace of mind.[9] While cognitive psychology recognizes that these "disturbances" occur and are essential for thinking and learning, cognitive models of writing fall short of crediting their affective aspects.

ETHICAL ORIENTATION

Given the link between cognitive maturity and critical thinking, a recent coupling has occurred between higher-level thought and moral maturity. Inspired in large part by Piaget (1956) and Erikson (1968), these theories depict ethical consciousness as developing through age-related stages. In their taxonomy of the affective domain, Krathwohl, Bloom, and Masia (1964) trace the formation of human character as individuals internalize progressively more abstract values. Kohlberg's (1975) six-stage model of cognitive-moral development is predicated on three levels of ethical orientation: premoral, conventional, and postconventional. As young people work through hypothetical dilemmas, they become increasingly clear about the values they hold. Ultimately they develop the capacity to reason about justice and universality. The Perry (1970) scheme identifies on a cognitive continuum positions of dualism, multiplism, and the highest position, contextual relativism, which are social, moral, and evaluative.

Notwithstanding Gilligan's (1982) eloquent departure from this perspective, these theorists contend that the more advanced the position, the more likely that reconciling ethical discrepancies requires formal reasoning. Because the upper reaches of ethical maturity require critical thinking, the potential of these typologies for assessing rhetorical sophistication was quickly recognized. The Wilkinson (1980) scales, for example, provide not only stylistic and cognitive but also moral or "affective" criteria for evaluating rhetorical development. One would think that the affective criteria for writing would tap our general emotional tendencies as well as our immediate feelings about writing. As it turns out, the criteria consist of a rank order of judgments about the self in relation to various domains of experience, with a movement toward greater awareness of experience (namely, from self to others, the environment, audience, and reality) and with objectivity as the highest order of judgment. When reified, Wilkinson's affective criteria thus rest on an idiomatic definition, one no more intrinsic to emotion than any other aspect of human experience. Winter, McClelland, and Stewart (1981) tested moral orientation and critical thinking by applying affective criteria to narratives. Again, the biases are clear. Emotional neutrality is considered morally the most advanced. The authors so much as say that their writing evaluation scale can actually be used to test the ability to remain aloof from one's emotions—presumably the hallmark of the liberally educated.

Morality, values, beliefs, attitudes, evaluation, preference; the circumlocutions become harder to ignore. At the risk of trivializing the issue, I would like for a moment to lay out a simple regression. If, in its most basic form, cognitive maturity may be measured by moral orientation (to take one theme), it can be traced to emotion. It would go something like this. If we are looking at critical thinking, we are also looking at moral orientation. If we are looking at moral orientation, we are looking at belief systems. If we are looking at belief systems, we are looking at attitudes. If we are looking at attitudes, we are looking at choice. If we are looking at choice, we are looking at the fundamental polarities of good and bad and are expected to choose the good over the bad. If we are deciding on the goodness or badness of things, we are trading in the affect.

CONSCIOUSNESS AND THE UNCONSCIOUS

Ordinarily consciousness, the unconscious, mind, and emotion are considered incompatible with hard science. Cognitive psychologists, however, do not ignore the constructs of consciousness and the mind as they do the unconscious and emotion. I want to look at the constructs of consciousness and the unconscious in terms of emotion, again stretching the limits set for this chapter.

According to cognitive psychologists, the things we are "working" on in our mental life are things we are conscious of. The cognitive process model of writing maintains that most of the work of writing occurs in verbal consciousness (Flower & Hayes, 1984), of which protocols are its manifestation. For this group, an unconscious component in writing per se does not seem to exist—a point of view Flower (1988) has recently retreated from. For others, the unconscious has been treated in several ways. Of course, it is the pivot on which psychoanalytic psychology has turned. If this form of the unconscious, with which uncontrollable passions have been affiliated, is part of human thought, cognitivists see it as a spoiler. More democratic about emotion, Piaget (1973) was apparently unwilling to rule out an affective unconscious. He treated it as a cross between a Freudian and a cognitive construct with comparable structures and status. In 1980 Neisser observed that psychologists have known for a long time that most of the work of thinking is unconscious.

Indeed, many psychologists agree that we "work" on things we are not conscious of. But they give it another name. This alternate form, also falling below the threshold of awareness, is called automatic to distinguish it from the motivational and derivative sort informing the depth psychologies.[10] To this group, these automatic processes occur effortlessly. They happen without attention, intention, choice, or interference from other mental processes (Posner & Snyder, 1975). Automatic processes do not use psychic energy like the defense system. Nor do they cost the cognitive system. But they are fully cognitive. And that, I suspect, means they are devoid of emotion.

Consciousness and the unconscious may be looked at from yet another perspective, one that also does away with the construct of the unconscious altogether (Blakeslee, 1980; De Bono, 1970). Consciousness is conceptualized as a continuum with a focus and fringe. Our attention is directed to the focus. What other theorists characterize as automatic or unconscious is now called the fringe. It is everything else that impinges on our attention but is not at its center. Rather, this "everything else" gradually diminishes from the focus until it is barely perceptible at any given moment. But it is part of consciousness all the same.

Such thinking intends to erase two obvious boundaries: one between conscious thought and thought to which we have limited access; and a second between verbal and nonverbal mental activity. What follows from this important shift is a conflation of human ways of thinking. Knowing through language is only one, albeit significant, form of thought impinging on writing. The planning and problem solving linked to conscious cognizing are the result of functions taking place simultaneously in the right hemisphere of the brain, the center of presentational thinking and the emotions. The traditional terminology used to describe consciousness has been skewed toward verbal, left-brain cognition to the exclusion of the nonverbal but important function of right-brain consciousness. Observing, intuiting, and imagining occur apart from verbalizing and remain that way unless they are translated into language or we act on them physically. Feelings figure strongly here, too. Adherents of this view maintain that we are continuously processing information in both modes with perhaps greater involvement of one modality over the other. With the seat of human emotion in the right brain, it is not surprising that its functions would be discounted. But it bears repeating. Even if words could be stripped of their feeling tones, other mental activities would reintroduce them.

MOTIVATION

I do not want to end this discussion without some words about motivation, about which Neisser again contends cognitive psychology has said too little and which, like the unconscious, is accompanied by great ambiguity, if not disdain. Historically, conscious processes were divided into three faculties: cognition, affection, and conation or will. Emotion was frequently bracketed with conation or will, which became linked to motivation. While all activity embodied some mix of these three classes of mental events, the whole of activity was believed directed by feeling or motivation.

Given the time-honored imprecision of its meaning, motivation seems constantly in danger of being mistaken for emotion, like an interchangeable part. This practice may be partially attributed to Piaget, who blurred affect and motivation, ranked both considerably below the intellect, and failed to address either beyond their energizing capabilities.[11] While I later mention two other views of emotion that Piaget held, he (Piaget & Inhelder, 1969) most often combined emotion and will or motivation and viewed them as some kind of energy. The prime motivation for intellectual development came from within the operative structure, markedly different from the mere acquisition of information.

In general, motivation has had to do with a sense of incompleteness accompanied by a wish to go beyond particular limits. During the twentieth century, motivation has been allied to psychoanalytic psychology particularly when such impulses became problematic—their sources fell below the threshold of awareness and corrupted behavior. At its best, Piaget attributes to motivation an intellectual energy that provides direction, sustains intellectual activity, and mobilizes for change.

In writing education, motivation has received perhaps more lip-service than emotion but equally scant systematic attention and clarification. Motivation is tucked, for example, in a corner of current disciplinary thinking (Bloom, 1985; Hayes & Flower, 1980, 1984) to be pulled out when other explanations fail and with which few can argue.[12] Emotions are often equated with anxiety, sometimes separated from temperament, and sometimes called motivation. Many researchers don't mention motivation at all. Or they mention it quickly, then crowd it out by more cognitive concepts. Or emotion and motivation are skirted by using such words as interpretation, evaluation, gist, or even goal-setting. In fact, the category of motivating cues that formed part of the original cognitive process model of writing was replaced in 1984 by the term exigencies, presumably ridding itself of any misreadings.

To the extent that exigencies are intentions or impulses to act, they are indeed motivations—which cognitivists do a better job of explaining in terms of goals than they do in terms of the more traditional definitions.[13]

From the cognitive perspective, motivation denotes the mechanism by which people choose goals in which to invest psychic energy and keep that energy focussed. To the extent that motivations are conscious sources of goals, in writing they may be fairly straightforward: grades, promotion, publication, satisfaction. For example: To get an "A" in this course I must argue against the Illinois Lottery in four pages. Short-term, subsidiary, and intermediate goals—procedural or substantive—are set all along the way to a final draft and take any number of forms which the cognitive point of view addresses comfortably.

Yet, as in the matter of human choice, the goal-setting process still mystifies. Cognitive psychologists study the representations of goals and the plans and paths that lead to them. But they have yet to account for their motivational properties: where goals come from, how they develop, and why (Warnock, 1984). What is unfortunate is that a crucial variable like motivation (over which cognition claims relatively little jurisdiction) seems to come out as, then why bother with it? Yet without it, learning simply would not take place.

END NOTES

The elaborations and refinements of the cognitive process model of writing have shed considerable light on composing. The model has endeavored to demystify the writing process by showing that composing has an underlying organization, though it may appear haphazard to casual observers or to writers themselves. The cognitive process model has not only identified more subprocesses of composing than earlier models; it has also introduced ideas about their continuous intermixing. It has described differences between the composing strategies of expert and apprentice writers and placed control of composing squarely with writers, which, at bottom, justifies continued pedagogical pursuits.

As a definitive paradigm for writing, however, the cognitive process model is premature, due in large part to its neglect of affective processes. One difficulty in reconciling the cognitive and affective constructs has to do with the cultural resistance we have inherited to treating emotion as a respectable phenomenon. Cognitive theorists come by their biases rightly. They represent the whole of our philosophical heritage, a topic addressed more fully in Chapter 4. Of similar concern is the pedagogical rigidity that thrives on such thinking. Recent history has demonstrated that when educators and scholars become alarmed by what they perceive is a relaxed, possibly frivolous nature of disciplinary theory and practice, they reach for the venerable critical thinking model. Once again, written discourse has become synonymous with critical thinking, which, for all intents and purposes, is the cognitive paradigm for writing.

Because tradition has given intellect the advantage, the cognitive position seems more grasping and imperialistic than other theoretical stances. The strict cognitive position appears to proceed from two premises: that emotion is not cognitive and therefore has no role in thought; or, that emotion is an inexorable (if not lawless) part of the cognitive apparatus. The extreme of this last position claims that all mental facts are cognitions. It is then not difficult to accept a cognitive component in every affect, for—as William James once observed—every feeling is undoubtedly a bit of information. Affect may exist, but it is administered by cognitive mechanisms and specifiable by a cognitive reference, leaving very little of itself left. Of course, the extreme subjective point of view would claim that all mental facts have feelings, a position also summarized in Chapter 4.

The truth is no doubt somewhere in between. It is not difficult to imagine certain facts existing without particular feeling tones. They are indeed "cold." It is perhaps more difficult to accept the idea that some emotions can bypass the thinking mind almost entirely. As one would expect, I am inclined to believe that real writing, like real thinking, is *rarely* just plain data. I have tried to show that cognitions are highly vulnerable to affective processing. Feeling is inherent in knowing. Knowing is inherent in feeling. Therefore, it is probably more accurate to say that feelings can know a lot or feelings can know a little.

Although emotional states may be represented in kinesthetic and perceptual structures as well as in cognitive ones, they are no less complicated. Cognitive mediation may well be necessary for interpreting emotions that cannot be reduced to simple positives or negatives. For example, cognitive capacities are clearly necessary (but not sufficient) to explain how shame, fear, or guilt develop (Cicchetti & Hesse, 1983). The evidence of frustration comes not directly from the senses but from the fact that the construct is a useful way of explaining certain behaviors and mental conditions.

But there is a difference between experiencing emotions and processing them cognitively. Piaget may be helpful here. He seems to have alternated between three views of emotion. In his first and most widely accepted view, emotion is defined as a discrete form of energy. (Piaget actually attributed to cognition not the energies themselves but the *interpretation* of those energies.) In his second position, emotions did not themselves become cognitive in the course of developing, but became increasingly embedded in cognitive structures. His last position suggested that emotions developed their own structures or organizations and labels (Cicchetti & Hesse, 1983).[14]

Whichever perspective is emphasized, the integrity of emotion is not lost. Identifying a verbal equivalent for a feeling allows us to classify and communicate it. Once a name is affixed to it, a cognitive process has been used. But it is the naming that is cognitive. The feeling itself remains affective. Beliefs, values, evaluations, and attitudes are generally considered useful cognitive surrogates for emotion (Hidi & Baird, 1986). If attitudes, values, and beliefs were divested of their cognitive properties, emotion would still be left. If we didn't have language, we would still have emotion. But just as no idea is fully formed until it is expressed, I suspect that emotions as we know them do not fully exist until language is found for them. As Langer advanced in 1972 and Berthoff (1981) agrees, it is the word that holds the concept. Words fix something in experience and become its nucleus.

In sum, language is cognition incarnate. But emotion exerts an influence over cognitive processes that cannot be disregarded. Emotions guide attention, perception, and arousal. We act in terms of them. Emotions provide direction, intensity, and tempo of activity. Emotions are an index of meaning and personal relevance. The meaning of events has to do with previous affective experiences. And this affect may well permeate human experience in ways that are not readily subsumed by cognitive structures. So, just what the boundaries of affect and cognition are cannot be answered casually.

NOTES

1. Other major activity in the cognitive psychology of writing is taking place at the Ontario Institute for Studies in Education. Derived principally from work with children, Bereiter and Scardamalia's (1987) knowledge-telling and knowledge-transforming models of writing are not covered here.

2. All citations in this section refer to Hayes and Flower (1980) and Flower and Hayes (1980).

3. All citations in this section refer to Flower et al. (1986).

4. The protocol for one page of a completed essay consisted of five pages of notes and fourteen pages of verbal transcript, which produced 916 language segments (Hayes & Flower, 1980). Another protocol recorded over fifty assessments of ideas, words, rhetorical plans, and composing procedures out of which was produced notes, but only the first sentence of an essay (LeFevre & Dickerson, 1981). Still another protocol showed a twenty-page transcript for a one-hour writing session (Flower & Hayes, 1981a).

5. Cognitivists reason that words give us considerable information because of the way their meaning is recoded and chunked. Words may also give us information because of the way they are retrieved. Either way, both the coding system and the recall process may well operate from subjective experience and so are also a hairbreadth away from emotional phenomena.

6. Although Zajonc contends that the presence of affect is not limited to social perceptions, interpersonal affects are specified in these theories. They would thus be consistent with the social constructionist school of composition theory. However, its leading proponent, Bruffee (1981), shies away from affective concerns.

7. Rather than being "computed from component beliefs" (that is, cognitions) each time they are activated, emotions may be stored under their category names or other organizing units and cue related cognitive material. They may be stored as integral parts of cognitive schemas. Access to affect summaries within other units is presumably more convenient and efficient than tapping into a fragmentary emotion stored with each event (Clark & Isen, 1982; Fiske & Linville, 1980). Other models are known for their network/node and spreading activation systems. In these organizations, emotions are scattered throughout the various schemas and reached through networks. Nodes exist where emotional states and content areas intersect (Gilligan & Bower, 1984). Festinger (1957) defined cognition so broadly as to include the bonding to words of emotional overtones.

8. This is especially important for ambiguous affective signals because they are apt to be interpreted in ways that are congruent with current emotional states (Gilligan & Bower, 1984).

9. See, for example, Elbow's *Embracing Contraries* (1986), Ghiselin's *The Creative Process* (1952), Rothenberg's "Creative Contradictions" (1979), and Taylor and Getzels' *Perspectives in Creativity* (1975).

10. In actuality, cognitive psychologists contend that it is not automatic processes that we are conscious of so much as those heeded, the attentional ones (Ericsson & Simon, 1984; Klatsky, 1980).

11. Recent work suggests that Piaget implied considerably more about the affective aspects of children's development than the literature has traditionally indicated (Cicchetti & Hesse, 1983).

12. Coincidentally, the topic for a writing episode submitted to protocol analysis was motivation and satisfaction with writing. But nothing of its affective processes appears gleaned from the text (Hayes & Flower, 1980).

13. The emotion of interestingness, just now coming under study (Hidi & Baird, 1986), is still defined in terms of increased intellectual activity, little different from the traditional Piagetian view of motivation. To my knowledge, research on interestingness has not yet accounted for differences in its quality, intensity, and origins.

14. Piaget seemed also to alternate between parallelism and epiphenomenalism in describing the relationship between cognitive and affective development. Each position is not without its inconsistencies.

4. *The Psychology of Emotion*

WESTERN THEORIES OF EMOTION

Emotion is as much a stepchild of contemporary psychology as it is of composition studies. With roots trailing back to antiquity, emotions have been associated with weak temperaments and chaotic or bestial behaviors. They have been relegated to the human organs below the neck—the farther down, the more bestial. These ideas had their origin in the early Western dichotomy between the

reasoned	and	impulsive
mature	and	childish
masculine	and	feminine
classical	and	romantic
scientific	and	poetic
modulated	and	impulsive
Apollonian	and	Dionysian

In this scheme, emotion was not specified beyond a vague polarity. Human behavior was believed regulated by impulses to increase what was pleasant and avoid what was not, a simple hedonic formula. Pleasant feelings were counterbalanced by unpleasant ones. People were emotional or they were not. Ideally, however, emotion and reason were not true opposites. To the extent that emotion complemented reason, it served true knowledge. Indeed, pleasure accompanied healthy activities and a life of such activities was synonymous with happiness.

According to Plato, humans were basically rational. But in order to sustain their rationality, they had to control their baser, emotional selves. Plato believed the human soul to be immaterial, superior in nature to the body but hindered by it. His story of the charioteer and the steeds became an object lesson. The charioteer, representing reason, drove two steeds. The white steed, standing for the will, was noble and easily controlled, and the dark one, representing the passions, was rude and unmanageable. It was the dark horse which continually impaired the charioteer's control of the chariot. Thus was created the idea of a tripartite division of the soul that survives today. The rational part of the soul was higher and commanded the psychology of the well-regulated person. Next was the spirited element of the soul, the seat of action and the virtues. In the lowest part resided the concupiscent or acquisitive element, which could only be brought under control by the virtues, principally temperance. The latter two parts of the soul were often combined and called irrational in contrast to the highest part.

Gradually, the core dualism between mental processes and bodily functions was established in Western thought. The higher-order emotions were separated from the tissue and appetitive passions, with the attendant preference for mind or reason over body and emotion. The "irascible soul" was placed in the visceral cavities where it would contaminate reason as little as possible. Emotion was further subdivided into superior and inferior functions. It was with the superior part that humans felt anger. It was with the inferior or appetitive part below the waist that humans craved food, drink, and sex.

In this tradition, the intellect was active and the emotions were passive. Human beings did not consciously initiate emotional experiences. They underwent them. Emotions happened to people. Accordingly, if humans reasoned through their impulses before they acted on them, they would not act on them. However, because humans did display undesirable behaviors, the way to account for them was to consider humans helpless in the face of whatever produced those behaviors. Once emotions were ruled out of conscious control, people could not be held responsible for the acts that resulted—in much the same way that animals couldn't be. And because these behaviors were animal-like, emotions were considered lower in nature and more properly applied to negative than to positive conditions.

Of course, Aristotle elaborated on this connection. His psychological treatise, *De Anima*, enunciated the continuity between animal and plant behavior. Living matter was composed of two related entities, the psyche (or soul) and the body. The psyche was a function of the body and was divided hierarchically by complexity. Nutrition was the simplest activity, belonging to all plants and animals, including humans. Sensory discrimination was the next level of functioning, again belonging to both animals and humans. Still more complex were the appetites or motivations. Following these was locomotion. Acts of reasoning, the highest form of activity, were exclusive to humans. The progression in this psychology was from processes which were wholly involuntary and base, to those which were vaguely or indirectly associated with bodily functions, to those which were completely voluntary and "disembodied" and called the active intellect.

The Western intellectual and ethical tradition that placed the rational soul in the head and linked the base cravings with the noncognitive soul was perpetuated through Cartesian dualism. Descartes' personal conflict between church dogma and the study of natural human phenomena did not prevent him from reaffirming the separation but interaction of a mechanically operated body and its "free," insubstantial soul or mind. By this time, the brain was firmly established as the locus of the mind. Human reasoning (or the soul) became identified with a separate entity that interacted with the body at the one unduplicated part of the brain, the pineal gland. Having located that point, Descartes named six primary passions. And because of their unfavorable contrast to reason, he too considered the emotions externally initiated and relegated them to lower bodily structures.

Such were the themes that ran through descriptions of the passions, as they were called, until the eighteenth century. The eighteenth-century Enlightenment philosopher Immanuel Kant named as irreducible three faculties of the mind: the cognitive, conative, and affective—in other words, thinking, willing, and feeling. Mental feelings or affections could be distinguished from their cognitive or volitional counterparts by their corporeal and animalistic qualities.

The work of nineteenth-century logician Bain (1875) marked a turning point in prescientific psychology. Bain aligned himself with philosophers on the one hand and physiologists on the other. Like the ancient philosophers, he supported the dualism that divided all psychological phenomena into pleasure and pain and physical and mental parts. Like the Enlightenment philosophers, he endorsed the tripartite division of the mind. Thought or intellect and volition or will constituted activity, but were directed by feeling—variously identified as pleasure, pain, emotion, passion, sentiment, or the affections. Like the physiologists, Bain looked upon the human senses as the building blocks of the higher mental functions. And anticipating the defenders of affective primacy, he held that affect preceded volition and influenced it. Like many psychologists to come, Bain believed that emotions continually sabotaged the "natural intellectual associations."

TWENTIETH-CENTURY PSYCHOLOGIES OF EMOTION

A self-conscious psychology founded at the turn of the century introduced another approach to the study of emotion: the analysis of personal experience. Physiologist Wilhelm Wundt (1896/1907) held that the subject matter of psychology was immediate experience that could be studied only through the precise reporting of introspections.[1] Wundt first advanced a unidimensional theory of feeling based on pleasantness or unpleasantness. Then he elaborated on it, cataloguing the data of emotion on three axes: pleasantness/unpleasantness, excitement/calmness, and tension/relaxation. Emotion could also be classified by three related principles: (1) its qualitative characteristics, (2) its intensity, and (3) its form of occurrence (sudden or gradual at onset; persistent or intermittent in duration). With these axes simple feelings could now be compounded, creating any number or combination of emotions—a potent influence on contemporary emotions theory. Like Bain, Wundt believed that feelings preceded acts of recognition and cognition. When a physical process rose above the threshold of consciousness, its affective elements were noticed before anything else. Emotion was thus always a companion to thought, whereas thought was not always a companion to emotion, another issue clearly not laid to rest.

Then the sequence of emotion-related behaviors became interesting. In classical and Darwinian theory the chain in human response was first, sensory stimulation; second, emotion; and third, bodily reaction. Challenging this idea, James (1884) and Lange theorized bodily changes following directly from perception of an existing event. The perception of these bodily changes was the emotion. The order was: we feel sorry because we cry; we feel happy because we smile. The behavior was, in effect, the source of the emotion. Cannon (1927) and Bard then reversed the James-Lange hypothesis. Instead of organic reactions bringing about emotions, Cannon argued that the environment stimulated the nervous system whose impulses then gave rise to emotions.

Until this time it had been common to speak of the emotions as passions. As physiological psychology became scientifically respectable, the word emotion or affect replaced the term passions, and empirical approaches to the study of its nature came into currency. Physiological research led Cannon and Bard to hypothesize emotions and their accompanying energy as organisms preparing for flight or fight—whichever was needed for survival. Because the Cannon-Bard position challenged the peripheral theory of James and Lange, it became known as the Centralist theory of emotion. Because the involuntary part of the autonomic nervous system figured prominently in this view, it also became known as the Emergency theory of emotion.

But at the end of the nineteenth century there was no better advocate of fundamental human emotions than Charles Darwin, who cast them with all other naturally endowed organismic events that spanned the entire phylogenetic range. Darwin's audacious theory of evolution furnished considerable evidence of the universal capacity for emotional response among all living things. Drawing on physiognomic similarities, Darwin enunciated the phylogenetic links between higher and lower animals. Emotion was the first link in the evolution of adaptive functions that differentiated plants from animals and eventually humans from all other organisms. Published in 1894, *The Expression of the Emotions in Man and Animals* formed the cornerstone for an entire tradition of inferring human emotion from facial expression, a line of inquiry still very much alive (Ekman, Friesen, & Ancoli, 1980).

If the adaptive view of the emotions was formulated by Darwin in the late nineteenth century and maintained through instinctivist McDougall early in the twentieth century, the maladaptive perspective gained momentum through the psychoanalytic model. Like the evolutionists, Freud (1915/1925, 1925) maintained that emotions were derived from basic biological units. But rather than rely for evidence on facial expression, Freud relied on introspection, the method introduced by Wundt but ultimately discredited by the profession. Most important, emotions in this psychology were not adaptive as advanced by proponents of evolutionary theory. Although instinctive in origin, emotions were, rather, a form of psychic energy that represented human disorganization. Emotions were regulated by the unconscious, the discharge of which were manifestations of primal conflict. Aggression, frustration, guilt, and anxiety represented tensions produced by these conflicts and motivated individuals to reduce them at all psychological cost. The repression used to suppress these emotions demanded an expenditure of energy. Anxiety, especially studied as a way of explaining emotion as pathological, occurred when those repressive forces weakened (Freud, 1936). Thus, emotions were considered compensatory responses and manifestations of human disorder. Early personality theorists Murphy (1947) and Young (1943) also perpetuated the notion of emotion as a disturbed human condition. Affective response drained the autonomic system, disrupted behavior, and interfered with normal human enterprise.

With the introduction of behaviorism at the beginning of the twentieth century, a polar alternative to the psychoanalytic and phenomenological psychologies emerged. A behavioristic psychology for studying emotion meant a shift from qualitative approaches to empirically verifiable physical and physiological ones. During the same period as Cannon, Watson (1929) provided the first clearly behavioristic theory of emotion. He defined it as an "hereditary pattern-reaction" involving profound changes in the bodily mechanism as a whole, but particularly in the visceral and glandular systems. He believed that emotional stimuli shocked organisms into temporary chaos, thereby keeping alive in professional circles the idea that the emotions were evidence of human disorganization.

As an outgrowth of Watson's atomism and a reaction to the depth psychologies, learning theory dominated mainstream psychology in the

1940s and 1950s. What was believed to be happening in the mind became drive-centered. Drives, not emotions, were now primary motives. Instincts became drives that provided the impulses for action. Emotions also represented bodily upset produced by the collision of those drives. Amsel (1962), Dollard, Doob, Miller, Mowrer, and Sears (1939), Miller (1951), and Mowrer (1960) redefined the affective domain in terms of a new nomenclature: drive induction or reduction, conditioned response, habit formation, partial reinforcement, avoidance learning, extinction effects, and instrumental control of emotion. Fear and anxiety were studied as unconditioned reflexes or unlearned psychological states. Frustration and aggression theory became psychological bywords. Emotions were subjected to new empirical scrutiny. Indeed, the greatest point in common between the behaviorists and learning theorists was that both depended on classical conditioning and observable behavior. And both subjected their data to minute quantification.

Particularizations of earlier nativist thinking also emerged. Taking propositions from Darwin, Cannon (1929/1953) researched the physiological properties of four fundamental and primitive emotional reactions that humans shared with lower animals: hunger, pain, fear, and rage. Although Watson (1929) believed that most emotions were learned, on the basis of his study of Little Albert, he postulated three primary emotions: (x) fear, (y) love, and (z) rage. McDougall (1928) identified as innate or primary the emotions of fear, disgust, wonder, anger, subjection, elation, and tenderness, distinguishing between them and complex emotions like anxiety, hope, and shame. Hate, for example, was a complex emotion that combined anger, fear, and disgust; scorn was a complex emotion that combined anger and disgust. Whereas primary emotions appeared early on the evolutionary tree and were shared in good Darwinian fashion by all organisms, complex emotions were restricted to humans. Human affect could also be distinguished by the increasing specificity of goals and increasing specialization of their corresponding behaviors. Ultimately, McDougall's schema offered a theoretical substrate for the psychoevolutionary model of emotion conceptualized by Plutchik (1962) and outlined later in this chapter.

Despite these disparate systems, psychologists seemed to agree on the following propositions:

1. Emotional phenomena were biologically based
2. Emotional phenomena had physiological and behavioral components
3. The subjective experience of emotion could be captured through introspective techniques
4. Emotions could vary by quality and intensity
5. Some emotions were innate or primary and others were derived or mixed

6. Although some emotions were involuntarily regulated, derivative emotions could come under voluntary control
7. Emotions were largely interfering, but motivated and had adaptive potential

At the same time, the psychology of emotion showed some striking lapses. The psychoanalytic and phenomenological schools were unable to establish scientific rigor from affective data reported strictly from consciousness. For all their quantification, behaviorists and learning theorists failed to provide a complete picture of mental phenomena by neglecting subjective data. Learning theorists acknowledged the force of instinct but rejected psychologies that were inspired by nativism. While learning theorists and psychoanalysts focussed on anxiety, frustration, and aggression, they failed to account for the positive emotions.

In fact, it became increasingly apparent that the debilitating view of emotion was a gross distortion of affective experience. The positive properties of emotions were recognized principally through the efforts of Robert W. Leeper (1948). He said in effect that emotion disorganized some behaviors but organized others—as in unpleasant reactions that were clearly positive and pleasant responses that were clearly negative. Emotion contributed to the integration of personality and was capable of arousing, sustaining, and directing positive activity. Emotion facilitated learning, augmented performance, guided decision making, and influenced thought content and sensory perception. Leeper particularly promoted the role of perception in emotion. Emotions reflected individuals' perception of the more enduring and significant aspects of their experience.

While later theorists softened the debilitating view of the emotions, the legacy remained. Even long-range, adaptive responses were considered preceded by a temporary loss of normally integrated emotion (Young, 1967). And, as I have pointed out, still threaded through contemporary psychology are assumptions about an intellect unaffected by emotion or about emotion as a complex disturbance, an interruption or defect in otherwise lawful, goal-directed mental processes (Ericsson & Simon, 1984; Larson, 1984). It is no wonder that anxiety, apprehension, and blocking immediately come to mind when writing specialists think of emotion.

CONTEMPORARY THEORIES OF EMOTION

Over the last few decades, several trends have occurred in studies of the emotions. First, the once rigidly evolutionary, psychoanalytic, or neurological theories have developed into ambitious attempts at integrating several traditional positions. They may emphasize motivational, behavioral, or adaptive phenomena, but they are set broadly enough to cut across theoretical boundaries. Second, contemporary theories have been realigned according to a fundamental distinction: those postulating differences in emotion by etiology and fundamental quality (Izard, 1971; Plutchik, 1962; Tomkins, 1962, 1963; and other primary emotions theorists); and those theories postulating qualitative differences between emotions based on levels of physiological arousal (Mandler, 1975, 1984; Schachter & Singer, 1962; Schlosberg, 1954).

Third, in response to cognitive science that has held sway across several other psychologies, earlier experiential paradigms have given way to more exacting mentalistic ones. In so doing, a mature cognitive psychology no longer concerns itself simply with linear thought but with a fuller range of human mental events. As a result, the cognitive mediation of emotion is espoused by psychologists of several theoretical persuasions.

In the next sections I first summarize general theories of emotion that emphasize the motivational, behavioral, social, or cognitive properties of emotion. These theories do a competent job of accounting for affective phenomena at the broad paradigmatic level. However, the utility of this level of proposition was limited for the empirical phase of this research. I needed to reify highly abstract theory because of its application to actual writing events. Middle level paradigms support the more hypothetical ones with lower level propositions. These are then tested by empirical manipulations that yield immediate and specific findings (Diesing, 1971). In the second section I present middle-range theories. It was at this level that I was able to gather data on emotion from writers in a reasonable and understandable way. There is overlap in theoretical perspective. Consequently, in some cases placement in a category may appear arbitrary.

Paradigmatic Level

Motivational, Arousal, and Activation Theories. One position assigns to emotion the responsibility of motivating and sustaining activity. Simple arousal involves physiological and/or behavioral changes independent of positive or negative coloring. However, when arousal motivates, sustains, or terminates activity according to a hedonic principle, it becomes emotional. Sharing this theoretical view, Tomkins (1962, 1963) and Izard (1971) divide human processes into systems. Cognition is the primary communication system, motor behavior is the primary action system, and emotion is the primary motivational system. Together they function as part of a central assembly structure which each theorist sets out to explain.

In Tomkins' thinking the construct of arousal alone is inadequate to distinguish between nonspecific amplification from any neural message and that from emotion. Rather, he hypothesized a neurological basis for activating affects and distinguished them by the density of neural firings. Emotions had differential ranges of intensity that changed their quality at certain levels. Emotions were capable of being activated either innately or through learning. Consequently, the same principle governed the "later-learned control of affect" whether it was mediated by perceptual, motoric, or by cognitive processes. What finally distinguished affect from its sensory, motor, and cognitive counterparts, said Tomkins, was its unique capacity to amplify information and make it urgent. Cognition without affect is weak. Affect without cognition is blind.

Izard forwarded a more elaborate system. He maintained that emotion had systemic properties, with expressive (facial), behavioral, and experiential components. Affects and cognitions were interrelated subsystems, but affects could exist in consciousness without being represented cognitively. Also positing a neurochemical source for affects, Izard contended that affective processes could be derived directly from it. However, as affect and cognition came to interact in consciousness, after Wundt's theory a century before, relationships developed into a virtually limitless number of affective-cognitive structures that formed the motivational experiences marking human consciousness and behavior. Moreover, the unique motivational qualities of emotion insured human adaptation and survival. This theory ultimately formed the basis for Izard's work on primary emotions and his Differential Emotions Scale (Izard, Dougherty, Bloxom, & Kotsch, 1974), which guided the development of an emotions scale for writers used in this research.

Behavioral and Evolutionary Theories. Some theorists of the emotions found behavioral orientations appealing because behavior is presumably unequivocal. Like theories based in physiology, behavioral models of emotion look at physical reactions that are organized toward approach and withdrawal. In 1970 Arnold defined emotions as the felt tendency toward anything appraised as good and away from anything appraised as bad. This movement involved real or symbolic objects in the environment to which humans were attracted or by which they were repelled.

One of the more comprehensive treatments of emotion in this context was presented by Plutchik (1962, 1980). Drawing on the work of Darwin and McDougall, Plutchik held that emotion is found in some form at all evolutionary levels. Primary emotions do not necessarily depend for their definition on particular neural structures, body parts like the face, or experiential data. Nor are they necessarily triggered by external stimuli. Human emotions can also occur in the absence of physiological arousal inasmuch as changes in the autonomic system are slow and often unavailable for introspection. Primary emotions are, however, defined in terms of goal-directed behavior.

From eight primary and bipolar emotions, Plutchik fashioned a multidimensional model of emotion. By approximating mixed or derivative emotions of the eight prototypes within a circular structure called a circumplex, his structural model presumably accounted for the entire affective domain. Based on the eight distinctive behaviors, Plutchik's chain reaction of emotions was arranged in this order:

stimulus event → cognitive interpretation or appraisal → subjective reaction or emotion → behavior → function or purpose

This process could occur slowly and in seriation. Or it could occur in such rapid succession that its components appeared simultaneous.

At bottom, Plutchik maintained that emotions prepared people to modify their behavior in order to increase adaptation. Cognitive evaluations were a by-product of thought. Behavioral responses were a by-product of feelings. Both had survival functions.

Social Construction Theory. Followers of this school (Averill, 1980a; Meichenbaum & Butler, 1980) stress the interaction between individuals and the sociocultural system. These theorists believe that emotions are not biologically assumed but socially constituted. In contrast to Darwin's belief in the universality of emotional expression, here emotional responses are relative constructs, varying from culture to culture. Thus, not only is culture a human product, but humans are cultural products.

In these theories emotions are role-driven. Social norms and rules govern individuals' appraisal of situations and the emotional expression that results. Conversely, the meanings that individuals attach to situations help shape larger social interactions. Therefore, because personal meaning systems differ, this perspective implies levels of mental activity that extend beyond both specific cognitions and subjective states to broader social themes and sensibilities.

Chapter 1 noted that social psychology has long been concerned with perceptions, attributions, attitudes, and emotions. In contrast to the pure cognitive perspective, a relatively young subdiscipline grounded in cognitive psychology has made it possible to bring at least part of emotion into mainstream cognitive thinking. Unlike Zajonc (1984) who grants power to emotions beyond social intercourse, cognitive social psychology attempts to clarify a role for interpersonal affect within cognitive borders. Hastorf and Isen (1982) and Fiske (1981) recognize an integrated cognitive, affective, and motivational system. In keeping with Schachter and Singer's seminal work, this group maintains that individuals recognize emotions by the situations in which they occur. Social context and accumulated experience thus provide the appropriate emotional labels— features of which include valence, intensity, and display. However, affect is subsumed under the cognitive organization and is the result of it. Prior cognitive structures organize and cue emotions at any given moment. Chapter 3 elaborated on some of these ideas.

Cognitive Theories. Most favored and certainly most relevant here are theories emphasizing cognitive processes. Represented principally by Lazarus, Averill, and Opton (1970), Lazarus, Kanner, and Folkman (1980), and Mandler (1975, 1984), this school places the higher mental activities squarely at the center of emotions processing. Despite a minority group partial to affective primacy—a position I summarize in the End Notes of this chapter—by and large, contemporary psychology considers affect postcognitive, not the other way around. Emotions are elicited only after information has been processed.

The thinking here is that situations in and of themselves have no meaning until people attach meaning to them. Nor are they intrinsically positive or negative. They are contextual. They are responses that imply objects. Emotions refer backward or forward to events, persons, objects, or ideas. Individuals love someone. They are angry over something. They are excited about something. In order to experience these feelings, people must know something about the object or situation. They must have recognized some of its discriminant features before they can feel something about it. And this is cognizing. The cognitive interpretive system is the primary way humans make meaning of the world. This process intervenes between stimulus events and feelings. It recognizes events, interprets them, and produces evaluations that lead to actions.

The key themes are interpretation and appraisal and call to mind Plutchik's chain reaction. First, we determine meaning. The meaning we impute to our environment refers to the way we construe and/or interpret it. Second, we judge it. Our appraisals are based on these construals or interpretations. Essentially, appraisals are evaluations of incoming stimuli—positive, negative, and then the more subtle feelings. At whatever level of awareness, this appraisal stimulates physiological changes. These are transformed into feeling states which are labeled good, bad, joyful, or frustrating, depending on the situation we believe is causing them. Finally, we react. Cognitive processes shape an emotional response out of a human and contextual interaction.

Lazarus divided appraisal into three forms: primary appraisal, secondary appraisal, and reappraisal. Primary appraisal is the first of many evaluations of a human-environmental transaction in terms of individuals' well-being. Secondary appraisal is the process of evaluating their coping resources and response options, and the process acts on feelings of self-worth and competence. Reappraisal is the feedback process whereby adaptive encounters bring about changes in the primary and secondary appraisals. Individuals never stop evaluating experience. As they react and the environment counterreacts, appraisals are continually altered, though these appraisals are often not conscious (see also Wilson, 1979). Original perceptions and evaluations feed back into all successive emotional states, color the original construals, and set up the conditions for further appraising.

In 1975 Mandler introduced a most elegant cognitive-interpretive paradigm for affective processing that endeavored to unite what might otherwise have been warring models of the emotions. He maintained that both affective experience and affective behavior were the interactive result of autonomic arousal and cognitive interpretation. Drawing first on human physiology, Mandler identified two adaptive functions of autonomic arousal. One function was embodied in the principles of homeostasis and physiological readiness. The other was a signal to the mental organization for attention, alertness, and scanning of the environment.

This second function addressed the cognitive-interpretive system because attention, alertness, and scanning required analysis and interpretation of the environment by the sensory and cognitive apparatus. By definition, this function was associated with positive or negative values and so was linked to emotion. The autonomic nervous system was therefore a signal system that not only entered into the evaluation of situations but also regulated emotional *intensity*. Thus, at the juncture of a specific cognitive state and arousal, a particular subjective state was produced. This ultimately became an evaluative cognition which defined the *quality* of the emotion. In short, valence plus arousal constituted feeling.

Meaning analysis is a core construct for Mandler (1984). He separated affective consciousness into arousal and value and posited cognitive mediation via meaning analysis, a term he preferred to appraisal because it did not invoke notions of badness or goodness. He contended that little in life existed without meaning. Meaning depended on individuals' mental structures and the requisites of the environment at any given moment. But the mental contents resulting from a particular meaning analysis did not necessarily refer to some labeled, stored, or genetically organized emotional system. Nor were meaning analyses and overt behavior necessarily correlated. Meaning analyses could also occur automatically. The results of meaning analyses, however, resided in our consciousness.

Time and again in twentieth-century psychology the concept of consciousness has been all but abandoned as an appropriate subject for experimental study. Mandler, however, gives consciousness special attention. He has contended that the conditions generating arousal led to conscious constructions. The subjective experience of emotion is a conscious construction that combines evaluative and arousal structures into a single construction. Affective consciousness develops first out of the *fundamental* and *general* processes involving arousal and cognition. Since conscious construction proceeds from the abstract to specific situations and evidence, the structures that "construct conscious emotional experiences" are themselves at a fairly high level of generality. One of the functions of an affective consciousness is to make efficient evaluations of the immediate environment and activity within it.

Consciousness is therefore not merely a window into the raw constituents of feeling. Events in consciousness are sensitive and idiomatic indices of the state of persons' mental organization, the output of which is frequently coded by language into culturally determined and socially sanctioned categories. While Mandler also acknowledged prior unconscious activity, the perception of arousal, together with its cognitive interpretation, were registered and integrated into consciousness and created emotional experience. In true cognitive fashion, emotions remain wholly part of the cognitive apparatus. And reminiscent of earlier psychologists, Mandler believes that the organizing functions of affective processes could outweigh their interfering ones.

Middle-Level Propositions

Just as psychologists came to question the wisdom of studying broad concepts of the mind exclusively and found it valuable to analyze component functions, emotion specialists found it meaningful to move from broad paradigms to detailed emotional phenomena. Middle-range propositions do just that. They differentiate affective data and attempt to characterize them fully enough so that they provide a useful empirical frame.

Emotions may be organized by category, dimension, or a combination of both. When they are arranged by category, affective data are treated as unordered and distinct entities. They fit into established groups and their classes are frequently unrelated. Primary emotion schemes fit here. Organizing the data by dimensions means identifying common characteristics or properties of certain categories of emotions. Such systems define the relationship of some emotions to other emotions in the domain, but not necessarily to all others. Systems that combine distinctive categories and dimensions of affective phenomena identify emotions by groups and relationships. By simultaneously differentiating and integrating features and hierarchical principles governing the data, these typologies attempt a comprehensive account of the affective domain.

Categorical Systems. The primary emotion theories of early psychologists gave research on emotion categorical form. Contemporary theorists continue to propose primary as well as secondary or mixed emotions. Tomkins (1962, 1963) distinguished nine primary emotions, which operated by stimulation increment, stimulation maintenance, and stimulation decrement. Two primary emotions were positive: interest/excitement and enjoyment/joy. Surprise/startle was neutral and had a resetting or channel-clearing effect. Five were negative: distress/anguish, disgust/contempt,[2] anger/rage, shame/humiliation, and fear/terror. Izard's (1977) Differential Emotions Theory named ten qualitatively distinct emotions: interest, joy, surprise, distress, fear, anger, disgust, contempt, shyness, and guilt. For instance, anger, disgust, and contempt often occurred in combination and might be called the hostility triad. Other emotions were mixed but often included a dominant or primary emotion. From these combinations, Izard contended, could be generated the entire spectrum of emotional experience, representing its true nature in human life.

Dimensional Systems. Taxonomic approaches enable specialists to organize emotions by properties. This has the obvious advantage of committing no one set of propositions to exact numbers or kinds of emotions. Rather, dimensions lay out categories that presumably exhaust the basic discriminations of the domain. Along the lines of Wundt's dimensions, Schlosberg (1954) postulated pleasantness/unpleasantness, attention/rejection, and activation/quiescence. Affective processes could vary by intensity, similarity, and polarity (Plutchik, 1970). Through an elaborate statistical procedure called the Semantic Differential, Osgood, Suci, and Tannenbaum (1957/1975) arranged 550 concepts including emotions according to three bipolar affective components of meaning. Evaluation refers to the goodness or badness of the term; potency refers to its strength or weakness; and activity refers to the degree to which the term implied activity or passivity. Emotions could be organized by factors: tension/anxiety, depression/dejection, anger/hostility, vigor/activity, fatigue/inertia, and confusion/bewilderment (McNair, Lorr, & Droppleman, 1971/1981). Emotions could vary by approach or withdrawal (Arnold, 1970) or by neurological gradient: Positive and negative emotions were activated by stimulation increase. Negative emotions were stimulated by unrelieved levels of nonoptimal stimulation. Only positive emotions were activated by stimulation decrease (Tomkins, 1981); or by a single index of physiological arousal (Schachter & Singer, 1962).

Categorical and Dimensional Systems. These systems delineate the affective domain by distinguishing among categories hierarchically and organizing them by inter- and intragroup relationships. Work by Plutchik and Davitz fit here.

Plutchik (1962, 1980) provided an amibitious model of the emotions. His psychoevolutionary theory maps primary and mixed emotions and constructs an elaborate hierarchy of dimensions through which all emotions may be described. First, Plutchik named eight primary emotions: acceptance, anger, anticipation, disgust, fear, joy, sadness, and surprise. These "pure" emotions could be conceptualized by polarities: joy was the opposite of sadness, acceptance was the opposite of disgust, and so on. The primary emotions could vary by degree of similarity to one another. They also had intensified forms, reflected in the distinctions, for example, between annoyance and rage and apprehension and terror.

Second, the existence of primary emotions could be inferred from subjective, behavioral, and adaptive evidence, and arranged by several "dimensional languages." The data obtained from self-reports are the subjective data. The data obtained from actions such as hitting and smiling are the behavioral data. And the data reflecting the ability to survive, such as mating, are the functional or adaptive behaviors.

Because Plutchik contended that emotions were most easily recognized by what people do, behavior is integral to his definition. Emotions are patterned bodily reactions of destruction, reproduction, incorporation, orientation, protection, deprivation/reintegration, rejection, or exploration. These adaptations may also be ordered by such polar opposites as destruction versus protection and orientation versus exploration. These functions also had their experiential and adaptive equivalents. The affective process itself could be traced from triggering event to its phylogenetic functions, which Plutchik charted as a chain reaction.

Having classified eight "pure" emotions, Plutchik addressed all other emotions, which in his system are synthesized from second- and third-order dyads and become increasingly complex and difficult to describe the farther they go from the single or dominant feeling. Plutchik found the analogue of this blending process in a color wheel. Just as opposite colors when mixed in equal intensity produce gray, when combinations of emotions opposing one another occur simultaneously and with equal intensity, greater conflict and paralysis result than with combinations of adjacent emotions. The entire conceptual system formed the basis of the Emotions Profile Index (Plutchik & Kellerman, 1974), a scale that measures twelve personality traits based on their affective counterparts.

Davitz (1964, 1969) mounted a far more modest endeavor than Plutchik. He did not specify a number or kind of primary emotions. Nor was his work heavily grounded in theory. Davitz simply set out to clarify the meaning of emotional states by compiling descriptions of them as people used the terms every day. He reasoned that, except in one's self, emotional experience cannot be observed directly but must be studied through linguistic labels. Each label represents a range of experiences about which there is consensus among members of the same language group.

As a first step, Davitz asked individuals what they meant when they said they were happy, sad, angry, and so on. Professional psychologists emphasized physiological responses, behaviors, and situational factors. Lay people usually referred to their subjective experience. As the work developed, the definition of certain emotional terms showed considerable overlap. When these terms were grouped, more precise distinctions could obviously be made between the groups than between emotion terms within the groups. Twelve descriptive categories emerged. The twelve categories fit into four major dimensions of reported emotional experience and three major clusters, thereby creating a matrix or hierarchical system. As a result of interviews and questionnaires, 556 items describing what people meant by common affective labels culminated in a dictionary of fifty state emotions and generated categories as well as a dimensional system for classifying the emotions.

Davitz's taxonomy avoided strong theoretical commitment and was derived from a population more general than the writers under study here. However, it had strong intuitive appeal because it was developed from everyday language and referred to emotions most accessible to consciousness. It delineated emotions with admirable clarity and simplicity. The taxonomy had historical precedence and made use of properties relevant to writing. Thus, at the paradigmatic level, the social and cognitive theories of emotion offered me a credible way of understanding how writing and emotion generally interact. Davitz's system provided a most workable typology for obtaining specific affective information.

END NOTES

The sovereignty of cognition has long been established. With the exception of the adaptive view, emotion has been envisioned as the uncontrolled, animal part of the mind and reason, the crowning human achievement. Nonetheless, periodically revived is the debate as to the independence or primacy of the two constructs (Lazarus, 1984; Zajonc, 1980, 1984). Insofar as this research explores the relative importance of cognition and emotion to writing, it touches on that issue.

Advocates of cognitive primacy insist on the cognitive mediation of affective processing. They can also track the bifurcation of cognition and emotion from the earliest cognitive processes of attending and perceiving. Attention and shifts in attention precede all other cognitive or affective responses. Perception is the second cognitive process, which also occurs before cognition and emotion separate. (To the extent that cognition and affect are indistinguishable at both these points is this idea similar to "proto-knowledge," a construct I mention later.) During the third or interpretative phase, cognition and emotion are cued by abstracted prior knowledge and expectation and begin to split. Once the information is fit into schemas, cognition and affect diverge (Fiske, 1981).

Advocates of affective primacy maintain that simple human preferences lend themselves to immediate evaluation. The emotion systems of the simplest forms of life are approach and avoidance responses. Basic human response is similar—though I again shrink from such dualisms. Emotional reactions of this type are undifferentiated and binary like good or bad, safe or dangerous. Because emotions at this level have close biological roots and survival functions, cognizing is considered unnecessary.

At the other end of the spectrum and derived from phylogenetic and ontogenetic differentiation, human emotions are also infinitely more complex than those necessary for mere physical survival. The parallel evolution of human intellectual and emotional capacities has brought about not simple enlargement but enormous structural differentiation and a profound complexity of *both* the cognitive and affective functions. Langer (1967) has maintained that our higher mental life is the result of such an elaborate emotion-laden system. From this fact is derived the distinctive human capacity for self-consciousness and symbolic manipulation that we identify with full-blown language. It is not without reason that in English the word feeling has connotations so broad as to include simple sensations as well as the most subtle of feelings. Cognitive processing takes place when rich complexes of emotions, qualitatively distinct from the basic binary ones, are virtually unable to reduce to that dichotomy.

Supporters of affective primacy like Broadbent (1977), Wilson (1979), and Zajonc (1980, 1984) contend that even some higher-level emotions can be experienced independently of cognizing. For example, some emotions can be totally impervious to cognition—as in various types of persuasive techniques. Emotional experiences may precede cognitive awareness of them—like anxiety or depression that people feel without knowing precisely what those feelings are about. In other instances, feelings may be so well learned that stimuli seem to by-pass cognitive processing altogether. Time collapses so that sense and feeling occur simultaneously. Last, emotion may run ahead of conscious cognitive processing and increase its efficiency. In other words, the participation of emotion in processing certain types of information may actually guide cognizing.

Still other theorists posit a kind of proto-knowledge. According to this view, a rich body of ineffable information resides within us. Polanyi (1967) called it tacit or personal knowledge, a process by which we become aware of subliminal processes inside our body while perceiving objects outside. Gendlin (1978) postulated a type of inchoate feeling state. He called this more oceanic sensibility a "felt sense." A felt sense is neither a cognition nor an affect but a bodily awareness that has meaning. It is preverbal and preconceptual—body and mind before they split apart. It encompasses everything we know and feel about a given subject at a given time, yet a felt sense by-passes the thinking mind almost entirely.

To be sure, human emotion depends internally on human biology and on prior knowledge and expectation, and externally on everything outside the human body impinging on the internal. This is the cognitivist's way of saying that human mental capacity, or potential, as Neisser (1980) put it, is the combined result of the "plant's" genetic endowment and the medium in which it grows.

I have tried to show that cognitive factors are powerful determiners of linguistic activity. But it is difficult to rule out emotional response that by-passes meaning analysis. Some environmental events are subject to virtually no meaning analysis. So rapid is the emotional response that individuals cannot distinguish the sensory experience from the feeling or the feeling from the thought. The feeling becomes the thought. Cognition and affect are so inextricably interdependent that investigations into written discourse are not served well by priority in either direction.

NOTES

1. Coming from roots similar to Wundt, Husserl (1913/1962) represented phenomenological psychology, the analyzing of consciousness to understand human knowledge, including emotion. This psychology never rose above vague speculation.

2. Tomkins has since given "contempt" separate status.

5. *Operational Framework for the Inquiry*

In Chapters 2, 3, and 4 I drew on the personal documents of accomplished writers, composition studies, theories of linguistic thought, and the psychology of emotions as background for my inquiry. This chapter defines key terms and traces my steps in developing a research program.

DEFINITIONS AND ASSUMPTIONS

Emotion

The term *emotion* refers to a complex inner or mental condition that has physiological and behavioral properties. However, while neurological and bodily involvement is recognized to the extent that writing cannot take place without either, the subjective quality of the inner experience constitutes its central feature, and it is called feeling or emotion. In this research, the terms *emotion* and *feeling* and the more scientific term *affect* are used interchangeably.

The properties of emotion may be inferred from three main categories of data: physiological, behavioral, and experiential. Emotions may be defined physiochemically. While some research links various biochemical patterns with different emotions, other research indicates that some emotions are not biochemically distinctive. Furthermore, some affective expression is independent of measurable physiological change altogether (Kagan, 1984).

Since no clear evidence exists for distinctive physiological reactions accompanying different affective conditions, researchers look to a second form of evidence that is derived from their behavioral qualities (Arnold, 1970; Davitz, 1969; Plutchik, 1962). With these data emotions are construed as action tendencies or related patterns of behavior. They involve widespread bodily changes like breathing, pulse rate, posture and impulses to act in particular ways. Sometimes they accelerate purposive activity. Sometimes they suppress activity. Sometimes they arrest activity completely. Again, it is not necessarily the action itself that constitutes the central emotional experience but the impulse to action.

Today most psychologists agree that emotion is not any one property alone. Rather, it is a complex phenomenon, having experiential qualities and involving heightened perception, bodily changes, and behavior organized toward approach or withdrawal—and all of these in conjunction with given eliciting conditions.

Over the last two decades, the cognitive perspective on emotion has catapulted into prominence. Theorists subscribing to this position see cognitive functions and emotion working together in at least two ways. First, because human language is considered cognitive, such cognitive activity allows people to label their emotions. Second, and more important, cognitive processes have an important interpretive function. Without the cognitive system people would be unable to link the objects of their emotions with the emotions themselves. Thus, it is possible to identify emotional states and distinguish between them only by taking into account all these components.

It is helpful to be aware of several other points. Psychologists agree that emotions are distinguished first and foremost by sign and intensity. Feelings may be pleasant or unpleasant, mild or intense. They may be transient or long-lasting, a property bordering on the difference between trait and state emotions (to be defined later in the chapter). Psychologists also distinguish emotion from phenomena such as hunger, thirst, and pain that share the physiological, behavioral, and subjective aspects of feelings but originate intraorganically and have no direct relation to the environment. Psychologists also distinguish between emotional experience felt and that symbolized or verbalized. We may "have" an emotion but be unaware of it. We may be aware of an emotion but not express it. We may express one emotion while symbolizing another.

Contemporary usage of the term *emotion* also reflects its elusive quality. I have already pointed out that *emotion* may mean excessive arousal at one time, motivation at another, or specific feelings at still another. The term *feeling* can refer to simple sensations as well as high-level emotions. The words "I feel" are often not intended to indicate emotion at all. Rather, they are an acceptable substitute for "I think" or "I believe." We also infer emotion from metaphor, imagery, and idiom. In this research I assume that at least some emotions are conscious, that is, experienced, and reportable. They may be differentially labeled and are amenable to expression. This expression may be registered on the face or skin. It may be registered in bodily activity. And, of course, emotions may be expressed in language.

Trait and State Emotions

Theories of emotion distinguish conceptually and empirically between trait emotions and state emotions. *Trait* emotions are affective characteristics of long standing. They predispose people to particular state emotions but do not have a locus in time. The construct of personality—the relatively permanent organization of people's behavior and responses—explains differences between individuals. In the sense that trait emotions are regularities of emotional response, they are associated with temperament and may be likened to personality characteristics (Spielberger, 1972).

Human emotion is rooted first in our biology. Our genetic heritage spells out our general functioning, intellectual potentials, and emotional predispositions. Searle (1984) has stated that our moment-to-moment mental states only function the way they do at any given instant because they function against a background of capacities, abilities, skills, habits, ways of doing things, and general stances toward the world. My writing this book must be supported not only by my skills and abilities, but also by my attitudes and tendencies in this direction—in a word, by my temperament. This is simply another way of saying that human enterprise depends on what individuals bring to it.

State emotions are characteristic of an individual's affective life at a given moment. They refer to temporary departures from the trait emotions, the more stable affective phenomena. Unlike the trait emotions, state emotions occur within specific points in time and have identifiable beginnings, middles, and ends. They tend to run through short characteristic courses and may vary widely in intensity. The construct of personality helps explain the relationship between trait and state emotions. Individuals can be irritable all the time or enraged once a year. General irritability would represent a personality characteristic as well as a trait emotion. Rage on a specific occasion would represent its state counterpart. General optimism would represent a trait emotion. Joy during a child's birthday would represent its state counterpart.

Emotions-Related Writing

When emotions are linked to writing, some might be negatively related to writing, some presumably empty of emotion, and some positively related to writing. Even simple transcriptive tasks, or what Applebee calls writing without composing (such as addressing invitations, signing checks, or preparing a shopping list)[1] may be charged with pleasure or treated with resignation.

When an emotion and the composing process are negatively related, emotions suppress writing. This results in a decrease, if not nonexistence, of text. It may be that no one emotion by itself is crucial to nonproduction but that particular combinations of feelings are. For example, inspiration may depress writing only when it is accompanied by shame. On the other side, it may not be the existence of certain feelings that is sufficiently salient to inhibit writing so much as the very absence of them. Perhaps particular levels of adventurousness or confusion are needed in order to compose. This study is interested in writing as an outcome. It is therefore concerned with the state emotions that are directly related to writing, that are involved in bringing it about, sustaining it, or carrying it to completion.

This issue brings up another important qualification. This research does not investigate the origins of writing-related emotions: what the reported emotions are a response to, the eliciting event or agent, text, writing process, or competency of the person engaging in it. If, however, a positive relationship is established between certain emotions and writing, a temporal relationship is implied. If certain emotions precede writing, I am suggesting that particular emotions elicit text. If emotions occur at the end of writing, I am suggesting that they are consequences of the process. It is also possible that individuals pass through entirely distinct sets of emotions (those that arise after writing begins and subside before it ends) from the ones that are involved at the beginning or the end of writing—which individuals may or may not be aware of. When writing intervenes between the emotions anticipating it and those following it, while the precise cause of the feelings are not identified, I suspect that those feelings and the writing somehow influence each other. The emotions will intensify, diminish, or stay the same during composing, and those changes will vary lawfully.

METHODS OF STUDYING EMOTIONS AND WRITING

Methods of Research on the Emotions

In an effort to describe the emotions associated with writing, I first turned to research on emotion. Descriptive studies of the emotions have a long and respected history that started with Darwin's observations of facial expression. As the study of emotion came within the purview of the human sciences, psychologists came to rely on similar field work as well as experiential approaches. The data for verbal descriptions of emotions currently come from interviews and checklists (Csikszentmihalyi &

Larson, 1984), repertory grids (Kelly, 1963), surveys and questionnaires (Davitz, 1969; Epstein, 1979), feeling "thermometers," and thought-sampling and thought-listening methods (Eysenck, Arnold, & Meili, 1972; Meichenbaum & Butler, 1980).

Self-reports are commonly used to measure the internal dimensions of emotion. They include retrospective accounts or daily recordings of emotional experiences as they occur. Csikszentmihalyi and Larson reported an experience-sampling method that outfits subjects with self-monitoring equipment and self-report forms and asks them to document representative psychological states at random moments. Several of these procedures take place in natural settings without supervision of the research team (Bower, 1981; Epstein, 1979).

However, because subjective methods of studying emotion have not always squared with scientific tradition, some investigators prefer carefully controlled experiments. A typical research program involves systematically manipulating conditions (for example, movie footage) designed to influence the emotions, often measured physiologically (Lazarus, Spiesman, Mordkoff & Davison, 1962; see also Schachter & Singer, 1962; Yarrow, 1979).

Methods of Writing Research

The study of written *products* has considerable precedence in composition research. A variety of written product data—syntactic features, stylistic factors, grammatical accuracy—has been examined across public school and college student populations as well as nonstudent adults (Applebee, Langer, & Mullis, n.d.; Braddock, Lloyd-Jones, & Schoer, 1963; Ebel, 1969; Godshalk, Swineford, & Coffman, 1966; Meckel, 1963; Sherwin, 1969).

Research on the writing *process* has a considerably shorter history. Descriptive studies use interviews, questionnaires, checklists (Brand, 1980; Emig, 1971; Stallard, 1974), and newer and more sophisticated approaches such as video-time monitored observations (Birnbaum, 1982; Matsuhashi & Cooper, 1978), think-aloud protocols (Berkenkotter, 1981; Flower & Hayes, 1981a; Flower & Hayes et al., 1986), invisible writing and draft sampling methods (Blau, 1983), contact-pencil techniques (Crawshaw & Ottaway, 1977), cued or stimulated recall (Rose, 1984b), and process logs (Faigley, Cherry, Jolliffe, & Skinner, 1985). Some discourse specialists believe that this research is preparadigmatic, a proto-science that is laying the groundwork for more objective verification. However, because composing language is dynamic and predominantly mentalistic, writing specialists such as Bizzell (1979), Connors (1983), Emig (1982), and Lindemann (1986/1987) agree that research in writing may only be amenable to descriptive, field, or case study approaches.

Methods of Studying Emotion and Writing

Despite the abundance of anecdotal information, no previous research exists to guide an inquiry on writing and emotion, except as it disrupts the process. Since the mid-1970s, considerable data have accrued on writing anxiety (Bloom, 1980; Holladay, 1981), writer's block (Rose, 1984b), writing apprehension and its academic correlates (Daly, 1978; Powers, Cook, & Meyer, 1979), writing apprehension and its personality correlates (Daly & Wilson, 1983), reducing writing apprehension (Fox, 1980; M.W. Smith, 1984), and scales measuring writing apprehension or blocking (Daly & Miller, 1975; Rose, 1984b). No research has been carried out on composing using a more balanced spectrum of emotions. No research describes the participation in writing of the positive emotions or the positive aspects of negative emotions. No research compares the emotions involved in required writing and self-initiated writing or the emotional profiles of skilled or unskilled writers.

Ideally, research combining evidence from life observation and laboratory settings should yield the strongest results. Life observation methods would monitor emotional involvement in the writing process and be relatively free of contrivances. Controlled experiments would manipulate relevant variables in laboratory settings. Given the paucity of empirical research, controlled experiments seemed premature. Protocol analysis seemed still more premature. Instead, I gravitated to an open, exploratory inquiry, understanding the obvious trade-off. I would sacrifice fewer contaminants and more powerful inferences for greater contextual validity. This method would enable me to establish some boundaries but, hopefully, would remain sensitive to ordinary experience (Diesing, 1971; Guba, 1978). Because some form of the basic self-report has been used not only in studies of emotion but also in cognitive psychology,[2] I decided on a verbal checklist in order to collect affective data experienced before, at a point during, and after writing. Individuals would check off how they felt as they went about the real-life business of writing—at school, at home, or anywhere else.

A review of measures of writing (Fagan, Cooper, & Jensen, 1975; Fagan, Jensen, & Cooper, 1985) indicated that, except for scales measuring apprehension and blocking, no instrument inventoried a balanced sample of items reflecting the affective domain. My next aim was to locate an emotions scale that was brief and portable, addressed a more complete set of emotions, and could be applied to writing tasks with small modifications in the instructions. Several commercial scales and scales constructed for research purposes were reviewed.[3]

Instruments were rejected when they failed to meet one or more criteria: They did not measure both trait and state emotions; they were preoccupied with negative emotions, ignoring the positive ones, both of which composing would be expected to elicit; they were too long; or they were apt to interfere with or discourage writing or produce their own emotions. Bearing my criteria in mind, I decided that of the instruments reviewed, the Differential Emotions Scale (Izard et al., 1974) had the greatest potential for adaptation to discursive tasks.

DEFINING THE RESEARCH GOALS OPERATIONALLY

So far, I could account for affective phenomena at a broad paradigmatic level. However, the utility of this level of theory was limited. I needed a way of organizing specific emotions data. Psychologists may differ on the fundamental locus of emotional events, but many agree that emotions are most easily recognized by what people do, and so bracket emotion and activity. I reasoned that we experience feelings. If we are rarely without them, we are equally likely to experience them when we write, although those feelings may last for only a moment and vary in clarity and intelligibility. While writing is first and foremost a mental process, it is also an activity (Purves & Purves, 1986; see also Zoellner, 1969).[4] What we observe of ourselves or others when we write is behavior (actual as well as its verbal surrogates), and we can track it over time. Common sense and personal experience tell us that feelings of sadness, inspiration, or boredom are linked by and large to different courses of action. They are also linked when writing. Feeling sad, inspired, or bored at various junctures during composing is apt to reflect different writing events.

This thinking pointed me to the structure of emotional meaning set forth by psychologist Davitz (1964, 1969) that is summarized in Chapter 4. Based on interviews with 300 psychologists and lay persons, Davitz generated a dictionary of emotional meaning. Table 5.1 summarizes the matrix of twelve dimensions of affective meaning within which fifty separate emotions are grouped. Briefly, Davitz distinguished by valence three factors of emotion, one positive and two negative factors—negative: type 1 and negative: type 2. Each factor is composed of four clusters: competence, hedonic tone, activation, and relatedness. Competence refers to the ability of individuals to cope with their environment. Hedonic tone defines emotional experience with respect to individuals' internal adjustment to stimuli. The last two dimensions, activation and relatedness, are behaviorally oriented. Activation refers to the level of activity without implying direction or sign and is composed of clusters *activation, hypoactivation,* and *hyperactivation.* Relatedness is composed of the *moving toward, moving away,* and *moving against* clusters. Relatedness refers to activity with respect to stimuli, thereby emphasizing directionality.

On the basis of his theoretical and empirical research, Davitz computed the cluster scores for the fifty individual emotions. These scores

Table 5.1
A Structural Analysis of Emotional Meaning

Dimensions of Emotional Meaning	Clusters		
	Positive	*Negative: Type 1 (Passive)*	*Negative: Type 2 (Active)*
Competence	Enhancement	Incompetence: Dissatisfaction	Inadequacy
Hedonic Tone	Comfort	Discomfort	Tension
Activation	Activation	Hypoactivation	Hyperactivation
Relatedness	Moving Toward	Moving Away	Moving Against

Source: Davitz, J. (1969). *The language of emotion* (p. 143). New York: Academic Press.

determined the purity of their positive and negative qualities, the extent to which the emotions had adaptive qualities, their level of activity, and the direction of that activity. The scores indicated not only the presence of the twelve clusters in the meaning of the emotion but also the degree to which each cluster was emphasized.

Since emotion is in part an impulse to act, I could hypothesize about composing on the basis of the activation and relatedness dimensions. According to Davitz, the pure positive and negative: type 2 emotions are linked to discernible activity. Emotions like joy and inspiration produce moderate to high activity toward objects and tend to bring people and things together in positive ways. The negative: type 2 emotion such as anger produces high activity, but it moves against objects. One emotion is positive. The other is negative, but both embody high levels of activity. Therefore, emotions like joy, inspiration, and anger that are composed of these properties would be expected to increase the occurrence of writing.

A closer look at Davitz's cluster scores, listed in Appendix A.1 for the emotions used here, provided more specific information. For example, the emotion anger yields a *hyperactivation* score of 53.0, a *moving against* score of 46.0, a *tension* score of 19.0, and an *inadequacy* score of 16.8. These values indicate that the predominant meaning of anger includes more than usual activity directed presumably against the source or object of the anger, although this is conjecture. This would suggest a good deal of writing—perhaps even negative writing, although this too would be conjecture.

The cluster scores for the term *affection* categorize it as a positive emotion. Its meaning embodies the notions of moderate *activity, moving toward* something, *comfort* and *enhancement*. A score of 47.0 makes *moving toward* its most prominent feature. This is followed in descending order by *comfort* with a score of 22.4, *activation* with a score of 15.4, and *enhancement* with a score of 4.0. Undertaken at a modulated tempo, composing from this emotional condition would be marked first by approach impulses and then by fulfilling and relaxed feelings. On the other hand, the 8.0 score for *moving against* behavior associated with anxiety is surrounded by stronger feelings of *inadequacy* and *tension* with respective scores of 20.0 and 18.2 and weaker feelings of *discomfort* and *incompetence: dissatisfaction* with respective scores of 7.2 and 4.2. This indicates that while aggressive behavior is part of what anxiety means, it is not the primary property of its meaning. In fact, anxiety carries with it an abiding sense of inferiority and distress such as is addressed in the apprehension literature.

These are textbook examples. And neat as they seem, they are counterbalanced by some equally paradoxical ones. For instance, Davitz classifies the emotions disgust and frustration as negative: type 2, or the agitative and lashing out emotions. However, according to the scores, disgust can produce two contradictory behaviors—more activity as well as less—with scores of 5.4 and 3.4, respectively. Only one syndrome would be expected to enhance writing. With the hyperactive form of disgust, we would expect writing to occur because activity was high. If writing diminished or ceased altogether, we would be inclined to say that the alternate syndrome was operating. Technically the emotion might not even be registered on a scale if it failed to produce any text.

A similar situation would exist for frustration. Frustration is also associated with behaviors that seem to cancel each other. According to the cluster scores, the *moving against* cluster at 7.2 is most highly associated with frustration. Less important but with almost equal scores are the *hyperactivity* and *hypoactivity* clusters at 4.8 and 4.6, respectively. While the *moving against* score in its pure form should go hand in hand with high activity against something, like disgust, the cluster scores reflect almost equal weight for high as well as low negative activity. This tells us that for about as many occasions as activity is destructively high, it can be destructively low. Thus, at times, frustration may actually enhance writing. At other times it may leave writers at an impasse.

The background readings of professional writers took me further. Just as the cluster scores rendered equivocal some of the negative: type 2 emotions, exactly how the negative: type 1 emotions worked seemed similarly equivocal. Contrary to Davitz's proposition that the inhibitory emotions embodied notions of moving away and less activity that would imply reduced or no writing, the personal documents of authors suggested that depression, in fact, prompted considerable writing. Then there was the matter of baseline personality. I wondered about writers who had a generally placid disposition or a pessimistic outlook on life. Perhaps some state emotions were more influential than others because of their relationship to temperament. In these cases it would be important to look at the trait emotions. I was also uncertain about the more neutral emotional states like interest, excitement, or surprise. Such feelings, which theorist Tomkins called the resetting emotions, were regarded as positive. But evidence led me to suspect that they might depend on context or other emotions to determine their relationship to writing.

Consequently, even the so-called "pure" emotions could easily become complicated. For example, anger is marked by singularly high activity against the environment. However, student writers may be angry at their composition instructors but feel anxious about that anger. The combination of anger and anxiety could neutralize expressive response—producing mediocre writing, reduced writing, or no writing at all. Where hyperactivity implied chaotic or disorganized behavior, writing might also diminish but, perhaps, only temporarily. When relaxation and moving away behaviors provided sufficient psychological distance for organized behaviors to take over, effective writing might indeed occur. The

Yerkes-Dodson law (1908) specifies moderate behavior as optimum. Clearly, there are ranges of emotional experience outside of which happiness paralyzes and depression mobilizes. The degree to which the state emotions mix and meanings appear incompatible may make idiosyncrasy more the rule than the exception—a possibility I had to live with.

DEVELOPING AN EMOTIONS SCALE FOR WRITERS

While Davitz's taxonomy did not track change in affective meaning (which becomes important in this work), it had two advantages: It enabled me to infer writing behavior from behavior in general; and it provided the basis for assigning to factors a priori the emotion items included on Izard's Differential Emotions Scale (which I planned to adapt for use with writing).

The Differential Emotions Scale is a unidimensional instrument consisting of thirty affective items grouped into ten primary emotion clusters (interest, joy, surprise, distress, fear, anger, disgust, contempt, shyness, and guilt).[5] It provides a trait and state form. Izard and his colleagues conceptualized a trait emotion as the frequency with which a feeling is experienced over time, and a state emotion as the intensity with which a feeling is experienced at any given moment.

During 1981-1982 the Differential Emotions Scale was administered to forty-one undergraduate creative writing students, graduate students, and writing faculty at an urban midwestern university. They completed the trait form of the scale that asks respondents to consider their general feelings, except that this time they were asked to describe their feelings about the writing process in general. Participants were also asked questions about the feelings they experienced whenever they wrote: Which emotions were most useful? Which seemed to sustain their writing longest? Their writing habits—frequency, favorite kinds of writing, preferred time of day, particular audiences, and special reasons for writing. They were then given a copy of the state form of the Differential Emotions Scale and asked to complete it before, at a point during, and after their next occasion of writing on their own, adding any emotions they experienced that were not listed on the scale. As a result of these responses, four terms—frustrated, lonely, bored, and inspired—were added to Izard's original items. Several narrative questions also seemed interesting enough to be included in the revised instrument.

In keeping with similar scales, a glossary was to be provided to limit idiosyncratic uses of the emotion terms. The revised list of items was compiled with synonyms drawn from the glossaries and key terms of various published and unpublished instruments[6] or from the 1980 edition of the *American Heritage Dictionary*, if the item was not represented on another scale.

The revised list was sent to a group of consultants composed of emotions and cognitive psychologists and writing specialists. They were asked to comment on the emotion terms and to recommend three synonyms that they felt were most understandable and commonly associated with each term. Responses were tallied and redundancies eliminated. With some items, the final synonyms emerged with an implicit range of intensities (for example: irritated, angry, enraged. A little anger was roughly equivalent to irritated; strong anger was roughly equivalent to enraged.). In other cases, the synonyms did not imply several levels of intensity (for example, timid and bashful).[7]

The taxonomy of the Differential Emotions Scale, which formed part of the original item bank, was updated according to the consultants' responses, and the glossary terms were selected. Accounts from writers suggested that they experience more negative or dissonant than positive emotions when writing. Both Averill (1980b) and Plutchik (1980) note that the English language makes available more negative than positive adjectives. Further, while finer discriminations may be rendered among the negative emotions, the consultants suggested equalizing the number of positively and negatively toned items.[8] The emotions excited and adventurous were added to the scale after they were corroborated in the literature.

This process resulted in a list of twenty single-word adjectives, all of which were represented in major work in the affective domain.[9] The items were provided with a five-step, unidirectional scale which was called the Brand Emotions Scale for Writers (BESW). The twenty BESW items are classified in Table 5.2 according to Davitz's three factors: positive, negative: type 1, and negative: type 2, the last two labels of which reflected a change to negative passive and negative active emotions, respectively.

Consistent with the Differential Emotions Scale, the BESW provides two forms as shown in Figures 5.1 and 5.2. The BESW Trait-When-Writing form is designed to assess the relatively stable affective characteristics or trait emotions that writers bring to the writing task. It is therefore concerned with how people feel in general when they write and asks about frequency of emotions. The BESW State form is designed to assess state emotions or transitory departures from baseline emotions that occur when composing actual pieces. It is therefore concerned with how people feel immediately before, after, and at specific points during particular writing episodes and asks about intensity of emotions at those times. The BESW includes one additional space to which respondents may assign an emotion not listed on the form, and a glossary defining each emotion in nontechnical language (see Appendix A.2). Both trait and state forms of

Table 5.2
BESW Emotion Items Grouped by A Priori Factors

Positive	Negative: Type 1 (Passive)	Negative: Type 2 (Active)
Adventurous	Ashamed	Afraid
Affectionate	Bored	Angry
Excited	Confused	Anxious
Happy	Depressed	Disgusted
Inspired	Lonely	Frustrated
Interested	Shy	
Relieved		
Satisfied		
Surprised		

the scale also include narrative questions. The narrative questions on the Trait-When-Writing form ask about the writing context and feelings when writing in general. The State form seeks this information in conjunction with a particular text.[10]

Because self-report measures like the BESW depend on subjective response, their limitations should be noted. As the argument goes, people are inaccurate when talking about their evaluations, sensations, and emotions (Nisbett & Wilson, 1977). Reporting affective experience is typically subject to the distortions characteristic of any self-report: leveling, sharpening, forgetting, and wishful thinking. Self-reports of emotion are also suspect because people tend to report socially acceptable emotions.[11]

The scales themselves may suggest emotions that respondents are not really feeling, or remind them of emotions that they were feeling but were not sufficiently salient to be reported spontaneously. Pure emotions may be assumed, but mixed emotions are more prevalent in human experience and more difficult to articulate. Furthermore, no matter how sophisticated a feeling state, people can report only those aspects of emotional experience for which they have language, which may not always capture the experience they are trying to describe. Even when feelings are

Figure 5.1
BESW TWW form

```
                                          Name _____
                                          Code No. _____
                                          Date _____ Time _____
```

From the list below, indicate the number that best describes how **Often** you feel that emotion when you <u>WRITE IN GENERAL</u>.

Answers: 5 = Almost Always
          4 = Quite Often
          3 = Moderately Often
          2 = Occasionally
          1 = Never

___ Adventurous	___ Confused	___ Interested
___ Affectionate	___ Depressed	___ Lonely
___ Afraid	___ Disgusted	___ Relieved
___ Angry	___ Excited	___ Satisfied
___ Anxious	___ Frustrated	___ Shy
___ Ashamed	___ Happy	___ Surprised
___ Bored	___ Inspired	___ Other: _____

Please answer the following questions:

1. How often do you write in the following forms?

          4 = Very often
          3 = Moderately often
          2 = Rarely
          1 = Never

___ Letters	___ Articles
___ Diary or Journal Entries	___ Reports
___ Notes	___ Academic Papers
___ Short Stories	___ Memos
___ Poetry	___ Research
	___ Other: _____

2. Are these writings usually: ___ 1. Finished products
                                 ___ 2. Drafts

3. When do you usually write? (check one)

   ___ 1. Mornings   ___ 4. Anytime
   ___ 2. Afternoons   ___ 5. Other special time: _____
   ___ 3. Evenings

Note: The BESW forms were put into booklet form for the convenience of respondents.

4. Where do you usually write? (check one)

    ___ 1. Home
    ___ 2. School
    ___ 3. Work
    ___ 4. Anywhere
    ___ 5. Other special place: _____

5. How often do you usually write? (check one)

    ___ 5. More than once a day
    ___ 4. Once a day
    ___ 3. Less than once a day but more than once a week
    ___ 2. Once a week
    ___ 1. Less than once a week

6. At any one time, for how long do you usually write? (check one)

    ___ 3. More than 2 hours
    ___ 2. 1-2 hours
    ___ 1. Less than 1 hour

7. What primary emotion is usually expressed in these writings? _____
    (If necessary, refer to the emotions listed on the previous page or the glossary.)

8. How strong is this emotion?   ___ 4. Very strong
                                    ___ 3. Strong
                                    ___ 2. Moderate
                                    ___ 1. Slight

9. To whom do you usually write? Someone in my: (check one)

    ___ 1. Personal life   ___ 5. Recreational life
    ___ 2. Family life   ___ 6. Professional life
    ___ 3. School life   ___ 7. Public life
    ___ 4. Social life   ___ 8. Or For me

10. Why do you usually write? _____
    _____

11. Which category best describes the theme of these writings? (check one)

    ___ 1. Personal Life   ___ 5. Recreational Life
    ___ 2. Family Life   ___ 6. Professional Life
    ___ 3. School Life   ___ 7. Public Life
    ___ 4. Social Life   ___ 8. Other: _____

12. Generally, how satisfied are you with these writings? (check one)

    ___ 4. Very Satisfied   ___ 2. Slightly
    ___ 3. Moderately   ___ 1. Not at all

Figure 5.2
BESW S form

```
                                    Ssw_____
                                    Required_____

                                    Name_____
                                    Code No._____
                                    Date_____Time_____
```

Immediately BEFORE you write, indicate the number from the list below that best describes how STRONGLY you feel each emotion NOW. The last space is left open for you to add an emotion that is not listed.

THERE ARE NO WRONG OR RIGHT ANSWERS. TAKE YOUR TIME AND TRY TO BE AS ACCURATE AS POSSIBLE.

Answers: 5 = Very Strongly
          4 = Strongly
          3 = Moderately
          2 = Slightly
          1 = Not at all

_____	Adventurous	_____	Excited
_____	Affectionate	_____	Frustrated
_____	Afraid	_____	Happy
_____	Angry	_____	Inspired
_____	Anxious	_____	Interested
_____	Ashamed	_____	Lonely
_____	Bored	_____	Relieved
_____	Confused	_____	Satisfied
_____	Depressed	_____	Shy
_____	Disgusted	_____	Surprised
		_____	Other: _____

Note: For the second page of the form, *all* instructions are replaced with: At this *VERY MOMENT*, indicate the number from the list below that best describes how *STRONGLY* you feel each emotion *NOW*.

For the last page of the form, *all* instructions are replaced with: Immediately *AFTER* you write, indicate the number from the list below that best describes how *STRONGLY* you feel each emotion *NOW*.

Please attach the writing to the scale and answer the following questions:

1. What form of writing was this?
   - ____ 1. Letter
   - ____ 2. Diary or Journal Entry
   - ____ 3. Notes
   - ____ 4. Short Story
   - ____ 5. Poem
   - ____ 6. Article
   - ____ 7. Other: _____

2. Was it a finished product?
   - ____ 1. Yes
   - ____ 2. No

3. What stage of writing was it in?
   - ____ 1. A first draft
   - ____ 2. A revision of a previous writing

4. When was it written?
   - ____ 1. Morning
   - ____ 2. Afternoon
   - ____ 3. Evening
   - ____ 4. Other special time period _____

5. Where was it written?
   - ____ 1. Home
   - ____ 2. School
   - ____ 3. Work
   - ____ 4. Other: _____

6. How long did the writing take?
   - ____ 3. More than 2 hours
   - ____ 2. 1-2 hours
   - ____ 1. Less than 1 hour

7. What was the primary emotion expressed in it? _____
   (If necessary, refer to the emotions listed on a previous page or the glossary.)

8. How strong was this emotion?
   - ____ 4. Very Strong
   - ____ 3. Strong
   - ____ 2. Moderate
   - ____ 1. Slight

9. Was it written to someone in your (check one):

   - ____ 1. Personal life
   - ____ 2. Family life
   - ____ 3. School life
   - ____ 4. Social life
   - ____ 5. Recreational life
   - ____ 6. Professional life
   - ____ 7. Public life
   - ____ 8. Or For yourself

10. Why did you write it? _____
_____
_____

```
11.   Which category best describes the theme of this writing?    (check one)
            1. Personal life                    5. Recreational life
            2. Family life                      6. Professional life
            3. School life                      7. Public life
            4. Social life                      8. Other: _____

12.   How satisfied are you with this writing?       4. Very satisfied
                                                     3. Moderately
                                                     2. Slightly
                                                     1. Not at all

13.   If you choose not to hand in your writing, please summarize the
      content in the space below:
      _____
      _____
      _____
      _____
```

conscious and reportable, some theorists believe that, at best, affective language reflects experience abstractly and imperfectly. Anomalous responses may also arise because emotion scales generally tap only a limited number of feelings. Last, even if all these constraints could be controlled, recording emotions while experiencing them has been thought to alter the very experience of them.

On the other side, if studying emotional experience means capturing some of the contents of consciousness, researchers have no direct access to such contents, however well trained they may be. According to Ericsson and Simon (1984) and Mischel (1981), investigators may infer emotions, but those inferences are by definition less accurate than reports made by cooperative subjects. Therefore, despite the presumed shortcomings of people as observers of themselves and as users of the language, the experiential aspects of emotion may be investigated most directly by using structured self-reports. Based on the assumption that people are able and willing to characterize their feelings honestly, the self-report thus provides the single most reasonable facsimile of internal events:

It ... can provide data on inner states that cannot be obtained by any other means. If self-report were to be abandoned, it would not be possible to study ... the subjective experience of emotions. It should be considered that, for some purposes, it is not even important that the self-report is veridical, but only that it reveals the construals of people. (Epstein, 1979, p. 51)

The BESW employs a number of techniques to help writers characterize their feelings accurately. Because people tend to be more accurate when their verbal accounts immediately follow the feelings experienced, the State form was designed so that respondents might assess their feeling states at particular points before, during, and after writing. Trait emotion information, to which State form information may be compared, would also stabilize anomalous affective data by serving as a check on reliability. Regarding candor of self-disclosure, people have been found willing to reveal their feelings while performing other tasks provided they are asked specific questions about those feelings (Nowlis, 1965; Ericsson & Simon, 1984). The BESW restricted responses to specific emotions and specific rhetorical information.

END NOTES

The first items on the BESW were originally identified as primary by emotion specialists. This list was modified when early field testing indicated that other state emotions were important to writers. A uniscale was chosen because it seemed easier to complete than a bipolar one and did not assume opposite values (Cattell, 1973). A survey of other scales indicates that, of the twenty BESW items and their glossary synonyms, all are included in major works in the domain. Not only was the total number of items kept within the limits set by other state scales, but because the state emotions are unstable by definition, a more thorough scale might prove less sensitive to affective variation. Two features make the BESW a more appropriate tool for this application than established instruments. First, it inventories a balanced sample of negative and positive emotions. Second, having been developed specifically for writers, it is expected to yield more accurate data about the emotions involved in composing.

For some time, a controversy has politely raged over whether or not there are primary emotions and if so, what they are. Even when research such as this relies on both discrete categories of primary emotions and on an open system of dimensions into which individual items may be slotted, there are several equally legitimate ways of organizing them. Whether taxonomic principles are derived from a single construct or an elaborate hierarchy, it is difficult to envision one best or penultimate organization. It is equally difficult to envision twenty emotions reflecting the richness and complexity of any human act, much less writing. A combination of information from emotions theory and research, writers' testimony, the Differential Emotions Scale, and the consultant panel explains how the emotions chosen for the BESW were derived.

But there was no distinct advantage in waiting for the perfect instrument—or, for that matter, the perfect research design—before starting, any more than educators would wait for the perfect curriculum before teaching. Just because the perfect study cannot be performed does not mean that it should not be approximated. There was also no distinct advantage in waiting for the best set of emotions to come along. The state emotions are enormously varied as our everyday language suggests. The problem of sampling feeling states is a complicated one. There are always more cross sections of affective meaning to cut, finer distinctions to make, and thus more subtle emotions to consider. It would doubtless be worthwhile to generate a more thorough catalog of psychological conditions from which to sample the ones associated with writing. But I proceeded with the items I had, expect to have missed some, and remain prepared to surrender old items for new.

NOTES

1. These tasks are excluded from the inquiry.
2. The status of the verbal report gained new prominence with the publication of Ericsson and Simon's book, *Protocol Analysis: Verbal Reports as Data* (1984). However, the relationship between the verbal report and emotional experience remains unexplored.
3. Single emotion scales: anxiety (Spielberger, 1972; Zuckerman, 1960), depression (Lubin, 1966); scales tapping several emotions: anxiety, depression, and hostility (Zuckerman & Lubin, 1965), anxiety, curiosity, and anger (Spielberger, 1979); mood inventories (McNair et al., 1971/1981; Nowlis, 1965); normed commercial instruments (Gough & Heilbrun, 1980; Plutchik & Kellerman, 1974); scales constructed for research purposes (H. Conte, pers. com., 1982; S. Epstein, pers. com., 1982; Izard et al., 1974); scales with equivalent state and trait formats (Izard et al., 1974; Spielberger, 1979; Zuckerman, 1977); trait and/or state emotion scales keyed to primary emotions (Izard et al., 1974; Plutchik & Kellerman, 1974); forced choice scales (S. Epstein, pers. com., 1982; McNair et al., 1971/1981; Plutchik & Kellerman, 1974); and scales measuring feeling and response tendencies keyed to stimulus situations (S. Epstein, pers. com., 1982; Zuckerman, 1977).
4. Curiously, Purves' recent espousal of writing as activity is linked to emotion through this work. This is actually not surprising given his earlier interest in reader-response theory.
5. Csikszentmihalyi and Larson (1984) report that because emotion items shame, guilt, and anxiety are subject to repression and denial, they are more difficult to assess. They are nonetheless found on many personality or emotion scales. Here, items shame and anxiety were retained from the original item pool.
6. H. Conte (pers. com., 1982); S. Epstein (pers. com., 1982); McNair et al., 1971/1981; Nowlis, 1965; and Plutchik & Kellerman, 1974.
7. At this point, this asymmetry did not seem to be an issue, since the State form of the scale provided a continuum along which emotions could be assessed by intensity when it was not suggested by the language itself.
8. In postulating between three and twelve primary emotions with considerable overlap, theorists also acknowledge a decided imbalance toward the negative emotions. Psychologists also pay most attention to them.

9. Fourteen items appear on the 50-item Davitz checklist (1969), with the remaining six items on the BESW extrapolated from Davitz's data (see Note for Appendix A.1). Nine items are included among Tomkins' (1962, 1963) primary emotions and eight are represented among items on the Differential Emotions Scale (Izard et al., 1974). Ten appear on the 65-item Profile of Mood States (McNair et al., 1971/1981) and eighteen more are similar. Three basic trait emotions and six "emotional components" are found on the Emotions Profile Index (Plutchik & Kellerman, 1974). Seven appear on the 300-item Adjective Check List (Gough & Heilbrun, 1980) and twenty-two more are similar. Fourteen out of 132 emotion items appear on the Multiple Affect Adjective Check List (Zuckerman & Lubin, 1965) and thirty-five more are similar.

10. The long forms of the BESW are shown for interested researchers, although not all questions were analyzed in this research.

11. By the same token, repression, for example, may create false negatives. No emotion is thought to exist because none is reported.

6. *The Research Program*

SCALE DEVELOPMENT STUDIES

Factor analysis of the BESW emotion items, reliability and correlational tests, and a construct validation were carried out during an early part of the research program.

Factor Analysis

Three separate analyses[1] were performed on the emotion items using the Trait-When-Writing form, the State form before writing, and the State form after writing. Responses were collected primarily from students enrolled in college writing classes. Additional samples included English teachers and nonstudent writers. This resulted in a total of 181, 173, and 117 responses to the Trait-When-Writing form, State form before writing, and State form after writing, respectively.

Factor analysis indicated that two factors, labelled positive emotions and negative emotions, explained 44%, 36%, and 42% of the variance in the Trait-When-Writing form, the State form before writing, and the State form after writing, respectively. The orthogonally rotated factor loadings for the three sets of responses are reported in Table 6.1. The first factor, accounting for the most covariance in the State form (both pre- and postwriting) was the negative factor, whereas the positive factor was the first factor in the Trait-When-Writing form.

A criterion level of .30 for a factor loading was used on the 60 items (20 items × 3 forms) to determine the makeup of the two components. Six items were found to be complex (loading .30 or greater on both factors) and one item was singular (loading less than .30 on both components).

Because the scale was designed to compare the emotions of writers at different points during composing, an attempt was made to find identical scales for each of the three forms of the BESW. When the .30 criterion level was used, five items were found to be singular or complex on two of the three scales. Fifteen of the twenty items loaded on the same factor in all three forms. The resulting makeup of the two factors included negative items confusion, depression, disgust, fear, frustration, loneliness, shame, and shyness. The positive items included adventurousness, affection, excitement, inspiration, interest, relief, and surprise.

A more subjective criterion was employed for the five items that did not meet the .30 criterion on all three scales, a criterion that took into account the similarity of factor loadings across the scales. When consistency on two of the three forms was used as a subjective criterion, items boredom and anger were added to the negative component and happiness was added to the positive component. Boredom was a singular item in the postwriting form but was a negative item in the other two forms. Anger was a complex item in the Trait form but was a negative item in the other two scales. Happiness was a complex item in the postwriting form but was loaded positively in the other two forms.

Items satisfaction and anxiety, however, were not easily categorized. Satisfaction has traditionally been theorized as positive and anxiety as negative. Satisfaction was positive on the Trait form but a complex item on both the pre- and postwriting forms. Anxiety was a negative item on the postwriting form but was a complex item on both the prewriting and Trait forms. After these two items had been eliminated, the resulting composition of the two factors included ten negative items: anger, boredom, confusion, depression, disgust, fear, frustration, loneliness, shame, and shyness; and eight positive items: adventurousness, affection, excitement, happiness, inspiration, interest, relief, and surprise.

The finding of two factors in each of the three forms of the BESW was not only inconsistent with Davitz's taxonomy, but was also inconsistent with the factor structures of other emotion scales. A glance back at Chapter 4 indicates that three-factor typologies of emotion dominate the emotions literature. Mehrabian (1980) summarized several studies on intermodality associations, synesthesia, physiological responses to stimuli, and the semantic differential, and determined that the most parsimonious description of emotional meaning were Osgood, Suci, and Tannenbaum's (1957/1975) three dimensions of pleasure, arousal, and dominance.

However, the findings were not incompatible with the position of some psychologists who question whether such scales are actually capable of measuring various dimensions of emotion or whether they reflect the dichotomous "good" versus "bad" (Arnold, 1970; Bradburn, 1969; Polivy, 1980). What is interesting about these findings is that "good" and "bad" feelings were not merely opposite ends of one dimension but different dimensions entirely. Three explanations may account for these results.

TABLE 6.1
Rotated Factor Pattern of the Three Forms of the BESW

	Loadings					
	Trait-When-Writing form[a]		Before Writing[b]		After Writing[c]	
			State form			
Item	Negative	Positive	Negative	Positive	Negative	Positive
Confused	.80	.11	.68	.03	.78	−.10
Disgusted	.69	−.03	.74	−.09	.78	−.10
Frustrated	.61	.12	.76	−.10	.75	−.23
Depressed	.62	−.06	.73	−.07	.75	−.20
Angry	.56	.31	.63	−.03	.75	−.14
Afraid	.59	.05	.55	.18	.56	.01
Lonely	.57	.06	.56	.07	.55	.09
Ashamed	.43	−.21	.54	.06	.59	−.10
Shy	.44	.18	.39	.16	.38	.05
Bored	.52	−.01	.40	−.21	.26	−.20
Interested	.01	.85	−.15	.71	−.09	.74
Excited	.07	.77	−.04	.76	−.14	.67
Inspired	−.01	.70	−.02	.67	−.09	.83
Happy	−.03	.75	−.28	.59	−.31	.72
Adventurous	.16	.59	.03	.58	.06	.64
Relieved	.10	.69	.03	.42	−.08	.36
Affectionate	−.05	.59	.14	.44	.04	.39
Surprised	.15	.56	.22	.40	.13	.40
Anxious	.50	.50	.32	.37	.60	.15
Satisfied	.04	.83	−.32	.36	−.45	.53

[a] $n = 117$
[b] $n = 181$
[c] $n = 173$

Although the factors are given opposite labels, a first possibility is that the items themselves do not have totally opposite meanings. One of the problems with bipolarity is that not all emotions have exact opposites (Cattell, 1973). This interpretation would seem to be the case for such items as affection, shame, and loneliness, which have no polar counterparts in the other factor. However, this explanation would only partially account for such a finding. Several items that did appear to be opposite in meaning were only moderately correlated negatively as in, for example, the average correlation in the three tests between interest and boredom ($r = .31, p < .001$).

A second explanation for the failure to achieve strong negative correlations between the negative and positive factors and items is the presence of a response set of acquiescence. Some subjects may have been inclined to checking off all 1s or 5s (Gough & Heilbrun, 1980). Bentler (1969) has argued that an adjective checklist format such as the BESW predisposes some respondents to an acquiescence bias or the perception of all adjectives as self-descriptive. An acquiescence bias would tend to raise the intercorrelations among items.

Third, the two-factor solution may be explained by the unique nature of the emotions experienced when writing. The format of the BESW is based on Izard's Differential Emotions Scale. As on the Trait form of the Differential Emotions Scale, the instructions accompanying the items ask writers to describe "how *often* you feel that emotion when you *write in general*." As on the State form of the Differential Emotions Scale, writers are asked to describe "how *strongly* you feel each emotion *now*." These instructions allow for experiencing and reporting several emotions when writing—both positive and negative, and both over the long haul and at any given moment. Thus, just because persons report feeling both positive and negative emotions strongly does not mean that they are acquiescing or responding inconsistently. Stronger positive emotions do not necessarily bring along with them weaker negative emotions. Individuals may feel, for example, anger and inspiration simultaneously. Indeed, anger and inspiration are not incompatible. This interpretation may account for results in some of the subsequent studies in which writers experienced increases in positive feelings after writing while not experiencing corresponding decreases in negative feelings.

The failure of items anxiety and satisfaction to load consistently on either the positive or negative component requires further explanation. The item anxiety was found to load on both negative and positive factors on the Trait-When-Writing form and on the State form before writing. However, it loaded only on the negative factor on the State form after writing. This means that respondents tended to mark anxiety the way they marked other positive and negative emotions when writing in general and before specific sessions. But, when they responded immediately after writing, anxiety felt negative. The anxiety associated with writing apparently consists of both positive and negative feelings. When subjects reported their feelings in general when writing or immediately before writing, anxiety may have referred not only to trepidation but also to a neutral or positive tension, or arousal. Perhaps writers anticipated the opportunity for expression and communication, or were reflecting optimism and doing well. However, the anxiety experienced after writing may have referred to the discomfort linked to completing a piece that would be evaluated.

The item, satisfaction, was weighted on the positive factor on the Trait-When-Writing form, but on both positive and negative components on the two State forms. The complex loadings on the State forms were associated with high negative correlations on the negative component. This outcome was unlike those of other positive items that were typically loaded near zero on the negative component. Perhaps satisfaction reflects true bidirectionality, whereas the other items reflect true unidirectionality. Low scores on items such as frustration, confusion, interest, and adventurousness may actually mean a lack of that particular emotion. On the other hand, responses with a low score on the term satisfaction may mean true dissatisfaction. This interpretation would also be consistent with the finding that satisfaction was a positive emotion in the Trait-When-Writing form but was not negatively correlated with the negative component. In this case, when respondents were asked how they felt in general when writing using frequency instead of intensity terms, a low score on the term satisfaction might actually have represented a lack of satisfaction rather than actual dissatisfaction.

Reliabilities

Although some methodologists argue that it is impossible to test the reliability of state emotions because they are in constant flux, whether or not the BESW registered emotional change dependably was tested. The internal consistency (alpha) coefficients for the sets of items defining both factors were calculated for each of the three forms. Six coefficients ranging from .79 to .88 indicated high internal consistency. The coefficient alphas averaged .84 for the negative component and .82 for the positive component. The average coefficient alpha was .85, .82, and .83 for the Trait-When-Writing form, State form before writing, and State form after writing, respectively.

Correlations between Forms

According to a procedure outlined by Gorsuch (1983), the relationship between factors was assessed across the forms of each of the domains. The resulting values between the positive factor scores from each form and between the negative factor scores from each form revealed correlations ranging from .32 to .65 (each $p < .01$).

Construct Validation

An early construct validation of the BESW was performed with two commercial scales, the Multiple Affect Adjective Check List (MAACL) (Zuckerman & Lubin, 1965), which is a trait scale measuring anxiety, depression, and hostility, and the Profile of Mood States (POMS) (McNair, Lorr, & Droppleman 1971/1981), which is a state scale measuring tension, depression, anger, vigor, fatigue, and confusion (Norton, 1985). With correlations significant at the .05 level or better, the procedure found weaker agreement between the MAACL and the Trait-When-Writing form on the negative passive ($r = .43$) and negative active ($r = .40$) emotions than it did between the POMS and its State form counterpart (negative passive correlations ranging between .61 and .84 and negative active correlations ranging between .69 and .87). But, as would be expected, only marginal agreement was found between the MAACL and the Trait-When-Writing form on the positive cluster ($r = .38$). Higher agreement on the positive cluster was found between the POMS and its State form counterpart (r's ranging from .60 to .67). Still higher agreement was found on the negative passive cluster (r's ranging from .61 to .84) and on the negative active cluster (r's ranging from .69 to .87). On the one hand, this confirms that, at any one moment, individuals are better able to evaluate their immediate feelings than their general ones. By the same token, the correlations also challenge the notion that because state emotions are in continual flux, reliabilities should be low.

PRELIMINARY STUDIES

Three small studies were carried out with forty-nine undergraduate student writers and nonstudent writers in order to test some basic properties of the BESW and refine the inquiry in general (Norton, 1985). First, I was interested in the direction and degree of change in the emotion clusters during writing and how they might differ under required or self-sponsored writing conditions. Second, I was interested in the relationship between the emotions *experienced* before or after writing and the *principal emotion* that respondents reported was *expressed* in it.[2]

Twenty-four individuals engaging in self-sponsored writing more than once a week participated in Preliminary Study 1. The respondents ranged in age from 14 to 63 and had been writing on their own for an average of twenty years. They completed the BESW before and after every self-sponsored writing session over a one-week period, producing 129 State forms. Of those sessions, only the sixty-three observations reporting emotions contained in the twenty-item BESW were considered. Preliminary Study 1 thus involved self-sponsored writing but did not restrict its form, content, or affective tone. On a separate occasion the same twenty-four writers were asked to write a letter to someone. Preliminary Study 2, therefore, involved required writing and restricted its form to letters. Preliminary Study 3 also involved required writing but restricted the emotion expressed in it. In this study twenty-five undergraduates ranging in age from 19 to 31 completed the emotions scale in conjunction with required, positively and negatively toned writing. The first week the students wrote about a pleasant experience. One week later they wrote about an unpleasant one.

The results of self-sponsored writing and required writing studies are not exactly comparable, but some generalizations may be made. For both the self-sponsored and required writing conditions, regardless of emotional tone, the emotions that respondents experienced before writing were directly related to those experienced after writing. If the individuals felt positive before writing, they were apt to feel positive after. By the same token, if they felt negative before writing, they could not write about anything, positive or negative, without experiencing some negative feelings after. Particular feelings might diminish or strengthen, but some intensity would still be registered on the scale.

While the results are influenced by a high proportion of positively toned material, they demonstrate two facts. Regardless of sponsorship or form of text, the writers in these samples overwhelmingly favored positive material. Moreover, writing about pleasant things provided the most powerful affective changes. When writers engaged in positively toned self-sponsored writing and required writing, increases in the positive emotions were strong and significant and were accompanied by significant decreases in the negative emotions. The very absence of statistically significant change in either negative emotion cluster during the negatively toned writing indicates that these emotions were stubborn, shifting only slightly according to the research conditions.

Sponsorship of writing was expected to have a differential effect on the emotions. I anticipated some constraints on increases in the positive emotions with writing imposed by an outside agent. I also expected negative impulses to be vented more freely with self-sponsored writing than with required writing and thus diminish more vigorously. Instead, whether the tone of the material was negative active or negative passive, the negative emotions barely budged. In fact, of the affective changes possible with either the negatively toned self-sponsored writing or required writing groups, the positive emotions increased significantly only for the self-sponsored writing with negative active tone. This suggests a special relationship between the positive emotions and the self-sponsored writing based in negative arousal, and would warrant a closer look.

While insufficient numbers of negatively toned material made confidence in trends inappropriate, I call attention to one trend because it provided a beginning sense of affective movement during writing. When the writers chose to write positively, their positive emotions intensified and their negative passive and negative active emotions decreased. Similarly, when the writers were required to write about something pleasant, their positive emotions increased and their negative passive and negative active emotions decreased. When the self-sponsored writing was negatively toned, the negative emotions resisted change, or weakened marginally. But when the writers were required to write about something unpleasant, their positive emotions tended to decrease, their negative passive emotions remained unchanged, but their negative active emotions tended to intensify.

If I can for a moment hypothesize a composite writer, a progression begins to emerge. Regardless of sponsorship or emotional tone of the material, the positive feelings of this composite writer are most amenable to increase, and negative feelings are not quite so amenable to decrease. As this writer moves from self-sponsored to required writing, the negative passive emotions remain unchanged, or weaken, and the negative active emotions tend to remain the same. But when required writing is compounded by writing about something negative active, this hypothetical writer tends to feel more negatively aroused.

An unsurprising pattern occurred when the principal emotion *expressed* in the writing was compared to its corresponding emotion cluster as the writers *experienced* it. Regardless of the initiating agent or tone of the writing, the intensity of the emotion expressed in it preempted the corresponding feeling both before and after writing, except in one instance. When students *chose* to write about a negative active experience, they felt more negatively aroused before writing than they expressed in it—which may be precisely why they chose to write. In all three studies respondents were asked to write either emotionally or personally. On the occasions that they were required to express specific emotional experiences in writing, it is clear that they did what they were told. But their feelings simply did not rise to the intensity of the emotions they were expected to express.

THE RESEARCH PROGRAM

Because there existed no established theory on the emotions of writing, nor was there a body of empirical findings from which hypotheses might be derived directly, my research plan drew on the ideas and methodologies of several fields. In an effort to formulate a starting point, I asked the following questions:

1. Which of the twenty BESW emotions most frequently accompany writing in general?
2. Which of the twenty emotions are experienced most intensely at the beginning of writing?
3. Which dissipate by the end of the process?
4. Which resist change?
5. Which emotions intensify?
6. What is their relationship across several writing sessions?

These questions raised others regarding the writers themselves and the writing tasks:

1. What is the relationship between the writers' twenty emotions and their personal and writing histories: their age, education, profession, baseline emotion or temperament, years of self-sponsored writing, writing skill, level of satisfaction with writing, and composing style?
2. What is the relationship between these emotions and particular rhetorical and situational features: the type of assignment, form of written text, thematic content, stage of production, sponsoring agent, and setting for the writing?

The Studies

In order to pursue the research questions, I chose populations of likely interest to researchers and practitioners and apt to manifest discernible emotional change during composing:

> English and psychology students
> Advanced expository writing students
> Professional writers
> English teachers
> Student poets

All participants were residents of an urban midwestern city. Except for some respondents in the English and psychology student groups, all students were enrolled at the public university.

The studies were not exact replicas of one another. Because I was trying to capture writers in their everyday situations, the conditions varied under which the BESW was administered. Most of the studies were carried out via university courses. The study with the practicing professionals took place in settings determined by the individual writer. Although, as the studies progressed, more variables came under scrutiny, not all data sets were consistently ample and amenable to statistical treatment. Thus, not all the research questions were probed in each study. Each research collaborator also had his or her favorite statistical approach. Some preferred *t*-tests. One used Spearman's rho. Some occasionally recruited percentages. One or two rounded off the probabilities while others retained exact values.

My plan in this chapter is to describe the general method for administering the BESW. Chapters 7 through 11 treat each study separately. A general discussion follows in Chapter 12.

Procedures

Method. The aim of the first contact with respondents was to introduce the study and its purpose. The terms, state and trait emotions, were defined in everyday language as were *self-sponsored* and *required* writing, if they were part of the study. Respondents completed a Demographic Data Sheet (see Appendix A.3) and received the BESW Glossary (see Appendix A.2). A Trait-When-Writing or State form was completed, including a Very Moment page[3] for the observation associated with a pause in writing, if it was part of the research plan.

Instructions for Respondents. The following general instructions were provided:

1. *Immediately before* you begin a writing session, fill out the Before section of the State form.
2. Start your writing.
3. If you are expected to complete a Very Moment (VM) page *on your own*, at a natural pause during the writing session, fill out the VM page of the booklet. Put an asterisk at the point in the writing that you paused. Then continue your writing. If you are in a class, when you are asked to pause during your writing, do the same thing.
4. *Immediately after* you finish writing, fill out the After section and answer the Questions at the back.
5. Be sure to date your form, answer all the questions, and check off Self-sponsored writing (Ssw) or Required writing on the front page.
6. Attach to the State form the original writing or a copy and return it to the researcher or your instructor.

When writers completed the BESW form in a class setting, most situational matters were accounted for. When the BESW—particularly the State form—was completed without supervision, the following instructions were provided:

If you are completing State forms on your own, please follow these guidelines:

Consider a writing session one that takes place at a relatively uninterrupted sitting, where distractions are momentary and some momentum is maintained. The ideal writing session for this study is uninterrupted and neatly bracketed by Before and After sections of the State form. Sadly that does not always occur. Note on your State form situations like telephone calls or family obligations that interrupt the writing session. Interferences or delays that get in the way of writing should be treated the way you would treat them were you not filling out a State form. However, please don't complete the After section of the State form several hours or even several minutes after you finish writing. In other words, treat the Before and After completions of the form as an integral part of your writing session, whatever happens. If an interruption is substantial, when you return to the writing, start where you left off but fill out a new Before form.

Don't overlook the VM page of the State form. However, if filling out the VM page is too intrusive, ignore it. Your writing is more important.

Follow the instructions as closely as possible. Please be accurate and honest. Your responses will be confidential. They will not be available to anyone, including your instructor (if applicable).

The Demographic Data Sheet and narrative questions on the BESW provided additional information about the writers when that information was not already known:

1. Age
2. Educational Status
3. Profession[4]
4. Writing Skill
   Self-rated; Instructor-rated[5]; Professional writers were considered skilled by definition
5. Years of Self-sponsored Writing Experience[6]
6. Age Beginning Self-sponsored Writing
7. Baseline Emotionality or Temperament
8. Level of Satisfaction with Writing
9. Type of Assignment (for example, personal experience, comparison/contrast, research)
10. Form of Writing (for example, prose, poetry)
11. Setting for the Writing: in-class, at home, or elsewhere
12. Sponsorship of the Writing: self or other
13. Composing Style[7]

END NOTES

The BESW attempts to chart the set of emotions most closely associated with writing. It is intended primarily as a research tool. It is not designed for evaluating personality or, for that matter, written text. The BESW is also not normed, but this should not materially invalidate its usefulness.

The factor analysis of the BESW items put in question the three-factor division of the affective domain. It supports the notion that we simplify our environments considerably when we think (Bradburn, 1969). We do not discriminate between negative passive and negative active emotions. Good is good and bad is bad, and that's all there is to it. Nonetheless, given some precedence for selecting affective clusters on a rational rather than factor-analytic basis (Zuckerman & Lubin, 1965), I used Davitz's three factors throughout the empirical phase of the inquiry. First, although people may not consciously distinguish between negative active and negative passive feelings, this does not mean that the two negative clusters are not operating differentially. A general negative factor would obscure those differences. Second, more accurate extrapolations might be made about a global negative cluster than might be interpolated from a global negative cluster. Put another way, sounder inferences might be made about the total negative factor by consolidating findings from the negative passive and negative active clusters than might be made about the negative passive and negative active clusters from a general negative factor.

Despite the assumption that scales of state emotions should not have high retest reliability, the BESW appears to be an instrument of promising internal consistency. The scale development procedures and preliminary studies indicate that the BESW rendered discriminations among the emotions at least as fine as, if not finer, than those made on common sense grounds.

Critics will no doubt contend that the affective domain is far too complex to yield to the simple analyses suggested by a scale as crude as the BESW. They are, of course, right. There should be no misunderstanding here. Neither the scale nor the methodological design is noteworthy for its originality or sophistication. The sample populations for four of the five experiments are standard class size. As bold as my voice may at times sound, I do not make grand claims about the studies. As for the data, readers may argue that the propositions wander and the variety of results bewilders. The consequence of running small studies is that some findings may be artifacts. Because nothing quite like this has been attempted before, I report perhaps more findings than I should to avoid throwing out some important ones. There is a coherence in the results, though perhaps not immediately apparent.

The preliminary studies confirmed that observing affective patterns is feasible. Emotions occur before writing, they change during writing, and those changes may be distinguished. Older adolescents and adults of normal intelligence seem to have no difficulty understanding and following the instructions on successive forms of the BESW, and these groups are capable of describing how they feel when writing in general and in conjunction with writing sessions. Completing the BESW does not appear to interfere with performance on the central writing task. However, the scale seems suited to short, episodic writing that may be completed, though not necessarily polished, at one sitting. It is also amenable for use over several writing sessions.

If anything is to be learned from the preliminary studies it is that, first, the writers gravitated to pleasant material. Second, writing personally is tantamount to writing emotionally. Third, negative points of view such as those expressed in persuasive writing make an impact on their authors, but it may depend on who initiates the writing. Next, emotions experienced when writing and emotions expressed in it may rise and fall similarly. But the emotional quality of the text appears to be a gauge of subjective experience. Last, although—or perhaps because—the positive emotions are most amenable to change, the negative emotions seem the more interesting to watch, particularly the negative active.

NOTES

1. A common factors method of factor extraction was used. In this method the initial communality estimates were set equal to the squared multiple correlation of each item with all other items in the scale (Gorsuch, 1983). Each analysis was followed by a scree test of the eigenvalues (Cattell, 1966) to determine the number of nontrivial factors for each set of data. A scree test was chosen because it is usually a more conservative determinant than the eigenvalue of the number of nontrivial factors greater than or equal to 1.0 criterion. However, both criteria indicated two nontrivial factors for each set of responses. An oblique rotation (PROMAX) of the two nontrivial factors revealed little correlation between them and contributed no additional clarification. Therefore, an orthogonal rotation (VARIMAX) was used.

2. The data on the emotions *experienced* or *felt* were obtained from the values that the students reported for the twenty emotions on the State form. The *principal emotion expressed* was obtained from question 7 of the narrative section.

3. Whether controlled by the instructor or by the writers themselves, the observation at the pause in writing had nothing in common with corresponding observations of other respondents except for the pause itself.

4. These data were collected independently of the Demographic Data Sheet and the BESW.

5. *Instructor-rated* skill was generally evaluated on a three-point scale: Highly skilled student writers received a grade of A (3); those moderately skilled received a grade of B (2); and those less skilled received grades of C or below (1). When a 2-point scale was used, skilled writers received grades of A or B (2), and unskilled students received grades of C or below (1).

6. Self-sponsored writing experience and sponsorship of writing are related constructs but should not be confused. Self-sponsored writing, as well as the age

that respondents began it, refers to the length of time between starting to write on one's own and the present. Sponsorship of writing refers to the sponsor or agent initiating the writing sessions.

7. These data were collected independently of the Demographic Data Sheet and BESW.

7. Study 1: College Writers

Among several ways of classifying written text is to group it by the stimulus that activates it. Because school writing is invariably assigned, often overlooked is a subtle but central component in the writer's psychological environment: the sponsor of the writing. One hypothesis underlying this research is that the emotional correlates of writing initiated on one's own differ from the emotional correlates of writing requested by others. Writing does not happen naturally. Nor is it a human imperative. It is a highly deliberate act. Bosses require it. Instructors assign it. In the absence of an external mandate to write is an internal mandate—but a mandate, nonetheless. This originates with the self.

When we are the stimulus that starts the process and keeps it going, the writing may be called self-sponsored (Emig, 1971). When writing is initiated or requested by others, it may be called required. Self-sponsored writing is often, but not always, independent of academic, job-related, or professional assignment. Common types are casual letters, letters to editors, journal entries, personal notes, poems, and fiction. Self-sponsored writing can also take the form of reviews or freelance and feature articles. Work-related and school writing is largely assigned. Common types of required writing on a job are memos, letters, and reports. Common types of writing in educational settings are essays, papers, and research. School-based writing in which the topic remains self-selected is still considered required in this inquiry. We often think of literary work as self-sponsored in that authors are not in a normal sense *required* by others to create works of art; rather, they are produced for their own sake or for the satisfaction of their authors. Insofar as literary work and other professional writing is part of a regular activity for which writers are paid and from whose proceeds they live, they are considered required here.

Let me qualify these last points. The fact that writing is mandated by others does not suggest that it is without expressive or artistic value. Nor does writing initiated by the self suggest that it is without instrumental value. Both required and self-sponsored writing can be fictional or nonfictional, public or private, planned or spontaneous, or instrumental or expressive. The deciding criteria are who sponsors the writing and under what stimulus conditions the text is being written.

My major interest in this first study was to track the basic movement of emotions during school writing because that's where the formal training in writing takes place. I also wanted to start gathering information about the feelings of individuals who wrote apart from an external mandate. What makes this study important is that it tapped the largest number of writers of all five groups, it tested the changes in individual emotions statistically, and it established baseline information to which other data could be calibrated.

PROCEDURE

Eighty-seven undergraduates participated in this study. Four elective English classes provided seventy writers. Seventeen additional respondents volunteered from an introductory psychology course. The median age was 22, and there were fifty-two females and thirty-five males. Over a two-week period the students completed a Demographic Data Sheet and at least one BESW State form immediately before and after in-class writing assignments that required them to write about their experiences from a particular emotional perspective. Fifty-three of the students completed the BESW during at least three sessions.[1] Twenty-six students also engaged in one extra required writing exercise and at least one out-of-class session of self-sponsored writing.

EFFECTS OF WRITING ON THE STATE EMOTIONS

Like the preliminary studies, this first study indicated that, in general, students' emotions changed significantly when they wrote. Table 7.1 shows that the positive emotions intensified from before to after writing. The negative passive emotions weakened during writing, but the negative active emotions remained unchanged.

While it is scientifically more correct to rely on several items to measure a single emotion, the rank order of individual affects began a pattern that generally repeated itself throughout the five studies. It is presented in Table 7.2. The overall strength of the individual items remained stable across the three writing episodes. However, within the upper and lower limits, the intensities of individual items shifted. Granted, some emotions

Table 7.1
Mean State Emotions and Differences of the College Writers across Three Writing Sessions

Emotion Clusters	Before Writing	After Writing	Difference
Positive	19.74	22.30	2.56***
Adventurous	2.31	2.28	− .03
Affectionate	2.22	2.34	.12
Excited	2.26	2.52	.26**
Happy	2.59	2.83	.24**
Inspired	2.15	2.47	.32***
Interested	2.79	2.87	.08
Relieved	1.59	2.73	1.14***
Satisfied	2.21	2.88	.67***
Surprised	1.60	1.68	.08
Negative Passive	9.63	8.94	− .69**
Ashamed	1.29	1.36	.07
Bored	1.69	1.40	− .29***
Confused	1.91	1.58	− .33***
Depressed	1.69	1.61	− .08*
Lonely	1.66	1.62	− .04
Shy	1.47	1.36	− .11*
Negative Active	9.10	8.82	− .28
Afraid	1.61	1.45	− .16*
Angry	1.63	1.67	.04
Anxious	2.36	2.14	− .22*
Disgusted	1.58	1.64	.06
Frustrated	2.05	1.96	− .09

Note: n = 85 to 87 for each factor and item.
*$p < .05$
**$p < .01$
***$p < .001$

Table 7.2
Rank Order of Means for the Individual Emotions of the College Writers across Three Writing Sessions

	State form		
Before Writing		After Writing	
Interested	2.79	Satisfied	2.88
Happy	2.59	Interested	2.87
Anxious	2.36	Happy	2.83
Adventurous	2.31	Relieved	2.73
Excited	2.26	Excited	2.52
Affectionate	2.22	Inspired	2.47
Satisfied	2.21	Affectionate	2.34
Inspired	2.15	Adventurous	2.28
Frustrated	2.05	Anxious	2.14
Confused	1.91	Frustrated	1.96
Bored	1.69	Surprised	1.68
Depressed	1.69	Angry	1.67
Lonely	1.66	Disgusted	1.64
Angry	1.63	Lonely	1.62
Afraid	1.61	Depressed	1.61
Surprised	1.60	Confused	1.58
Relieved	1.59	Afraid	1.45
Disgusted	1.58	Bored	1.40
Shy	1.47	Ashamed	1.36
Ashamed	1.29	Shy	1.36

Note: The means in all tables presenting rank orders were rounded to the hundredths place. In case of a tie, the items were arranged alphabetically. $n = 87$.

change as a function of change in others. The students, nonetheless, felt significantly more inspired, excited, happy, relieved, and satisfied over the writing sessions. Relief showed greater gains in both rank and value than satisfaction. But it was still preempted by satisfaction, relatively high in rank to begin with. In fact this was the only group in which satisfaction prevailed over the ranks of all other positive emotions after writing, including relief.

Two means of verifying change in the individual emotions were available in this work: Davitz's taxonomy and the factor analysis. Designating emotion in part as a behavior made Davitz's taxonomy well suited for this work. If an emotion had a high cluster score on Davitz's activation dimensions, the emotion would be expected to rank high in relation to the writing activity. If an emotion had a low cluster score on the activation dimensions, the emotion would be expected to rank lower in relation to it.

Davitz's respondents bracketed happiness with the highest levels of enhancing activity and excitement and inspiration with moderate to high levels of enhancing behaviors. The rank orders generally agreed with the cluster scores. In this study, these emotions ranked high, remained high, or intensified during writing. Although activity was part of what relief and satisfaction meant to Davitz's respondents, it was not a primary property of their meaning.[2] The cluster scores identified both satisfaction and relief as fairly static but highly comforting emotions. The results here indicated considerable movement over the writing sessions at the end of which students experienced a heightened sense of closure and release.

Satisfaction and happiness, unequivocally positive in Davitz's scheme and intensifying significantly here, were found to be complex on the factor analysis. This means that writers tended to think of these two positive items the way they thought of negative items at certain points in the writing session. Satisfaction embodied negative components at both pre- and postwriting. Happiness shared this weighting at postwriting. Before writing, some ambivalence is understandable for any population; writers have written nothing yet, and they don't always know how well it will turn out. Given an academic context, ambivalence after writing is even more understandable. The prospect of evaluation could certainly introduce negative coloring into a theoretically "pure" satisfaction and happiness.

Of the negative passive emotions experienced during writing, the items loneliness and depression were only exceeded by shame and shyness at the low end of the intensity distribution. These findings also draw support from Davitz's cluster scores. All four emotions are marked by moving away and high levels of low activity, and so would tend to be only marginally involved in producing text. In contrast, most sensitive to change were the negative passive emotions, confusion and boredom. Although Davitz did not calculate cluster scores for confusion (see Note in Appendix A.1), boredom was marked by high levels of low activity. In this study confusion and boredom ranked virtually the same and were the highest-ranking negative passive emotions experienced before writing. Moreover, not only were they capable of dropping in intensity, but they dropped in rank almost equally. It seems that both boredom and confusion are moderately strong concomitants of writing, at least before school-based tasks.

The negative active emotions were expected to be not only intense but highly volatile. The negative active emotions remained moderately intense as a cluster. However, the students felt significantly less fearful and anxious by the end of writing, regardless of writing sponsor or skill level.

I want to explore these findings in relation to Davitz's cluster scores. Davitz's scores indicate that fear is associated with considerable hyperactivity. This means that when the larger nonwriting public thinks about fear, they think of running, fleeing, hitting, and so on. Although the college writers felt less afraid by the end of the writing sessions, fear was far less involved in the sessions, if rank order and intensity are any indication of emotional priority.

Anxiety, on the other hand, ranked high among the positive, or what I call the "approach" emotions, before writing and dropped in intensity and rank to the middle of the distribution after writing. This time Davitz's scores are called into question for the opposite reason. The cluster scores show anxiety to mean moderate levels of inadequacy first, followed by slightly lower levels of tension, and only then by low levels of moving against activity. The primary emphasis on inadequacy is in keeping with the apprehension research and would be reasonable for student writers. But to be compatible with the data here, Davitz's scores for anxiety should have reflected moderately high activity.

Furthermore, the scores do not square with the factor analysis. Factor analysis indicated that anxiety reflected a positive element when composing in general and before writing. In other words, it found that anxiety was marked along with other negative emotions *only* as a postwriting state. It is again eminently reasonable that the postwriting anxiety is problematic for student writers because writing is seen in terms of grades. And unsuccessful experiences with writing are powerful teachers. But it also demonstrates that anxiety has positive elements for writers that a general population might be less sensitive to.

A look at the negative active emotions of frustration and anger is also valuable. According to Davitz's cluster scores, frustration is marked by extremely high tension. It is also marked by extremely low but equal levels of high and low activity. The college writers felt moderately strong frustration, and this feeling remained stable across the writing sessions. It cannot even be said that their level of frustration came about fortuitously by splitting the difference between the two activity scores; for its intensity never dipped below moderate. On the face of it, then, these findings run counter to Davitz's values. However, if the definition of bodily activity is widened to include internal arousal or agitation, it would raise and remain mute to one inconsistency but solve another. This expanded definition of frustration would not help explain why these writers felt so anxious, despite Davitz's low tension score. But it would help reconcile the students' moderately intense frustration and Davitz's high tension score. Interpreted this way, frustration as tension would be a characteristic shared by both the general public and college writers.

In contrast, anger is characterized by hyperactivity. Anger would thus be expected to hold a high position in the rank orders of these college writers. This was not the case. The students felt low moderate anger which, like frustration, was equally tenacious. This result is open to two interpretations. First, it is possible that students simply did not feel very hostile while writing. At the other end, the consistently intermediate levels of anger *reported* might represent considerably less hostility than what the writers actually *experienced*. On balance, it seems that over the writing sessions students' confusion, boredom, anxiety, and fear diminished more than their shame, anger, frustration, and other negative feelings. The subsequent studies corroborate several of these findings.

WRITING SKILL

Writing skill influenced emotional intensity in this study, but this infuence depended on whether the skill was determined by the instructor or by the individual student. Although information on writing skill was unavailable for the psychology students, the instructor of the English students judged forty-three students as skilled writers and twenty-five as unskilled. Of the same group seven students considered themselves less skilled than their peers, thirty-six responded that they were about as skilled as their peers, and twenty-four responded that they were more skilled than their peers. These two measures of skill showed a strong but imperfect relationship between them ($r = .32$; $p < .05$), suggesting considerable overlap but also a disparity.

Instructor-rated skill was a significant predictor of positive emotional change. When rated unskilled by their instructors, these students felt much less positive than the skilled writers before writing. After writing, the positive emotions of the instructor-rated unskilled writers intensified to the level of their skilled counterparts. Obviously, before writing, unskilled college writers would be apt to feel less adventurous, inspired, and surely less excited about or interested in writing. Afterward, relief and satisfaction intensified to the level of their skilled counterparts which resulted in significantly greater positive feelings.

These increases, however, were not accompanied by corresponding changes in the negative emotions. The unskilled writers did not feel any more negatively aroused or inhibited before writing than the skilled writers. Nor did the instructor rated skilled writers feel any less negative during the writing task than the unskilled writers. It seems that just because writers start feeling good during writing does not necessarily mean that they stop feeling bad.

When the data were analyzed using the self-ratings of writing ability, students perceiving themselves as more skilled than their peers generally showed changes in emotion similar to those considering themselves unskilled or moderately skilled. However, one difference in emotional intensity was found between the self-rated skilled and unskilled writers. Students rating themselves as less skilled experienced stronger negative passive emotions than their skilled counterparts. In other words, writers seeing themselves as skilled as or more skilled than their peers felt less bored, confused, shy, and so on than their unskilled counterparts both before and after writing. Perhaps writers who consider themselves skilled become more immediately engaged in composing and thus experience less withdrawal and intellectual disarray as they move through the process. What this finding may also mean is that a more discriminating picture of emotion results when writing skill is determined by students themselves.

At first glance it thus appears that the negative passive emotions have *more* to do with distinguishing writing competence than was previously believed. In addition, the negative active emotions frustration and anxiety seem to have a good deal to do with writing but *less* to do with distinguishing competence than was previously believed (Daly, 1978; Faigley, Daly, & Witte, 1981). It is true that unskilled writers may experience anxiety or frustration because they are undertaking a task at which they feel inept. But, it is also true that skilled writers may experience apprehension or frustration because they have high standards for themselves. An additional explanation is that feelings of agitation and/or negative arousal may mean different things as student writers move through a writing session. While the bodily state and label remain the same, the cause of such feelings may shift during composing. Postwriting anxiety, for example, could be as much linked to competence and a grade expectation as it could be linked to feelings about the subject matter or sponsor of the writing.

SPONSORSHIP OF WRITING

On the supposition that self-sponsored writing could alter the relationship between writing and the emotions, an analysis compared the emotions of twenty-six student writers involved in an extra required writing session with those emotions experienced during their first self-sponsored writing session. While I expected that, regardless of skill, students would react hostilely when forced to write, identification of the writing sponsor did predict change in intensity in the negative active emotions, but in the opposite direction. When the students moved from required to self-sponsored writing, they reported stronger negative active feelings. Indeed, students may feel more comfortable with the instructor-sponsored topics because student-selected topics run the risk of displeasing their instructors. They may also be better able to express negative arousal or lashing-out impulses when writing on their own than in school settings where evaluation is endemic and docility inspires instructors' favor. The matter of choosing topics in school writing tasks also confounds this interpretation, as does the order of the writing events.[3]

Overall, most of these findings do not seem surprising. Skilled writers would be expected to feel more positive before writing than unskilled writers. Skilled writers would tend to feel less bored or upset by school writing tasks than writers judging themselves as unskilled. Weak writers would tend to feel confused by an assignment and bored while doing it. Feelings of relief traditionally accompany the end of writing. Anxiety, typically related to writer's block and apprehension and counterbalanced by relief, was found to weaken. However, considering anxiety the principal negative emotion involved in writing, or relief the principal positive outcome, is a short-sighted view of what happens affectively when students compose.

NOTES

1. A repeated-measures analysis of variance for each of the three clusters determined that the emotions from the first session were stable across the second and third sessions. This indicates that the actual difference between the pre- and postwriting emotions was unaffected by the sequence of the sessions themselves. The sessions were therefore combined to produce one pre- and one postwriting mean response for each student on each individual emotion item and cluster. Subsequent analyses were based on the combined mean values.

2. The lack of activity indicated by Davitz's scores and these findings are not necessarily incompatible. Davitz's study was not tied to task performance or time-focussed. Rather, respondents performed a kind of psychological arithmetic by averaging emotional meaning over the long haul, much like the trait emotion data collected in Studies 2 to 5.

3. Although the order of the writing sessions may be just as relevant as their sponsors, because the scale was completed in conjunction with regular course work, it was not possible to counterbalance the order of instructor-assigned and student-initiated writing sessions.

8. Study 2: Advanced Expository Writers

Jockeying the wording of assignments with the amount, type, and form of written response can dramatically alter it (Crowhurst & Piche, 1979; Smith, Hull, et al., 1985). In an effort to counteract the unreliable if not unintended discursive results from hastily conceived assignments, the design and sequence of assignment prompts have come under scrutiny. The cornerstone of assignment design is invariably considerations of audience and purpose. Regardless of focus (for example, rhetorical, epistemic, thematic), assignments must also be realistic and relevant and pay attention to mode of development.

Beyond that, a wide range of recommendations for developing and ordering assignments has proliferated, with such discourse specialists as Moffett (1968), Young, Becker, and Pike (1970), and Kinneavy (1971) as theoretical touchstones. Assignments appropriate for large-scale proficiency and placement tests have recently become established in conventional wisdom (Brossell, 1985; Lloyd-Jones, 1977; White, 1985). In addition, issues of writing assignment design and sequence have spilled over into other disciplines (Dittmer, 1986; Raimes, 1980; Tchudi, 1986).

For classrooms, authorities advise specific rhetorical and lexical criteria against which instructors can test their own assignments (Bartholomae, 1983; Larson, 1981; Lindemann, 1987). In some applications, assignments reflect nonacademic subject matter (Macrorie, 1976). In others, case studies or situations become the assignment vehicle (Woodson, 1982), or maneuvering the textual elements like audience, emotional tone, or setting may be pivotal. But by far the most popular typology for developing assignments is rhetorical mode of development, typically narration, description, exposition, analysis (which may be subdivided into classification/partitioning, comparison/contrast, cause/effect, and process analysis), and argumentation.

The theoretical options that guide the design of assignments also provide insights into the ways they may interlock and develop hierarchically from one another (Kiniry & Strenski, 1985; L.Z. Smith, 1984). One of the more familiar student-centered models for sequencing assignments starts by helping students "discover themselves," hence the requisite personal experience papers at the beginning of the semester. The narrative and descriptive strands of personal experience writing are particularly defended as the most natural and, thus, the first rhetorical blocks on which all other written discourse builds (Britton et al., 1975; see also Chapter 3).

Students advance quickly to more complex academic writing. Analysis is introduced. The backbone of exposition, analytic writing assignments exercise critical thinking at the same time as they help writers move toward increasingly abstract and hypothetical matters. Students learn to evaluate, arrive at reasonable conclusions, and predict. Explanatory prose is followed by persuasive writing and argumentation, which exercise students' propositional thinking. The presumed jewel in the crown is research.

Study 2 examined not only a more homogeneous group of student writers but the emotional impact of a sequence of affective personal,[1] rhetorically based, and research writing assignments typically required in college composition courses. Because a longitudinal element is introduced here, the findings provide an especially typical picture of the emotions of classroom writers.

PROCEDURE

Twenty-four students were drawn from a lower-division, required advanced expository writing course. Eighteen students were under 25 years of age. Ten were female and fourteen were male. Over an eight-week summer semester, the group completed a Demographic Data Sheet, three Trait-When-Writing forms, and a State form immediately before and after nine writing sessions. The students were also asked to pause during some sessions to complete a Very Moment or VM page of the BESW. While a general category of assignment was predetermined for all the writing episodes, except for analyzing the word "real," students selected specific content. The writing schedule follows:

Week 1: Trait-When-Writing form: State form about a Confusing experience
Week 2: State form with a Descriptive essay
Week 3: State form with an Analytic essay
Week 4: Trait-When-Writing form: State form about an Adventurous experience
Week 5: State form with an early Draft of a Research paper

Week 6: State form about a Boring experience
Week 7: Trait-When-Writing form: State form with a Comparison/Contrast essay
Week 8: State form with an Explanation of the word "real" or "really":
State form with the Final Research paper

CHANGES IN THE STATE EMOTIONS

Overall, the students reported experiencing their emotions less and less intensely as the semester progressed. Appendix A.4 lists the means and standard deviations of the three emotion clusters within and across the nine writing sessions. The decline was expecially sharp early in the semester. The remaining intensities leveled off but plummeted during the boring experience writing session. By session nine the students felt dramatically less positive than they did during writing session one. A similar gradient was observed for the pre- and postwriting values of the negative passive and negative active clusters. Again, the negative slope was temporarily interrupted during the boring experience essay.

Accompanying these decreases were affective changes within the writing sessions themselves. State emotions are expected to be in continual flux. The data indicated that the students were, in fact, experiencing the composite emotions differently as they moved through the various writing exercises. Table 8.1 indicates uniformly direct and relatively strong changes in the positive emotions. Students' positive feelings intensified by the end of seven of the nine writing sessions, regardless of type of assignment. Except for the emotions reported for the boring experience essay, changes in the negative passive emotions were inverse and moderate. Students experienced weaker retreating and depressive emotions during three of the nine writing sessions. And shifts in the negative active emotions were mixed and weak. Students reported less nervous arousal or striking out impulses, but only after the description.

The rank order of the emotion items across the nine sessions listed in Table 8.2 provided a check on patterns established statistically in Study 1 and is interesting in its own right.[2] Unlike Study 1 in which the overall range of values for the individual emotions remained stable during writing, the values rose here, particularly at the upper level of the distribution and particularly for the positive emotions. Relief rose in rank across the observations, becoming the most intensely experienced emotion after writing. Satisfaction followed. Interest, happiness, and adventurousness maintained high ranks throughout the sessions.

Item for item, the negative passive emotions were either unaffected by the writing or displaced by the positive emotions. The students felt moderately confused and bored before writing; both feelings fell in rank after. Confusion dropped in rank until the pause, while boredom remained

Table 8.1
Mean Differences for the Three Emotion Clusters of the Advanced Expository Writers across Three Trait Observations and Nine Writing Sessions

	Positive		Negative Passive		Negative Active	
	Difference	t	Difference	t	Difference	t
Trait Observations						
Third–First	−5.8	−4.04**	−2.2	−2.14*	−2.1	−2.28*
Second–First	−3.5	−2.87**	−2.0	−2.18*	−1.7	−2.03
Third–Second	−2.3	−2.51*	−0.2	−0.00	−0.4	−0.16
Writing Sessions						
Confused						
After–Before	4.8	2.78*	−0.2	−0.25	0.1	0.09
Description						
After–Before	4.6	2.91**	−1.8	−2.67*	−.2.3	−3.07**
Analysis						
After–Before	3.5	2.82*	−0.1	−0.22	−0.5	−0.69

Adventurous						
After–Before	6.0	4.74**	−1.4	−2.90**	−0.7	−1.36
At a Pause–Before	3.7	3.64**	−1.2	−2.32*	0.3	0.45
After–At a Pause	2.3	2.65*	−0.2	−0.88	−1.0	−1.97
Research Draft						
After–Before	4.0	2.65*	−0.5	−1.27	0.1	0.10
Boring						
After–Before	0.9	0.64	0.5	0.69	−0.1	−0.16
At a Pause–Before	0.2	−0.25	−0.1	−0.25	0.7	1.07
After–At a Pause	1.1	1.41	0.6	0.88	−0.8	−1.97
Comparison/Contrast						
After–Before	2.9	2.37*	−0.7	−2.43*	0.1	0.14
Real						
After–Before	4.6	2.71*	−0.2	−0.84	0.4	0.88
At a Pause–Before	3.8	2.29*	0.0	0.00	0.5	1.24
After–At a Pause	0.8	0.69	−0.2	−0.70	−0.1	−0.26
Research Final						
After–Before	4.4	2.11	−0.3	−0.76	−0.5	−0.98

Note: $n = 16$ to 24.
*$p < .05$
**$p < .01$

Table 8.2
Rank Order of Means for the Individual Emotions of the Advanced Expository Writers across Nine Writing Sessions

	State form				
Before Writing		At a Pause		After Writing	
Interested	2.40	Interested	2.40	Relieved	3.02
Happy	2.25	Adventurous	2.27	Satisfied	2.72
Adventurous	2.20	Inspired	2.17	Interested	2.66
Excited	2.06	Happy	2.15	Happy	2.64
Anxious	2.05	Excited	2.08	Adventurous	2.28
Inspired	2.02	Anxious	2.02	Excited	2.28
Satisfied	1.80	Satisfied	1.98	Inspired	2.26
Confused	1.78	Frustrated	1.77	Affectionate	1.94
Affectionate	1.76	Relieved	1.67	Anxious	1.90
Frustrated	1.68	Bored	1.62	Surprised	1.67
Bored	1.53	Affectionate	1.56	Frustrated	1.63
Afraid	1.53	Surprised	1.48	Confused	1.44
Relieved	1.51	Disgusted	1.37	Angry	1.41
Depressed	1.41	Confused	1.33	Depressed	1.41
Disgusted	1.41	Depressed	1.31	Disgusted	1.40
Angry	1.35	Afraid	1.31	Bored	1.33
Shy	1.33	Lonely	1.25	Lonely	1.33
Surprised	1.31	Angry	1.21	Afraid	1.27
Lonely	1.26	Ashamed	1.13	Ashamed	1.24
Ashamed	1.13	Shy	1.12	Shy	1.19

Note: n = 19.

stable until the pause then dropped in rank after writing. Given the intensity of the instruction and the number of scale administrations, the students might have experienced not less but more hostile impulses. Again, this was not the case. The negative active emotions were equally if not more stubborn than the negative passive ones. Anxiety, ranking moderately high before writing, declined more in rank than in intensity. Anger, ranking in the bottom quarter of the distribution before writing, rose slightly. Frustration and disgust remained stable in the middle of the distribution.

Nonetheless, the four top-ranking emotions before writing were positive. After writing the number of positive items doubled as the highest ranking items. To be sure, this phenomenon occurs because, as individual items composing the positive cluster move up in rank, they displace items composing the negative clusters. With only one temporary but profound exception in the boring episode, the classroom experiences of these students were apparently anesthesizing and positive.

Positive feelings at the end of writing seem to refer to a complex of pleasant emotions of which relief and satisfaction are a central part. Relief, of course, does not necessarily refer to release from a negative situation. First, a certain amount of natural, if not neutral, physiological tension arises when we mobilize for any task. Relief may thus be linked to the sense of completion or closure when that task is done, regardless of the quality of performance. In fact, students' satisfaction with their text was directly related to pleasant feelings after writing, regardless of the nature of the assignment or students' skill in completing it. Moreover, except for the Research sessions, satisfaction was inversely related to the negative active state emotions experienced after writing. Consequently, on the face of it, good writing seems linked to good feelings and weak writing linked to bad, providing the evaluations are made by able judges.

But there was a crucial imbalance. At the outset of the semester, students' perception of their writing skill approximated the normal curve. Six students rated themselves more skilled than their peers, thirteen rated themselves as skilled as their peers, and five rated themselves less skilled. By the end of the semester the instructor rated only six students as skilled, making the correlation between the two skill ratings at best marginal ($r = .38$, $p < .08$) and the group freighted with unskilled writers.

Clearly, pleasant feelings and quality writing are not synonymous. A high number of unskilled writers participated in this study; by definition they do not do satisfactory work however easily satisfied with it they may be (Hayes and Flower, 1980). Weak writers would be expected to exercise poor judgment about what constitutes their best writing. Perhaps they reason that, because they work hardest at it in composition classes, their writing ought to be good, regardless of its actual merit.

CHANGES IN THE TRAIT EMOTIONS

Baseline temperament or trait emotions were tracked at three points during the semester. Much like the state emotions, the trait emotions decreased steadily over the semester. The largest differences occurred between Trait Observations 1 and 3, and the differences were of course negative. But how amenable to change the emotion clusters themselves were, formed a familiar pattern. The students felt positive less frequently on all comparisons of those emotions. They felt negative passive less frequently on 66% of the comparisons of those emotions. But they felt negative active less frequently on only 33% of the comparisons of those emotions, again signaling the recalcitrance of the negative emotions.

Like the state emotions, the positions of the trait emotions were generally stable within the rank orders and are shown in Table 8.3. The positive emotions ranked at the high end of the spectrum. The negative active emotions held ranks in the middle of the distribution, and the negative passive emotions held ranks at the low end. But the ranks of individual items within the three clusters appeared more chaotic than would be expected for trait emotions. The traits adventurousness, anxiety, disgust, satisfaction, and surprise produced the greatest fluctuations in rank. Anxiety rose in rank by Trait Observation 2 before dropping back in rank by Trait Observation 3, creating a bell-shaped curve. Satisfaction followed an equivalent but opposite pattern. Other positive items were more stable. Negative passive item, boredom, followed the movement of satisfaction at a lower rank. Feelings of inspiration, while declining in frequency, rose slightly in rank. By the third trait observation, students experienced boredom, confusion, and anger no more often than earlier in the semester. But they also experienced inspiration, relief, and satisfaction less often. All in all, these students seemed to feel no better about writing and more numb than they did at the beginning of the course.

Trait emotions are theoretically stable. Their mutability here, however, suggests otherwise. One explanation is that writing-linked trait emotions change as exposure to writing increases. Another perhaps more plausible explanation is that a practice effect was operating on students' responses that generalized to both the state and trait conditions. A related and equally reasonable explanation for the persistently eroding emotions is attitudinal.

This study was conducted during a summer session in which sixteen weeks of regular semester work were condensed into eight. The pace and the quantity of writing could easily induce exhaustion. The entire group consisted of six skilled writers and eighteen unskilled writers. Clearly, unskilled writers would be expected to feel negative about a required writing course. But even strong writers can suffer enervation, though perhaps for different reasons. Although no emotion item on the BESW

Table 8.3
Rank Order of Means for the Individual Emotions of the Advanced Expository Writers across Three Trait Observations

Trait Emotions					
1		2		3	
Interested	3.50	Interested	3.19	Interested	2.84
Satisfied	3.38	Adventurous	2.90	Inspired	2.63
Excited	3.08	Inspired	2.76	Adventurous	2.47
Inspired	3.04	Excited	2.71	Happy	2.47
Happy	3.00	Anxious	2.52	Satisfied	2.44
Frustrated	2.96	Frustrated	2.52	Frustrated	2.42
Adventurous	2.88	Happy	2.52	Excited	2.32
Relieved	2.71	Satisfied	2.48	Anxious	2.22
Anxious	2.46	Confused	2.33	Confused	2.21
Affectionate	2.42	Relieved	2.33	Disgusted	2.00
Confused	2.25	Affectionate	2.14	Relieved	2.00
Afraid	2.25	Angry	2.10	Affectionate	1.95
Angry	2.25	Surprised	1.86	Angry	1.95
Bored	2.13	Afraid	1.76	Bored	1.95
Disgusted	2.13	Depressed	1.76	Afraid	1.58
Depressed	2.08	Disgusted	1.67	Depressed	1.54
Surprised	2.04	Bored	1.62	Surprised	1.47
Lonely	2.00	Shy	1.48	Ashamed	1.42
Shy	1.83	Lonely	1.43	Shy	1.42
Ashamed	1.50	Ashamed	1.38	Lonely	1.26

Note: n = 24 to 19.

specifically represented fatigue and burnout, what was found seemed to be a combination of the last two explanations: a desensitization of students to their feelings from repeated exposure to the BESW (much like any relatively routine activity) and school-induced burnout. Within each writing session and item for item the students felt better as they completed each writing task—less negative and more positive—than they did about writing as a whole. Boredom is considered the prototypical emotion of underarousal. But across the semester they did not even feel increasingly bored.[3] They simply felt less.

AFFECTIVELY TONED PERSONAL ESSAYS, TRADITIONAL EXPOSITION, AND RESEARCH WRITING

The nine writing assignments were grouped into three categories: Those based on personal experience and limited by emotional tone—confusion, adventurousness, and boredom; those based on traditional rhetorical modes of development—description, analysis, comparison/contrast, and explanation of the words "real" and "really"; and those requiring research—research draft and final research paper.[4]

Of the nine assignments, students experienced the greatest increase in their positive feelings when writing the affectively toned personal essays, specifically about adventurous and confused experiences. They felt less negative passive only when engaged in the adventurous assignment, and experienced the least change in both negative passive and negative active feelings on the boring experience essay. Moreover, the boring experience exercise was the only assignment for which there was no statistically significant increase in positive feelings and for which there was a numerical increase in negative passive ones.

While the results from the boring experience essay provide a reason to doubt the impact of affective personal assignments on positive feelings, regardless of the position of the assignment in the semester, the positive emotions intensified. Irrespective of its middle position in the assignment sequence, writing about an adventurous experience produced the greatest positive increase. Even the confused assignment produced more intense positive feelings, although its position as first in the sequence confounds this finding.

Of the four standard rhetorical assignments, the description stood apart from the others in one important way. It was the only writing episode in which the students experienced changes in all three emotion clusters. The description tied with the "real" assignment in producing the third highest increase in positive emotion. But the description ranked highest in producing weaker negative passive and negative active emotions. The comparison/contrast essay was the only other traditional rhetorical exercise in which the students felt significantly less negative passive.

Both research assignments ranked in the middle of the distribution in magnitude of increased positive emotions. Interestingly, students' feelings improved more after working on the research draft than after completing the final product. Perhaps this finding reflects the phase in the writing process during which revision is heaviest and so would likely produce substantial relief for writers once it was over.[5] There was also some indication that the group felt less negative passive and negative active after completing the final research paper than after the research draft, but neither pattern was confirmed statistically.

Despite the flattening effect of the emotions across the sessions, I believed the affectively toned assignments would elicit emotional disarray. There was little evidence for this. In terms of net change, only in the sense that before writing several emotions connected to the affective personal material ranked higher (or were felt more intensely) than the corresponding emotions in the other categories did greater affective fluctuations occur when emotions were embedded in the instructions.

The rank order distributions provided in Appendixes A.5, A.6, and A.7 indicate that shyness, confusion, fear, and anxiety ranked higher before students wrote the affective experiential papers than before they wrote in the other two assignment categories. Of these, shyness seems the least disorganizing. This would leave confusion, fear, and anxiety. Confusion and fear remained more intense after the emotionally toned essays. However, all three items dropped in rank to their counterparts in the traditional essays.

Other feelings typically linked to emotional chaos, like frustration and anger, were virtual equivalents in the research and traditional assignments both before and after writing. Frustration shared ranks with its counterparts in the affective personal essays, while anger ranked substantially lower on those essays.

Of all three categories, the positive emotions associated with the traditional exposition and research intensified most at the very highest levels of the distribution. Satisfaction rose more in rank and intensity after these two assignment types. I thought students would enjoy the greatest relief after undertaking the research exercises, perhaps the most arduous of the nine assignments. Relief did move up to rank 1 after all three types of assignments, but the students felt the greatest relief after the traditional exposition. While other high ranking positive emotions intensified more during the affectively toned essays, students felt them no more intensely after writing the affective experiential papers than they did after writing the traditional papers.

At the lower end of the distribution, students felt somewhat more negative passive after writing the affective experiential essays. However, there was little difference among the three assignment categories in their corresponding ranks. The distributions, in fact, indicate a narrower range of emotional intensities during the affective personal essays than during the traditional rhetorical exercises, especially after writing. The students experienced no less anxiety, fear, shyness, confusion, or boredom when writing personal, emotionally toned papers but also no greater interest, excitement, inspiration, relief, or satisfaction. All in all, at least for this group, writing from a personal affective perspective seemed neither therapeutic nor challenging.

TYPE OF ASSIGNMENT AND WRITING SKILL

Other results showed that the instructor-rated skilled writers experienced stronger negative emotions for all assignments but the research. The instructor-rated skilled writers reported stronger negative passive emotions on 33% of the affective experiential observations, while their self-rated counterparts reported stronger negative passive emotions on only 17% of them. These same writers reported more intense negative passive emotions on 50% of the traditional expository observations, while their self-rated counterparts reported more intense negative passive feelings on only 12% of them. In addition, the instructor-rated skilled writers reported stronger negative active emotions on 38% of the traditional exposition, while the self-rated skilled students experienced stronger negative active emotions on only 25%.

Only on the research assignments were the percentages reversed. The self-rated skilled writers reported stronger negative passive emotions on 75% of the observations, whereas their instructor-rated counterparts reported stronger negative passive emotions on 50% of them. What this suggests is that when the locus of evaluation lies outside of the students themselves—as in their instructors—skilled student writers tend to be negatively disposed to the very assignments that emanate from them.

Lynn. Lynn is a good example. She was considered a skilled writer by her instructor but regarded herself as only average, rarely writing apart from notes or occasional letters. She saw herself as moderately emotional. In fact, her negative feelings surfaced repeatedly throughout the writing sessions.

Before the first writing exercise on a confusing experience, Lynn experienced little confusion but stronger anger and still stronger interest. By the end of the session, she felt more confused and still angrier. At the same time, she experienced her strongest sense of release after that assignment—as well as after the research. For Lynn, writing research papers was accompanied by unusually severe hostility and disgust. But, again, extremely powerful interest "saved" her emotionally. By the time she wrote the comparison/contrast paper, her confusion and anger had disappeared after writing. But her interest did not, as her piece on Geraldine Ferraro attests:

Geraldine Ferraro and the Democratic party have made history. Mrs. Ferraro's nomination to run on the Democratic ticket as its vice presidential candidate ends forever the cultural notion that a woman's place has a limitation. The final step of women's suffrage has been taken but not without some skepticism.

There are those who say that Ferraro is merely a symbolic gesture meant to placate the feminist movement. However, symbols, when they are well qualified, can be considered pioneers in breaking barriers that have been placed before the disenfranchised. Jackie Robinson, the first black man to play major league baseball, was a token who led the way for blacks as Mrs. Ferraro will lead the way for women.

It is true that one woman is not going to change the nature of the government, but the selection of a woman as the vice presidential nominee will stimulate other women to become involved in all levels of government. When more women are mayors, city council members, state representatives and senators, or members of the United States Congress, then women, not one woman, can influence the nature of government.

Mrs. Ferraro has been criticized while being compared to Vice President George Bush. On the one hand, Bush, a former ambassador to the United Nations, Central Intelligence Agency director, and envoy to China, has an extensive background in foreign policy. On the other hand, Ferraro has dealt almost exclusively with domestic issues. Despite this, she should not be considered a liability to the Democratic ticket because George Bush is the Republican exception rather than the rule. In 1964 when William Miller ran with Barry Goldwater and again in 1968 when Spiro Agnew ran with Richard Nixon, the Republican party chose vice presidential candidates who had no more foreign policy expertise than Mrs. Ferraro has now. . . .

Some feel that a risk is being taken by nominating a woman with so little national level campaigning experience. They are afraid that any slip she makes or any problems that occur will be magnified by the press. On the contrary, any slight risk is overshadowed by the immense gain in publicity that Mrs. Ferraro's candidacy brings to the Democratic ticket.

In terms of strong writing perhaps the most illuminating emotional profiles were obtained from the assignment on "real." The prompt read:

We all make certain distinctions when we use the word real or really: for example, housework versus a "real" job; school versus the "real" world; the person everyone knows and the "real" me; what I really mean; this is really great.

When people use quoted words this way, they seem to be saying, I'm using this word in a special way. When people use really for emphasis, they may be saying, I'm at a loss for a better word but you know what I mean.

What in fact do we mean by the term real? Explain the distinctions we try to make when we use "real" or really.

There was little guidance from the prompt itself as to the best inroads into the topic. But by week eight this did not faze Lynn. In fact, unlike the Ferraro piece, she felt fairly bored before beginning. But she grew less bored until it dropped out of her profile entirely. Rather, she felt a good deal of surprise and as much relief as she felt after the first essay. Even though the research and the "real" assignment were sequentially contiguous, the "real" assignment did not elicit harsh feelings. Yet Lynn did not feel very satisfied, and with good reason. Her paper paled in comparison to her knowledgeable and robust essay on Ferraro:

Real and really are words that are overused in the English language. Although we hear them frequently, their overuse does not stem merely from hearing them used often but from not hearing them used correctly.

According to Webster's Dictionary, real is an adjective which means existent as a thing; have actuality; as real events. We seldom hear real used to mean existence. Instead, real is used as a term to imply a standard of achievement or behavior. We are told that "real" men don't eat quiche; if we follow Webster's definition, men who do eat quiche must cease to exist since they are no longer real. The "real" world has come to mean the work world; does it follow then that millions of students, housewives, unemployed, and retirees are living in a nonexistent world simply because they do not work? I think not. In order to use "real" correctly and with a clearer meaning, we should use real to describe things that actually exist. I am sitting in a real desk; it exists. I am writing on real paper with a real pencil; they simply exist. . . .

Really, an adverb meaning "in a real manner or actually," loses all significance when it is used to modify an adjective. A movie is really great; the weather is really cold; that mountain is really tall. Instead of its literal meaning, to an excessive degree has become the new definition of really. The movie is excessively great; the weather excessively cold; the mountain excessively tall. . . . What is excessively cold to one person may be merely chilly to another. Really is more clearly and properly used to modify a verb. For example, Neil Armstrong really landed on the moon. The literal definition of really can now be used as a synonym. Neil Armstrong actually landed on the moon.

The preciseness of our language can be preserved by the elimination of abstract modifiers. Real and really stand at the top of the list for eradication.

Anita. While Lynn completed her academic training during the "preprocess" years, the fallout from such training was not as evident in her writing as it was in Anita's. Younger than Lynn, Anita had decided on a career in medicine. She saw herself as a skilled writer but did not often write on her own. Having written since childhood "to share things with friends," Anita was confident about her ability to handle the semester's work.

She characterized herself as moderately emotional, and her trait scales substantiated it. Unlike the group as a whole, her emotional disposition showed remarkable stability. Academic writing for Anita produced occasional anger, anxiety, fear, and frustration, but it was also accompanied by frequent feelings of interest, inspiration, relief, and satisfaction.

Like Lynn, Anita believed research writing was the most loathsome. It was during both research sessions that Anita felt strongest negative arousal. Anything other than research had to mean an improvement in those feelings, to wit, the "real" exercise. In an otherwise placid psychological condition, she felt moderately afraid and anxious before writing. Except for moderate interest, by the end of the session, her profile indicated nothing more than the slightest of feelings—her weakest throughout the study.

Her essay mirrored that limpness. She knew how to lace her topic sentences with examples and render her organization transparent with connectives. Like Lynn's, Anita's paper was sensible and unimaginative:

We use the term real in many ways. One way in which we use the term is to describe something authentic—such as real pearls, a real Izod, or real Nike shoes. Americans are caught up in a craze of designer fashions. ... In order to make a quick buck, people capitalize on this craze by producing imitations of the designer items. Hence, the public's curiosity in knowing whether the product they are buying is real or an imitation.

The term real is also used to describe a person—the "real" me. I have trouble with this phrase because of its ambiguity. First of all, whose perspective are we using? The facade that I present to the world would most likely be the real me to anyone who knows me. But I would say that the real me is the person deep inside of me that no one else sees. Secondly, what is meant by the "real" me? Are we talking about my emotions, my actions, my thoughts, or a combination of any one of these? And lastly, who's to say that any one person's opinion is any better or any more correct than another's? I would avoid using the expression, the "real" me, to describe a person. It doesn't mean anything. It only serves to raise unanswered questions.

A third way in which we use the term real is to describe something extraordinary. I use the word describe loosely. Generally speaking, we use "real" and "really" when we are too lazy to find another word to express our opinion. To say a movie is really good doesn't say as much as the movie was filled with lots of adventure, gorgeous men, tropical scenery, creative acting, and a happy ending. The second description, however, takes more thought than the first, which the speaker may be unwilling to expend.

Yet another way in which we use the word real, is to say "the real world." This phrase has always bothered me. It seemed to make my time spent in school seem worthless. I felt as though all the homework and classtime were being belittled. How dare someone say that the business world is the "real" world. What am I living in now—a dream world? And what about professors, are they people destined to spend their lives in a fantasy? Is their work any less important or real than an accountant's?

I find it hard to believe that the first twenty to seventy-five years of my life don't count. Even if those first years are only spent learning the rules of the "real" world, they must amount to something. Is it possible to skip the preliminaries and get right into the "real" world? Is it worth it? Or can one only enter the "real" world through a tragedy such as abandonment, running away from home, or death of one's relatives? The "real" world always seems to have negative connotations associated with it—such as the big, bad world or the cold, cruel world. Is it any wonder that one would rather stay in the world of dreams?

Mike. Contrary to his instructor's rating, Mike saw himself as more skilled than his peers. He completed two years of college and felt strongly "creative and imaginative," noting that he was working on a book. Despite his uneven grades, he was one of two members of the group who invariably felt most satisfied with their output.

Though he had some lucid moments, Mike's thinking was most confused during the "real" assignment. He was unable to maintain control of the rhetorical maneuvers demanded by the subject. Mike's paper is a vivid example of how skills can deteriorate when a topic of subtlety is introduced:

If I had to describe the word "real" in one short sentence, I would use it as an example in the form of a statement, "What is real." I do not wish this to be expressed in question form since that is, in essence, what we are asking. . . . Real is a term used by every one to punctuate their ideas, any idea they may express. . . .

The word real is as philosophical a term as any that Plato himself may have muttered. Yet today, we use the term "real" to give something substance, to give something meaning. We use it as a measuring stick for our descriptions. . . .

Real is also used to give something authenticity, to make it genuine. This is a 1912 Winchester, now this is a real gun. Obviously any gun that shoots or doesn't shoot is real, but by using it in this way we know that the 1912 Winchester is a rifle that must have been made very well, shot very true, it must have been a *really* good rifle. . . .

Real . . . has caused many people to spend a great deal of time trying to decipher its meaning. What is the difference between "very" good and "real" good. It seems as if real is often used in place of "very." That is the very sword Gen. Custer owned. That is the real sword that belonged to Gen. Custer. While "real" is most often used as a descriptive term, it is also used another way. Back to the original question, only approached philosophically this time, "What is real?" We find a great deal of controversy. This, however, is not a philosophy paper and I will not try to make it sound like one. It just seems very obvious that everything in one way or another is real. . . .

Philosophically, real is an abstract concept. Yet, what is real is something tangible, even if it is only a concept. . . . Real can be turned into a vicious circle of definitions if we are not careful. Suffice it to say that real is whatever we make it, whatever we choose it to be. . . .

Nevertheless, Mike remained unruffled after this essay. His positive feelings demonstrated considerable resilience. And this profile was supported by his trait profile. It showed some variability but only within the positive cluster. Other than that, only moderate anxiety appeared with regularity.

While Mike was not as confident in his writing by the end of the semester, his state emotions ran true to form. He felt anxious. But excitement, happiness, and satisfaction dominated his state profiles, because, like his response to the "real" paper, he remained unaware of the rhetorical circles he wound himself into. Mike did not seem destined for literary acclaim, but he was clearly in touch with his feelings.

Len. For this same assignment, Len displayed a rare (and for some instructors, I suppose, inappropriate) virtuosity. Educated beyond the bachelor's degree, Len had some experience writing for local newspapers. Most of his day-to-day writing was professional and technical. His emotional profile indicated that he was aware of no more than "occasional" feelings of any kind when he was involved in writing at work. But he also admitted to an emotion he routinely experienced that he called "methodically controlled." Apparently he felt more than he could express.

He reported two basic responses when writing: "either cold and business-like or sarcastic," but neither registered with any regularity on the scale. After writing, Len experienced consistently moderate positive feelings. Before writing, his feelings were well curbed. On only 7 out of 180 before-writing opportunities did he report any feelings over "slight" intensity. However, the writings themselves were replete with cynicism and ridicule. He admitted to sarcasm, but not to the strain of hostility he indicated when writing in general. If he felt it, it was preempted by stronger excitement, happiness, interest, and of course relief and satisfaction.

His "real" essay punctuates the discrepancy between emotional expression and emotional experience:

The drone of her alarm clock disturbs a peaceful dream of sylvan solitude. Opening her eyes, she saw, not trees swaying in the breeze, but the slow rotation of simulated-wood-grained fan blades. After dragging herself up and into the bathroom, she was ready to prepare herself for another day. She inserted her tinted contact lenses and applied her makeup, taking care to gently powder her surgically bobbed nose. The recent "face lift" was most successful. Moving to her dressing area she chose the polyester suit. It was most flattering to her "augmented" breasts. She vowed to complete and send that letter of gratitude to her plastic surgeon. With her "refined" appearance, she even felt comfortable wearing the cubic zirconium "diamonds" and the synthetic pearls. Only time enough for a glass of Tang instant breakfast drink, a breakfast bar, and a cup of freeze-dried instant coffee lightened with Cremora. Out the front door for the start of another day, out in the "real" world.

Is it any wonder that one of today's most sincere compliments is to be considered a "real" person? Our lives are saturated with synthetic imitations, from the clothes we wear, to the food we eat, to our very bodies themselves. What you see may be what you get, but it ain't necessarily what you got when you started! Surrounded by imitations, it is not surprising that we regularly use the words "real" and "really."

Ed Sullivan's "really big show" may have started it, but our overuse of these words is the result of America's infatuation with plastic perfection.

Len's essay failed to follow the guidelines for successful expository writing in the traditional sense. It read more like an introduction to a freelance article with its catchy lead and angle, a trademark of feature writing. But like the "real" exercise, Len's research, analytic, and comparison/contrast papers demonstrated that he could respond to deadly academic exercises as well as Anita and have more fun.

WRITING ABOUT A BORING EXPERIENCE

The pattern of emotions associated with the boring experience episode appeared dramatically different from that of all other tasks, emotionally toned or otherwise. Students were not only asked to write about a boring experience, but the term itself appeared on the BESW. It is not surprising that this essay ranked last in increased positive feelings and was the only session that resulted in stronger negative passive ones.

Tina. Tina was typical. Her flaccid emotional profile reflected the prevailing reaction to writing about boredom. Nonetheless, even she, an unskilled writer, tried to rise above the boredom that she was asked to write about. Initially she reported feeling sleepy. This moderated to feeling "mellow and relaxed" at the pause, which then culminated in "strong amusement." She started:

Boredom to me is sitting through a poor orchestra performance. What I mean by poor is anyone with ears in the audience could hear squeaks in the instruments, wrong notes playing, and anything else that goes with bad playing. It was so boring that after each piece the orchestra played, I clapped very loud because that meant I had one less piece to hear. ...

She concludes:

I enjoyed the performance as much as I like walking on nails. ...
Boredom is not so bad when you have someone to share it with.

That she managed to interject some silly ironies into an otherwise uneventful paper coincided with pleasant feelings by the end of the piece.

Ruth Anne. Ruth Anne's writing was weak and showed little improvement over the semester. She declared herself an intensely emotional person "inwardly." Her three trait forms reflected wide emotional fluctuations over the semester. On the credit side, her fear diminished. On the debit side, her interest, happiness, and excitement also abated. Her anger and frustration doubled.

Ruth Anne's feelings surrounding the boredom exercise corroborated those emotional proclivities. Her fairly neutral profile entering the session turned into her most intense negative profile after it. Not only did she feel negative active, she felt monumentally bored. She reported nothing else:

Boredom is an experience when I am obligated to stay somewhere without activity. . . .

Boredom is a state of mind. One can convince themselves a project is dull and not have any fun or interest. However, anything can be fascinating if conceived in the right perspective. . . .

Boredom is easy to be, especially if you are not interested in what is going on around you. . . .

I feel boredom is simply a state of mind and any uneventful occurrence or dull occurrence can be livened up with thought perspective upon the topic.

Like Mike, Ruth Anne initially indicated that she was moderately satisfied with her writing. However, unlike Mike, there was a dramatic change in her profile as the semester progressed. By week four she reported never feeling satisfied with her writing. By week seven she felt only occasionally satisfied with it and was totally unsatisfied with her boredom piece produced the week before. It is well recognized that some novice writers get worse before they get better. But Ruth Anne's writing never rose above the predictable and commonplace. She did not like to write, and she knew she wasn't doing it well. But she seemed more responsive than Mike to the quality of her work.

Len. Len was exceptional. He continued to transcend the conventional structure of academic discourse with social satire. As a result, he was never bored. By the middle of this particular session, his interest, happiness, and excitement increased three and four times. By the end of it, his level of inspiration increased threefold and his satisfaction and surprise increased fourfold. He felt as adventurous as he did when writing the "adventurous" paper, and his boredom disappeared entirely. It is easy to see why:

Boredom, as a topic of discussion, not surprisingly, could be this course's most lifeless exercise. To concentrate and focus upon boredom is antithetical to the production of provocative prose. Were this not the case, boredom would not be boring. And, needless to say it is. . . .

With a clever turn of phrase or an uncanny third eye, ennui can be transformed to whoopee, Dullsville to Gotham. . . .

He elaborates about cities and ends up on the West Coast:

It is no wonder that San Francisco is the home of the world's first commercial center for the rental of isolation. . . . Only in a place bustling with grand diversity would questionably sane people pay to be enclosed in silent darkness.

Anita. Anita's essay on boring differed in emotional response from her others in that her writing and feelings tended to reflect those of the unskilled group. Her piece was indeed boring, and she was bored by it. Further, at this point she expressed mild resentment toward writing:

Boredom is an emotion I often feel. . . . Another example would be daydreaming in church. . . . Another problem associated with boredom is the alleviation of this feeling. Many times I feel bored because I don't have anything to do. . . . In order to relieve my boredom, I need to find something to do. The problem with this is that the things I need to do didn't interest me in the first place and that is why I am bored. . . . Boredom afflicts most everyone.

Yet unlike the unskilled writers, she knew how to stretch the limits of her topic. Though the order of her ideas was haphazard, she was capable of wringing the topic of its potential. Her introductory sentences for those ideas show that capability:

I think being bored with a person is even harder than being bored with an event. . . .
I need to make jobs I need to do interesting or undertake a task which does not need to be done but one which would stir my interest. . . .
Boredom can linger or expire after a short period of time. . . .
A bored person gets a distinctive expression on his face. . . .

Her confusion, frustration, and surprise during this essay gave way to anger, boredom, and depression. By the end of the session, these feelings gave way to relief and satisfaction, as well as boredom and fatigue, clear from the piece itself.

Contrary to other emotionally linked exercises, writing about something boring seemed to induce boredom for the majority of students, skilled or unskilled. In 1971 Emig observed that even competent student writers working on topics unrelated to boredom found little satisfaction when contemplating their finished work. Students view finishing writing like starting, as a mundane moment devoid of any affect but indifference and the mildest of satisfactions. Emig further explained that this lack of emotion might reflect an impoverished affective vocabulary. If this were the case, providing students with that language would free them to self-disclose. The BESW gave them positive and negative emotion items alike, and students reported feeling more positive, clearly the more respectable of the two sets of emotions.

TYPE OF ASSIGNMENT AND ADDITIONAL DESCRIPTIVE DATA

The assignment categories lined up a little differently when self-sponsored writing experience was considered. In general, the longer students had been writing on their own, the more positive they tended to feel before and after they wrote. These students also felt less hostile and passive to the formal school activity, a finding that agrees with Study 1. This result seems to rest on traditional rhetorical essays like the description which, similar to self-sponsored writing, would likely tap personal experience. Of all three assignment categories, those students with considerable experience writing on their own reported stronger positive emotions on 50% of the traditional assignment observations, stronger negative passive emotions on only 12% of them, but no stronger negative active emotions at all. In addition, the self-sponsored writers felt more positive and less negative passive and negative active on the research draft and the final research paper. It seems as if students with more experience writing on their own feel better on all fronts when it comes to academic writing, even research.

Students' satisfaction with the work they had completed was only loosely linked to types of assignments. Students more satisfied with their affective personal and traditional essays felt consistently more positive and less negative passive and negative active. I argued earlier that the group as a whole tended to resist research writing. They also had a hard time being satisfied with their research. Except for the boring-experience assignment, the research episodes prompted the most negative response. The final research paper also ranked fifth in increase of positive emotion. Yet, three of the four writing episodes before it were accompanied by statistically significant but smaller increases in positive feelings. Like the boring-experience assignment, data accompanying the final research session were available from only sixteen students, the lowest level of participation in the study. Had the mean increase held constant, with several more respondents, the increase in positive emotion during the final research episode might have reached statistical significance. In contrast, even if all twenty-four students had been present during the boring episode, with the same mean increase, significance would not have been reached.

The conclusions that may be drawn from these findings are: first, self-sponsored student writers are better able to withstand school-based writing; and second, when students believe themselves competent in writing, they seem, indeed, to find writing less objectionable and distressing. But, it may be in forms of writing other than research that they are so rewarded. The evidence suggests that research engenders ambivalence, if not distress. Clearly, magnitude of emotional change is not the only factor determining salience. Sequence of assignment has potential importance, as does type of assignment. Emotions are guided not only by the content of the writing task and type of assignment but also by students' very participation in it. The adequacy of these findings needs to be tested further.

Emotionality and one emotion cluster established a relationship that proved religious in its consistency throughout the studies. Those students perceiving themselves as highly emotional felt more intensely negative active on 89% of the nine writing sessions. In contrast to the placid students, these students also felt stronger positive emotions on 33% of the affective experiential observations, stronger negative passive on 67% of them, and stronger negative active emotions on 83% of them. In addition, the more emotional students felt more intensely positive and negative passive on 62% of the traditional essay observations and more intensely negative active on 88% of them. The dominant effect in this study was positive, no doubt, because students have learned that it is socially unacceptable in school to reveal negative feelings, particularly the aggressive ones. But it is all too clear that they associated emotionality with nervous agitation and hostile feelings, reminding us once again that emotion carries with it a very bad name.

NOTES

1. While not synonymous, the terms personal experience, affectively toned, and affective experiential essays and personal, free, and expressive writing overlap conceptually, and so are interchanged throughout the book.

2. Changes in the individual emotion items were not analyzed for statistical significance here or in the subsequent studies. Thus, any shifts discussed are meant to support results obtained statistically in Study 1, or call them into question.

3. The boredom scale is an especially good example of a psychometric anomaly and response set cited in Chapter 5. By every indication, the students did not associate the increasing boredom that they were apparently feeling during the semester with a higher score on the State form. Rather, they checked off a lower score. A lower score on the scale should mean less boredom—and thus more interest, if those emotions are polar opposites. However, I suspect that the students did not associate the less boredom that they checked off with less actual boredom. Were they truly following instructions, their boredom scores should have increased, representing heightened boredom. Factor analysis confirms this anomaly insofar as the item did not load on either cluster after writing.

4. Although the research paper is clearly an expository writing assignment, because it was a longer, more complicated undertaking, it was treated separately.

5. Unfortunately these values are lost because the intensities of the individual emotion items for the two research sessions were averaged.

9. Study 3: Professional Writers

The fields of composition and literature have long used the work of professionals as models of quality. Of mounting interest are insights into their writing habits (Emig, 1971; Murray, 1968; Turner, 1977, 1985). Those individuals, for whom writing is a chosen career, are a highly self-selected group. Professional writers write more. They do it better. They are expected to have had a high rate of self-sponsored writing at one time in their lives, if not currently. And, as far as emotions are concerned, there may be something special to be learned from working professionals because, unlike other individuals who write, they *want* to.

In Chapter 2 I tried to show that the emotions of accomplished writers are plentiful and diverse. When pleasant emotions occur, they occur when writing begins; but they also occur when writing ends in the form of validation and closure. Personal documents, however, corroborate the presence of a good many unpleasant emotions. The excitory and striking out types of emotions diminish or are replaced by feelings of relief after writing. Established writers seem able to turn even depressed psychological states associated with diminished activity into powerful motives for writing. The number of references to psychological arousal suggests a special capacity of a generalized affect to mobilize for writing and to sustain it. The number of statements that bring positive and negative emotions into relation supports a utility in composing from dissonant feelings. Writers would be that much more compelled to write as a way of reducing such dissonance. This study was designed to examine the emotions of professional writers, those whose careers are based on the ability to formulate and communicate ideas in writing. This group also included experienced and actively publishing writers for whom writing is a regular, personal or professional necessity, but whose means of support may not necessarily depend on payment for publication.

PROCEDURE

In order to sample this group, area writers' groups were contacted. Other contacts were made personally or through recommendation. Each writer was interviewed. The study was explained and voluntary participation solicited. The resulting group consisted of twenty-four professional writers: seven full-time English professors, four organizational staff writers, four full-time fiction writers, three business people, two full-time freelance writers, and one each of the following—an historian, lawyer, college instructor and small press publisher, and freelance writer and business person. The ages of the participants ranged from 25 to 70 years, with an average age of 40. Fourteen participants were male and ten were female. All the respondents had some college background, although the extent of that background varied. Four had doctoral degrees, seven had completed master's degrees, five had taken course work beyond the bachelor's degree, four had completed bachelor's degrees, and four had some college education. Eleven primarily wrote poetry, six wrote fiction, and seven wrote nonfiction, including scholarly work. All were experienced writers and were actively publishing.

Once the writers agreed to participate, they were given a set of materials with an information sheet which is excerpted below.

Your Schedule

To determine how often you should fill out the State forms, use the following criteria:
1. If you generally write 1 to 2 times a week you should complete the S-form for *every* writing session over a 4-week period.
2. If you write between 3 and 5 times a week, you should complete the scale for every *other* writing session or every *other* week for 3 weeks.
3. If you write between 6 and 10 times in a week, you should complete the scale for every *other* writing session during one, 1-week period.

Your *Schedule* should look like this:

Day 1:
1. Fill out the Demographic Data Sheet.
2. Complete the Trait-When-Writing form that asks how you feel *In General* when you write.
3. Send both of these back to me in the envelope provided.

From Day 1 to the Middle of your Schedule:
Fill out the State forms with your writing according to the appropriate schedule outlined above.

Middle Day:

Continue filling out the State form, and fill out 1 Trait-When-Writing form.

From the Middle Day to Last Day of your Schedule:

Continue filling out the State forms with your writing.

Last Week:

Fill out 1 Trait-When-Writing form.

In addition to the general procedures outlined in Chapter 6, the professionals received the following suggestions:

When you decide on your writing schedule, include work that may crop up apart from your regular professional writing. If, for example, in between drafts of an article, you write a letter to your mother, this constitutes writing of the self-sponsored sort. And it should be counted as one of your writing sessions.

Please follow the appropriate State form schedule whether you are consciously feeling some emotions or not. Each session is especially important because your profile should accurately represent the proportion of emotion-linked to nonemotion-linked writing. The thinking behind this is that, because not all writing occurs in conjunction with conscious emotion, the no-cases must be allowed to occur so that they may be recorded.

Consider the minimum size for completing a State form a standard paragraph or four lines of a genre like poetry. Making shopping lists, copying recipes, or drafting checks are not considered writing for the purposes of this study.

Keep your State forms with your writing materials, to be *as* available as they are—at the proverbial moment's notice. If you are apt to write at places other than your desk, keep some State forms there too. The same thing applies if you use a word processor.

Assignments or events precipitating your writing need not have occurred immediately preceding it. They can have occurred in the distant past. A whole chain of predisposing events as well as feelings may intervene before your writing actually begins.

Over the course of your participation, you may write some first drafts, revise some drafts, and create some finished products. Your writing portfolio can therefore consist of entirely different work or one work continually revised. More than likely, it will consist of both.

Another note about self-sponsored and required writing. Your writings can be either self-sponsored or required. It is not always easy to tell. One way to determine whether your writing is initiated by you or by someone else is to ask who prompted it. If you, yourself, decided to write, then it is self-sponsored. If your boss, editor, or an outside agent requested it as part of a job or assignment, then it is required. Another way to decide is by asking yourself whether or not you live from the publication of that writing. If it is part of a regular activity for which you are paid and from whose proceeds you are supported, consider it required.

A work may change its category over the course of its development. If you start a piece on your own and for its own sake, the first or early drafts would be self-sponsored. If *The New Yorker* accepts it with revisions, at that point it becomes "work for hire" or required (by the editor).

Regarding the work itself, you also have the option of substituting a summary on the back of the State form for any fully written text.

The completed data sets were more uneven than I anticipated. There was considerable variation in the number of Trait-When-Writing and State forms completed by each respondent as well as variation in the time intervening between each writing session. Because of these inconsistencies, I examined only the first set of trait and state observations completed by each writer. However, an analysis of variance was performed on the first four sets of state observations to demonstrate that the first set was not substantially different from the remaining ones. The results of these tests suggested that, on balance, the emotion clusters remained the same across the writing sessions.[1]

THE STATE EMOTIONS

This study undermines some of the stereotypes of professional writers. Contrary to the literature and the more popular accounts that I noted in both Chapters 2 and 11, these professionals did not report great mood swings when they wrote. Nor were they fighting off bouts of distress, rage, or other debilitating emotions. Echoing the earlier studies, if the professionals felt positive before they wrote, they tended to feel positive after, and vice versa. Taken together, emotional intensity did not vary during the writing session. The writers felt more positive and less negative passive after writing than before writing or at the pause, but these patterns were not statistically significant. The negative active emotions resisted change altogether. Appendix A.8 lists these means and standard deviations.

Table 9.1 shows the rank order of the means of the individual state emotions. The rank order generally approximated those of Studies 1 and 2. There was not, however, quite the identical displacement of the most intensely experienced positive emotions as occurred in Study 1. By the end of their writing sessions, the college writers felt more satisfied than relieved. Here, the professionals were more relieved than satisfied—in keeping with the advanced expository writers of Study 2. However, unlike both Studies 1 and 2, the satisfaction of these practicing writers moved up in rank through the writing session, but failed to unseat interest or happiness.

In my discussion so far, I explained that, because students as apprentice writers knew so little about writing, they would be more readily satisfied with their work than experienced writers. This finding is confirmed here from the other vantage point. These working writers may have felt least satisfied (of the groups described thus far), because they knew too much. Profiles of Mark and Ted farther along in the chapter illustrate this point.

Table 9.1
Rank Order of Means for the Individual Emotions of the Professional Writers across One Trait Observation and One Writing Session

Trait Emotions		Before Writing		State Emotions At a Pause		After Writing	
Interested	4.00	Interested	3.38	Interested	3.25	Relieved	3.42
Excited	3.38	Excited	2.42	Inspired	2.70	Interested	3.17
Happy	2.96	Happy	2.42	Excited	2.65	Happy	3.04
Inspired	2.96	Adventurous	2.29	Happy	2.60	Satisfied	2.92
Affectionate	2.86	Anxious	2.29	Adventurous	2.55	Inspired	2.58
Adventurous	2.83	Inspired	2.21	Satisfied	2.50	Excited	2.54
Anxious	2.83	Affectionate	2.17	Relieved	2.40	Affectionate	2.50
Satisfied	2.78	Frustrated	2.17	Affectionate	2.30	Adventurous	2.25
Confused	2.70	Lonely	2.17	Frustrated	2.15	Frustrated	2.04
Frustrated	2.65	Satisfied	2.08	Anxious	2.10	Anxious	1.83
Relieved	2.46	Afraid	1.92	Confused	1.95	Depressed	1.75
Surprised	2.41	Depressed	1.92	Lonely	1.90	Confused	1.71
Afraid	2.36	Confused	1.88	Afraid	1.65	Lonely	1.71
Lonely	2.30	Relieved	1.71	Depressed	1.65	Surprised	1.63
Depressed	2.18	Angry	1.67	Angry	1.60	Afraid	1.58
Angry	2.09	Bored	1.54	Surprised	1.55	Angry	1.54
Disgusted	1.73	Disgusted	1.50	Ashamed	1.30	Ashamed	1.33
Bored	1.64	Ashamed	1.25	Bored	1.30	Disgusted	1.29
Ashamed	1.41	Shy	1.25	Disgusted	1.20	Bored	1.21
Shy	1.32	Surprised	1.21	Shy	1.10	Shy	1.21

Note: $n = 24$.

While inspiration tended to increase among the student writers discussed earlier, the related emotion of surprise held the lowest rank before writing of all the positive emotions of the professionals (as well as among all five studies). But it moved steadily toward the middle of the distribution by the end of writing. Writing for these professionals seemed to leave little room for the unexpected which, if it came at all, came after composing began.

Because writer's block, a severe and global writing dysfunction, has been associated with such emotions as anxiety, frustration, anger, and confusion, the negative active emotions have been thought to sabotage writing. Overall, the negative active emotions of both the student writers and professionals were moderate but largely unaffected by composing. Certainly, students could feel negative active throughout the process by virtue of their inexperience with it and their concerns about grades. But, the fact that the same pattern occurred with the professional group supports a rival point of view; that particular negative active emotions are an important affective concomitant of composing (Cheshire, 1984).

The negative active emotions of the professionals took two paths during writing. The ranks of some items remained stable through the process. Others started off at the high end of the distribution but dropped in rank during writing. Frustration followed the first course. Anxiety and fear followed the second course. Anxiety was the one negative emotion that was experienced with considerable intensity by the college students in Study 1 and by the advanced expository writers in Study 2. The rank order of anxiety for the professionals was similar both when writing in general and before the session. Echoing the factor analysis, anxiety dominated all the negative emotions yet stood out among the positive emotions at those two points. Anxiety ranked moderately high before writing. It lost considerable rank until the pause, then leveled off. While continuing to decline in intensity, by the end of the writing, anxiety actually exchanged ranks with frustration. However, both anxiety and frustration still retained their positions as highest among the negative emotions. More important, anxiety and frustration ranked high among the traditional "approach" or positive emotions. Considering the reputation associated with these negative active feelings, it is comforting to know that, at least for these working writers, a certain intensity of these feelings empowers composing.

The negative passive emotions are also important to follow. Like the earlier studies, the negative passive emotions generally hugged the lower ranks. The exceptions were confusion and boredom. Like frustration, confusion remained moderate throughout the writing session. Boredom followed that pattern at a lower rank. Although the professionals felt as confused before composing as the college students, boredom did not follow on its heels before writing as it did for the college writers. Their boredom ranked immediately below confusion as the highest negative passive emotion they experienced, and both dropped equally during writing. Several ranks lower than confusion, boredom played a distinctly minor role for the professionals. Confusion held its ground in the middle of the distribution throughout composing. But these practicing writers were simply not bored like their student counterparts.

Let me stress one point concerning the state emotions. That these practicing writers failed to experience more positive emotions after the actual writing sessions is not a trivial finding. My sense is that the psychological environment of these writers was far from lackluster. In contrast to Eastman's observation that professionals train themselves to tolerate a high level of boredom so that they can keep at their writing, there were perhaps few high peaks in their work from day to day. There were perhaps no major barriers to scale. Working in a professional climate on a regular basis, these writers could not afford to indulge their emotions. Rather, their very survival necessitated the ability to stay under emotional control. But, as the trait emotions confirm, this was apparently independent of an unflagging interest and enjoyment in what they did. That's when people decide to write for a living.

Jack. Jack is a good example of this kind of professional. Writing for twenty-five years, he had some undergraduate training but did not appear at all impeded by not completing his bachelor's degree. As an author of short and full-length mystery fiction, he was the most notable of the group. With eight novels to his credit, short stories published in *Ellery Queen's Mystery Magazine* and *Alfred Hitchcock's Mystery Magazine*, and awards for his work, he had good reason to feel superior to his peers and confident in his ability.

Perhaps that is why his emotional profile was among the most stable of the group. During the course of the study, his writings divided themselves into three categories: book reviews, evaluative commentary to some of his students about their fiction, and chapters of a novel in progress. The emotional distinctions between writing reviews and instructional responses were inconsequential. He maintained a strong interest and willingness to explore during composing, and relief and satisfaction increased to moderate intensities afterward. Yet, he appeared to have considerable mastery over any feelings that might curb his productivity.

A close look at his emotional responses indicated that Jack's emotions intensifed across the board when working on his novel. His excitement, interest, and adventurousness started strong and stayed strong. Relief and satisfaction made among the greatest gains. On one occasion he experienced somewhat more anxiety at the pause in the session, but it subsided before the end. In fact this was the one time Jack became mildly bored. Although he continued to work on the novel in subsequent sessions, that level of anxiety never resurfaced. The asterisk indicates an ostensibly inauspicious point in the dialogue that Jack reported the stronger anxiety.

Livingston, a captain with the New Orleans Police Department, questions Nudger, a sleuth who is being tailed and who "knew it was time to get cooperative" about jazz pianist Willy Hollister:

"Hollister makes women disappear," he said. Livingston was unimpressed by this vague revelation. "He does magic? I thought he was a musician." His voice had taken on the same sharp flintiness as his eyes.

"With a certain type of woman, he does magic," Nudger said. "They fall hard for him, have a passionate affair, then drop out of sight."

"You're saying Hollister has something to do with their disappearances?" Livingston asked. A coplike question, to the point and phrased to suggest the answer.

"There's nothing to indicate that," Nudger said. He decided to give Hollister the benefit of the doubt in this conversation with Livingston.* After all, Nudger hadn't any real proof that the man had done anything in the slightest illegal. "Maybe his women just get tired of being around all that ego," he said. "They might be surprised when they're caught in a love triangle: Hollister, the woman, and Hollister."

CHANGE IN THE TRAIT EMOTIONS

Whereas the analyses indicated that this group felt no change in their state emotions across the writing episode, they felt the positive trait emotions more often than either the negative passive or negative active when writing in general.

Table 9.1 lists the rank order of the individual trait emotions. Similar to its state counterpart, the rank order indicated that the professionals felt positive—interested, excited, happy, and inspired—most often when they wrote. Items occupying the middle range of the distribution included positive emotions satisfied, relieved, and surprised; negative active emotions anxious, frustrated, and afraid; and negative passive emotion confused. These writers were almost never bored.

The ranks of the negative emotions are especially instructive, given the interest of composition studies in writing apprehension. Like its state counterpart, trait anxiety was the most frequently experienced negative emotion, ranking sixth highest in the distribution. Although the intensity and frequency of emotions (as well as immediate and retrospective accounts of them) are not exact equivalents, the overall values of the trait emotions were substantially higher when the professionals considered them in general and in retrospect, than when they were immediately experienced during the actual writing session. Recollected feelings are, of course, subject to considerable distortion. But it is interesting to note that when these values and the state and trait values for the advanced expository group were compared, their good feelings got better in relation to writing in general, so to speak, but the bad got worse. For these practicing writers the good feelings also got better when writing in general, but the bad did not get worse; they resisted change. The net result is that the professionals appear to be in considerably better emotional shape than the student writers.

Roger. A representative case is Roger. With only one or two exceptions, Roger's optimism during composing was reflected in the upbeat quality of his articles.

Roger had been writing for considerably fewer years than Jack: ten years on his own and less than three professionally. He specialized in business, science, and health subjects and had published in *The Boston Globe, Construction News and Review, International Wildlife,* and *National Audubon Society Publications*. He had a broader repertoire than Jack, as his titles illustrate: The Silent War Against America's #1 Killer (heart disease), Miracle Technologies of the Eighties, How to Motivate Children, Look Mom, No More Braces! The Best Kept Secret in Dental Health, and a "fluff" interview with a local restaurateur, which made him angry—an emotion otherwise nonexistent in his profile.

Most of the time Roger's criteria for a subject were "interest and importance." His feelings tended to vary according to the subject matter. But the harder the piece, the more excited he was. His article about gazelles, "Managed Inbreeding: Better than Extinction," fell into this category. It required extensive research and far more than a passing knowledge of geography and genetics. Initially he expressed strong excitement and confusion. While confusion dropped off sharply as he wrote, his excitement remained high.

Roger was most fully aroused during the study before writing an article on aging. His lead suggests why:

Janie's gaze drifted out the front window to the frozen trees and the icy stillness outside her comfortable Arkansas home. "I have mixed emotions about D.C.," she said softly. "There's anger, yes, but I feel sorry for him too." The detached look in her eyes was very different from her usual smiling personality, like a protective veil she pulled over her real feelings. ... In a flicker Janie was joking about D.C.'s quirks once more, making it all seem light. ...

D.C. is Janie's father. He is 85 years old. Few memories of him remain from her childhood. When Janie was 8 years old, D.C. walked out on his family. Eventually Janie's mother divorced him. Janie was raised by her stepfather, a man she loved and admired.

For 50 years, D.C. lived alone in a small trailer, a borderline alcoholic. ...

Ultimately the article worked into a checklist for planning care for the elderly. Although Roger's ending was strictly informative, he was left with a residue of "compassion and sadness."

These sobering feelings stood in sharp contrast to joyful, childlike ones when he wrote about the future for a general audience. The following excerpt from his piece, "Life in the Year 2000 A.D.," reflected that playful side:

We are approaching a milestone in the history of civilization—the dawn of a new century, the birth of the Third Millennium, A.D. Who can help but wonder what the world will be like?

Just for fun, take a moment and write down your age and your spouse's age. Don't forget the children. Now add fifteen to each of the ages you have written down. That is how old you will be in the year 2000. Imagine how old you and your family will look in fifteen years. . . .

All set? Now let's take a peek at how scientists and futurists describe the rest of your world in the year 2000 A.D. Hold on to your hats, everything may not be as you suspect.

Roger reported the "wonder," "awe," and adventurousness he wanted to elicit from his readers. By the end of the session Roger was still strongly excited, only moderately interested, but he was completely finished feeling adventurous and marked the emotion items accordingly.

That the writing experiences in general for the professionals were stable and positive is a most visible and impressive finding. Again, negative passive feelings were particularly rare and weak. If we want to believe that writers harbor tumultuous or disconsolate feelings and find solace or release in their writing, we would not find it with this group, given the weak intensities of negative passive feelings observed here. This tendency did not, however, hold up when the group was examined by type of writer.

THE POETS AND PROSE WRITERS

Type of writer appeared to have little impact on the emotions experienced during the actual writing sessions, with one striking exception: the poets. While the sample size made it inappropriate to subdivide the writers into poets, nonfiction writers, and fiction writers, the group was divided into poets and prose writers. For the analyses using the state emotions, there were eight poets and twelve prose writers. For the trait emotion analyses, there were ten poets and twelve prose writers.

The Poets

Although no differences were found between the two groups of writers for the positive and negative passive trait items, the poets reported experiencing negative active trait emotions more often than the prose writers.

Paula. Take Paula. Characterizing herself as intensely emotional, Paula brimmed with negative active feelings both when writing in general and during specific writing episodes. But they were frequently matched by positive feelings. It was not uncommon to find her excitement, interest, and frustration or her anger and affection running neck-and-neck. Paula's feelings seemed magnifications of her material. If the material was neutral, she felt modestly aroused. If the subject was sensitive—as most were—her emotions were extravagant. Revising was different. An inveterate revisor, she pounded away at her letters, notes, poetry, and articles. Each successive intermediary draft was accompanied by more pronounced relief and satisfaction and weakening negative feelings.

Over the course of the study, her writings concerned her recent second marriage, a battle for custody of a stepdaughter, and her experiences teaching English in an urban high school. She was "frustrated and disgusted about racism and laziness, eager, motivated," but not sure "how to use [her material] in class."

Advice

Hey, Li'l Bro,
How c'n I tell you
whats in my soul?
Even yo momma ain't tole you
what it be like out here.

Archie Bunker?
He be on instant replay
Live an' in person
on the block
in the stores
an' (Oh, Lord!) in the church.
He be running scared.

He be feared you marry his
chile
you knife him
wi' some sharp folk talk
you rape his woman
wif yo eyes. ...

I be tellin' you, Bro,
You c'n beat the system
good as any white boy—
You jes gotta work
harderfastersmarterlonger.

On Trying to Read "Barn Burning" to 2nd Hr.

Whadda YOU know, Honky Teacher,
try'na tell me who I am?

You suborned, subhuman,
subterrestrial sub!
What's that f__r Faulkner know
about real rage
(rude and restless and rolling
under this smooth, cool
  (REAL COOL)
Surface)?
Yo grandma probly a slaver.
Yo ma cou'n hanie no real stud
  like ME.
Don't talk t'me bout no
Gwendolyn Brooks no
Nikki Giovanni no
Dunbar/Hughes/Angelou no
Martin Luther King no
  DREAM no
LIT-ER-A-TURE. . . .

You wanna know 'bout
  BLACK PRIDE?
I be Proud to sit back here
On my Jordached butt
an' tell you sumthin':
You ain't got nothin' to say
  to ME!

Cecily. Unlike Paula, Cecily's writing found its emotional source in more contemplative states. A poet, president of the local poetry society, and an English teacher, Cecily also coordinated scholastic and academic affairs at her high school and wrote on several school-related matters during the study. Each was marked by the same affective pattern, disciplined but rising positive feelings. Her trait emotions were similarly stable and evenly divided between positive and negative feelings experienced at occasional or moderate frequencies.

It was her poetry that evoked negative passive feelings. Confusion, depression, and loneliness alternated at highest intensities across the sessions, more often before than after composing. Her material was nostalgic—lonely or sad, triggered by a scene, a sermon, or some passing reminiscence. Something apparently stopped her, gave her pause, triggered other associations which rose into text. Except for interest and inspiration (to which she added curiosity and awe), before writing her positive feelings clung to the lowest intensities. They gradually intensified through the pause until happiness, inspiration, interest, and surprise took over at the end.

Childhood Visits to a Great Aunt

Perhaps had I a daughter
I would call her Kate,
Remembering town-summer afternoons
Where in a tree-shaded, drape-drawn room
You served us coca-cola
In the only bottles made then. ...

Galway Concert

I
Silhouetted fox
Races raging horizon
To die at the world's edge,
White bones melting in the moonlight
Before the baying has begun.

II
Climb the ladder of my fingertips
Cling to the promises
Grasp each bent joint in
this hand of hope
See how each joint forms a "V"
That eludes the open hand. ...

III
. ...
A lone leaf floats down.

The deterioration of Cecily's mother was becoming a problem to the family at this time:

Mother and the Christmas Tree

She was seventy-eight
And though neither of us knew it
In any conscious way,
This was to be her last tree
Cut from fringes of the Ozark hills.
I sat mid-day with the tree,
Seeing it sadly as a straggly sample of cedar.
Wondered why she had stuck pieces of bottle cotton on it,
Where the tinsel had gone,
And why the plastic angel with broken wings and missing halo
Was still there.

Cecily's emotional profile was markedly different when she had to defend decisions about the welfare of her mother, telling Aunt Eudora in effect "to mind her own business." She claimed she expressed "controlled anger." But she was not thrown by her feelings. On the contrary. From the looks of her letter she maintained a starched civility. But after writing she declared herself both "disgusted and relieved."

Dear Eudora,
   Mom received your card Friday. Thanks for taking the time to write. ...
   Tommy and I discussed at length the suggestion about Mom spending some time in White Plains—the apartment idea. We both agree that while it would be nice to have some "time off," ultimately we're better off to keep her here.

Cecily spells out her reasons and ends:

We do hope, of course, that you'll plan to stop here on your way down to visit with her and with us. But to invite her along, we believe, is asking only for future problems. If she were able, maybe a week at your place during nice weather would be good for her—I really don't know though. The ... problem is very real, and it changes her and our outlook on a lot of things.
   We hope all is going well with you, knowing this certainly isn't an easy time. Take care.

Curiously, the poets most noticeably resembled Paula's negative active inclinations over Cecily's sense of social rectitude. But it was their trait emotions that were more negative active, not their state emotions. In other words, these feelings did not occur when these poets were actually writing, but rather when they thought about writing from an aesthetically and psychologically safe vantage point. It may be easier for writers to disclose negative feelings in connection with their work in general rather than to associate them with specific texts. One critical variable in affective response is distance (Bower, cited in Flammer & Kintsch, 1982). The more proximate the emotion and behavior, the higher their correspondence. Put another way, the closer an event is perceived to relate to the self, the more intense the emotional experience. But these feelings could endanger the writing and so would likely be kept at bay. In view of the outcome emotions for the group as a whole, perhaps the writing process itself enables poets to come to symbolic terms with those negative emotions without having to feel them fully again.

Rich. Rich is an especially good case in point. Writing for forty or more years, Rich was professor of English at a community college and a Ph.D. candidate. He was also a local theater critic and book reviewer. In addition to publishing nationally, he wrote extensively for his own satisfaction.

Out of what was to have been a plum assignment to interview "John"—a noted literary figure—came Rich's story behind the story. Occupying two full writing sessions of three hours each, Rich wrote a twenty-four-page narrative that had apparently taken place over a decade before. At the time of the interview, John was just beginning his parabolic arc, his brilliant if not eccentric popular success before his academic disgrace, personal disaster, and sudden death.

During a first contact John suggested that Rich stay over. Rich, preferring to make a weekend of it with his wife, planned to do the interview but take a motel room instead. It was decided that the two wives would find something to occupy themselves while the interview took place.

After a pastoral opening:

The afternoon of our drive to C__dale was crisp and lightly overcast; the bare pecan trees stood solitary and gaunt in the low fields to the west of the highway. . . .

Introductions and a tour of John's house follows:

How shall I begin to describe the interior. . .? The words "open" and "warm" and "woodtone" spring immediately to mind. . . .

This room was some thirty feet square, an amalgam of finished raw wood, red quarry tile, and house plants of every description. . . . Three sides of the room were windows, and below them was a sort of window-seat arrangement, fully the width of a single bed, extending almost three-quarters of the perimeter of the room. The cushions were water filled—a remarkable circumstance in those days. . . . I sat . . . and found the water-pillow uncomfortable. My curiosity was piqued. The obvious conclusion was that this provided plenty of sleeping space for surprise guests, but it occurred to me that this particular arrangement, and the almost total isolation of the house . . . might also be indicative of bizarre sexual practices.

John brings out drinks and "sat beside me on the window seat and squeezed my right knee familiarly. . . ." Rich "hefts his ornate beer stein . . . to catch . . . the figures engraved on it: bodies engaged in sexual congress." John explains his interest in "quite ancient illustrations for the Kama-Sutra."

John's wife and his wife's lover, a guest at the house, took Rich's wife out to dinner so that the interview could proceed undisturbed—triggering in Rich passing fears about his wife's sexual safety and questioning his own. The group departed, leaving Rich struggling to regain his focus on the interview.

John got himself into a multiple martini state and the conversation took "an unfortunate turn." He off-handedly remarked that the sitting room was built "for people to pass out when the party is too good to leave. They are also great for fucking if that's what catches your fancy." John described the colorful history of the house, a former hideaway of some Chicago mafia, his occasional wish to kill his wife and her lover. He disclosed his responsibility for the accidental death of his brother.

The tables indeed turned. John took control, testing Rich's intellectual and emotional mettle, snickering about Mensa to which Rich belonged, and ranting about his own misunderstood creativity, the poet versus the common man, he—the poet, Rich—a ditch digger:

Or, finally, Richardditchdigger, let us suppose that you are the groundskeeper, the janitor of a tank containing a beautiful sleek pair of bottle-nosed dolphins, at a park like Sea World. You know how to touch them, to pet them; you play familiarly with them. ... And ... all day long and all night you hear them making their clicks and whistles, singing their song, and perhaps you know enough to know that they are also making noises that you can't hear because they are outside your auditory range. But suppose, Richardtikins, just suppose that these beautiful creatures are in fact speaking to each other. ... A language in which all is poetry and all is truth? And you, you are blissfully unaware of its existence? ... You sweep up the ground around the tank, you sieve out the feces. ... [But] you never, never even suspect what is going on all around you. ..."

"And I," he said at last. ... "I am the fucking dolphin. The only trouble is that there's only one of me."

"And so you write books," I offered. "To reach out for the others who might be there to listen."

He fixed me with a glare. ... "You are an asshole, aren't you. ... Writing books is jumping through a fucking hoop—I do it so people will know I'm alive."

Tears flow down John's cheeks. Rich extends his handkerchief and offers to make some coffee. Then what seems like the beginning of a proposition by John deteriorates into a vomit-filled sleep, leaving Rich to wander the house until the group returns. John is revived by his wife. John kisses Rich full on the mouth as Rich and his wife leave.

Rich's responses on the scale clearly did not rise to the full emotional measure of the experience. Whereas, when several respondents needed to, they extended the scale with as many as four emotion items, Rich did not. He simply recorded anger, depression, and frustration at slight or moderate levels. In addition, he did not identify the primary emotion his pieces elicited nor did he express any apparent reasons for writing.

I think this may be explained by the temporal gap between Rich's actual experience and the writing. It was as if the gap protected him the way insulation protects people from the full shock of live wire. He experienced feelings that he did not want to pinpoint further but seemed none the worse for it. In general, Rich described himself as moderately emotional. His negative feelings in fact outstripped their positive counterparts. Depression, anger, confusion, and frustration stood out on his trait as well as his state profiles. He experienced fear and anxiety at weaker levels. Rich thus exhibited a fertile conflation of negative active and negative passive feelings that did not jeopardize his output. Rather, he was all the more able to write about the interview in an absorbing if not artful way.

OTHER PERSONAL VARIABLES

Taken together, when the professionals rated their temperament, there was a discernible skew in the direction of greater emotionality. Three of the professional writers considered themselves easy-going, fourteen believed themselves moderately emotional, and seven considered themselves highly emotional. In fact, 84% of the group rated themselves as moderately or intensely emotional. Furthermore, that emotionality was linked not simply to negative emotions, but to negative active state emotions before writing and at the pause, and both negative active and negative passive emotions as traits. Once again, the negative active emotions are implicated, making it increasingly clear that feelings are characterized by unpleasant and maladaptive connotations.

The relationship between the skill of these writers and their feelings, however, turns out to be more constructive. Study 1 found that the college writers experienced low to moderately intense negative passive emotions during writing. Of that group, those considering themselves skilled enjoyed weaker inhibitory or blunting emotions when writing than their unskilled counterparts. That result was confirmed here on the basis of the skill variable. These professional writers also experienced less frequent and lower intensities of negative passive feelings than they did the positive or negative active ones. This finding is further strengthened by an analysis of the skill-ratings that the professionals gave themselves within the "high skill" rating I had already designated for them. Seven of the writers perceived themselves at least as skilled as their peers, and seventeen perceived themselves as more skilled than their peers. And the more skilled the professionals envisioned themselves, the less often they felt depressed, bored, shy, and lonely when writing in general.

These results go hand in hand with self-sponsored writing experience. The number of years these writers had been writing on their own ranged between three and forty-eight with an average of twenty-five. The longer the professionals had been engaged in self-initiated writing, the less negative passive they felt before writing. Given the proverbial distaste that students have for academic writing, the professional writers were expected to experience emotions distinct from those experienced by students because, unlike students, professionals wrote for money, glory, or themselves. This was not confirmed. Although the professional group wrote approximately twice as many self-sponsored as required pieces, sponsorship of writing did not influence either their trait or state emotions.

One possible explanation is that required writing means something different to students and professional writers. "Required" writing for professionals may mean an activity which they do every day, which they have selected, and for which they are paid. So, regardless of its form, the writing feels *as if* it was self-sponsored. School is not self-selected. Nor are composition courses. Nor is course-related writing. "Required" writing for students means that instructors assign it. The writing often has little value beyond a grade, and the rewards are both inconsequential and impalpable. As a result, commitment to writing between the two groups would differ markedly.

In keeping with these findings, seventeen professionals reported feeling moderately or strongly satisfied with their work, while five were only slightly satisfied with it. Before writing, satisfaction with their work was unrelated to any positive emotions and negatively related to the negative ones, as would be anticipated. Skilled writers are surely expected to come up with satisfactory products but not before they are generated. After writing, this satisfaction was directly related to the positive emotions and inversely related to the negative emotions—also reasonable.

Factor analysis found satisfaction to embody both positive and negative components during the actual writing. As I pointed out, there is good reason to expect less frequent and intense satisfaction from professional writers. The negative relationship between satisfaction and the negative emotions before writing, of course, also implies a positive response. After writing, the professionals reported considerable satisfaction of the positive sort, for it was accompanied by stronger good feelings as well as weaker bad feelings.

THE EFFECTS OF FORMAL EDUCATION

The relationship of satisfaction to schooling further indicates the complex role that satisfaction plays in writers' affective experience. The more formal education the professional writers had completed, the less satisfied they felt about their work. This effect makes some sense if schools teach students the criteria of quality writing and calibrate students' work in those terms. Professional writers would be that much harder on themselves than students.

A competing explanation for this result has to do with the paradoxical but not improbable role that English education plays. If we place on a continuum the path that individuals travel toward careers in writing, formal instruction first facilitates and encourages: an "A" in a creative writing class, the school essay prize, the first blush of publication in a student literary magazine, an article in the campus newspaper. Such events give budding writers a supportive but perhaps unrealistic sense of their potential. Those students whose writing stops with graduation may have glowing retrospective accounts of their writing skill but little day-to-day brush with the profession. Ignorance is indeed bliss. What may happen is akin to the adage, the more we know, the more [we know what] we don't know. Those writers gaining entry into the community of practicing professionals often find how little formal education has actually taught them when compared to the real world of publishing. It is not unusual for professionals to claim that their best instruction in writing came not from their teachers but their editors.

Mark. Mark was highly schooled. A graduate of Amherst College several years before, Mark was completing his M.F.A. in a nationally acclaimed writer's program. Despite his publishing record, his nagging dissatisfaction with his work was actually quite plausible. Mark was doubtless calibrating his work to the creative output of his peers in a highly competitive literary market.

Mark generally worked from inspiration, seeking "to enchant, discover, and uncover in as intense and human manner [as] possible," a lofty if not overblown sentiment. But there was an unmistakable discrepancy between that sentiment and his feelings when actually writing. For example, Mark volunteered to write a review as he put it, "to celebrate the work of a friend," at the same time as "get another credit and make some pin money." Before writing, his negative feelings outweighed the positive by two and three times. Despite the congratulatory nature of the review, those negative feelings persisted. By the end of the session his relief improved, but he remained just as hostile, anxious, ashamed, and dissatisfied with the product:

Philip Graham's *The Art of the Knock* is not simply a collection of stories, but a coherent invention of strange, funny, and sometimes frightening domestic lives. . . .
 We are, however, conscious of a gentle, reassuring presence in these stories. Graham does not beat us over the head with problems. He is often funny and always delightfully inventive. . . .
 As the last line of this passage suggests, the funny things slide into the serious things like jokes that tickle us into sobriety. Graham investigates and celebrates human intimacy. . . . He makes the reader laugh at the characters' idiosyncrasies, grow sober at their problems, but he leaves the reader wiser to human predicaments, to the baffling ways we hide from one another, and the frightful loneliness that results. This is a book you will remember with fondness.

Primarily a short fiction writer, Mark considered himself intensely emotional and, in fact, reported almost always feeling one set of emotions or another. No emotion was ever *not* experienced. Regardless of the sponsoring agent, his emotions were highly volatile. A week later Mark composed parts of a short story, "In the Red Zone," a piece he was under no obligation to write. None of the hostility and negative arousal appeared when he started. However, in less than one-half hour, a break occurred in his writing (at the asterisk) at which point he filled out a form reporting his frustration. He spent only twenty minutes more on the piece, after which he checked off slight intensities of all feelings—except for stronger depression and yet stronger frustration. To the narrative question about his primary emotion, he answered "lots." He was annoyed with himself and totally unsatisfied. "A story is there somewhere; I haven't gotten to it yet."

Ted. Few in the group had delusions of literary grandeur, least of all Ted. With a doctoral degree and a scholarly book to his credit, Ted was a staff writer for a local hospital as well as a freelancer and instructor of college composition. Ted regarded his professional writing as merely a way

Figure 9.1
Evidence of Mark's Frustration

IN THE RED ZONE

At 3:57 he saw the ~~the~~ ^miles of^ clearcut spruce and cedar, the slopes of Mount St. Helens razed by Weyerhauser:

"I'm going to puke," he said to Leonardo, who smiled and threw him an Olympia.

"Here. Piggyback the beer on that bourbon and you won't." Leonardo shut the motor down and stepped outside the ~~riding~~ cab of the truck, where he stripped away ~~began taxiing~~ his shirt and ~~began~~ cleared his throat. "Oh beautiful for spacious skies,..." He started laughing. "The fuck of it is, Henry, you can't tell the difference between what the volcano did and what Weyerhuaser did. Kind of makes me think we're on the right track, doing what nature does." ~~Maybe," he started laughing again. "There wasn't any eruption."~~ This tickled him to know end, and he began to roll himself on top of the ~~2~~ 3 3/4 ton hood. "... for amber waves of...✗ doesn't that just tickle your Kwakiutl blood, Hank?"

~~Hank marvelled at Leonardo's ability to indiscriminate and shook his head.~~

Leonardo stifled a smile and said, "Above all, Hank, you got to admit I'm an asshole."

"You want to be pisshead, but you're BLM, so ..."

"So," Leonardo began roaring with laughter, "I'm...", he choked, "an asshole with a conscience." He began rolling on the head again. "I'll be a janitor in heaven." With this he could speak no more, marvelling at his own mixture of profundity, humor, and inebriation.

✗From his half-drunk position, Hank was mildly sympathetic though he felt a stream of irritation migrating up his spine, tingling the neurons which fired his impulsive temperament. He leaned over and turned ~~impulsiveness~~ the ~~key~~ ignition key without depressing the clutch. The ~~car~~ truck lurched forward, sending Leonardo (in ^a^ half-pike with a quarter twist,) diving off the hood.

to make money. His ambition was to write fiction, but he did not feel very proficient at it. A letter to a friend shows how dispirited he had become:

I am still trying to write, although I have half-admitted to myself that it will never amount to anything. I have improved, but at each crucial spot on the page where I cast out the net for that exactly right phrase, image, or turn of action, rather than bobbing to the surface I see a grey haze. People with good fictional imaginations, I fear, see something and write it down. I must say that writing even as a hopeless amateur is a good discipline for the spirit and hygiene for one's point of view; I mean, it makes you look at life and yourself in relationship to life.

Despite the depressing content, there was little emotional difference between these letters and his hospital writing. Neither activity represented the means to his end—fiction writing. So, emotionally, he just lumped them together, his state feelings remaining flat and stable. But, when writing parts of his novel, he experienced more frustration and shame, especially at the beginning of one episode:

Marjorie was white skin, teeth and tongue, padded hips, which had their own logic. These intertwined themselves around the scaffolding of his reasoning so that by 2:45 a.m., he convinced himself to subordinate himself to that whiteness, at least for a while.

And so for the next several weeks, as spring peacefully became summer, David drew upon the inexhaustible fund of patience which has been strengthened by many years of deprivation. When he encountered Marjorie, he acted as if they shared a secret, fixing his features in an agreeable expression. Alone in his cubicle, though, or when observing her without her knowledge, he was cast over by a sense of duplicity and desperation. When her telephone rang and she used that oozing voice that made David miserable, he closed his door and told himself: "It's only for two months." He knew that he was inhabited by a stranger and yet could not get rid of the stranger.

Charles. These writers seemed to be an all-or-none group. Either they submitted voluminous copy or barely a scrap. Charles belonged to the first group. He had recently received his doctorate in English. His original interest in fiction writing in graduate school quickly shifted to composition studies. Most of his writing was related to his position as an assistant professor. Except for one professional memo, his sessions consisted of successive revisions of an article that he was preparing to send out for "professional advancement."

Charles was living proof that the more educated writers are, the higher their expectations and the more tolerance they have for revision. Charles' drafts showed him to be a fastidious and proud revisor. Charles started off feeling "professionally enthusiastic." Unlike Mark or Ted, his feelings of satisfaction increased with successive drafts but not before he proceeded through several deep revisions. He seemed to understand the process he

Figure 9.2
Charles' Struggle to "Say Something Significant"

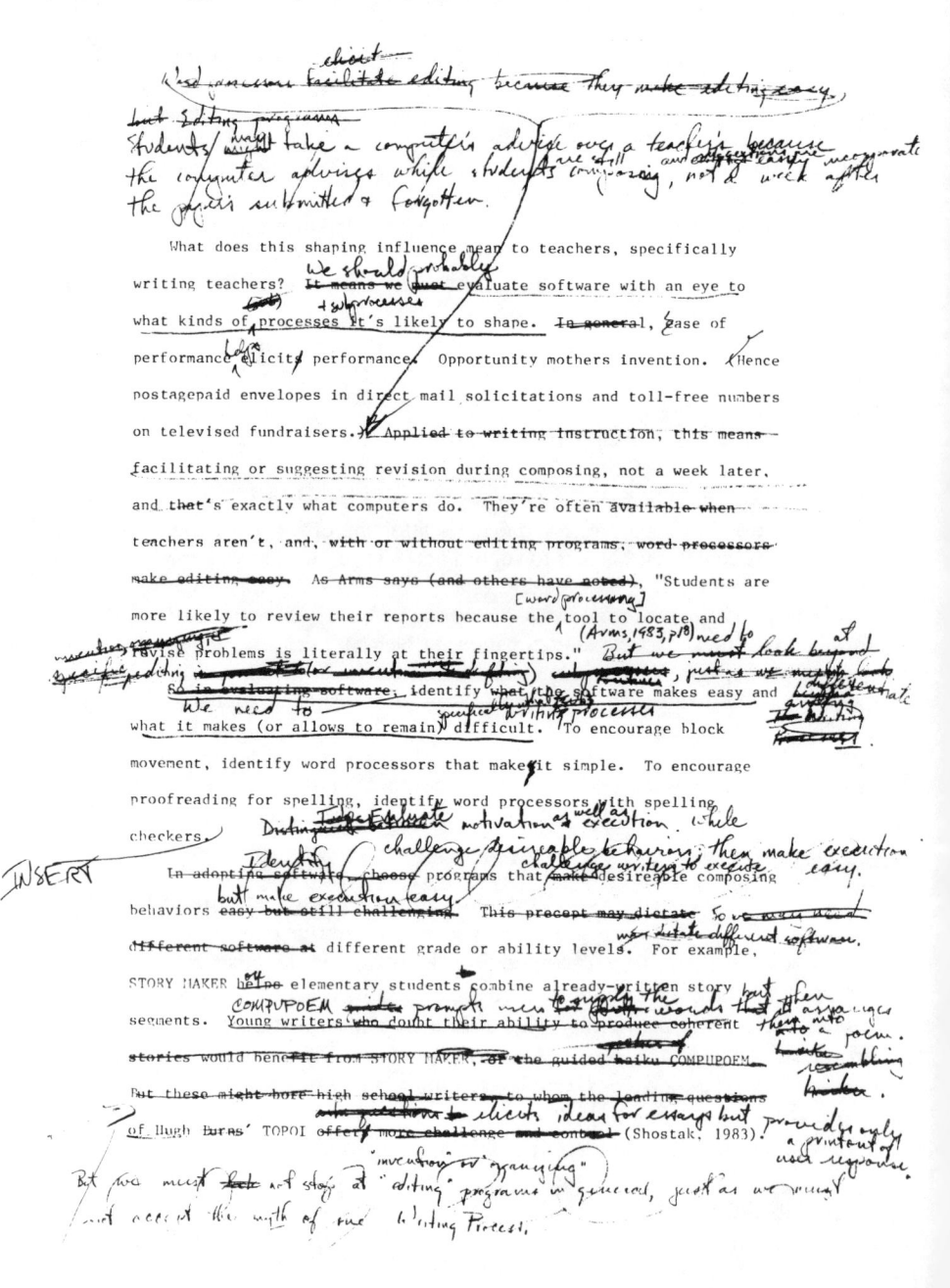

[Handwritten edits at top, partially legible:]
"...elicit... editing because they make editing easy..."
"Students might take a computer's advice over a teacher's because the computer advises while students are composing, not a week after the [paper is] submitted & forgotten."

What does this shaping influence mean to teachers, specifically writing teachers? ~~It means we must~~ We should probably evaluate software with an eye to what kinds of processes [& subprocesses] it's likely to shape. ~~In general,~~ Ease of performance [before] elicits performance. Opportunity mothers invention. Hence postagepaid envelopes in direct mail solicitations and toll-free numbers on televised fundraisers. ~~Applied to writing instruction, this means~~ facilitating or suggesting revision during composing, not a week later, and ~~that's~~ exactly what computers do. They're often available ~~when teachers aren't, and, with or without editing programs, word processors make editing easy~~. As Arms says (and others have noted), [word processing] "Students are more likely to review their reports because the tool to locate and revise problems is literally at their fingertips." (Arms, 1983, p18) [need to look at]

~~So in evaluating software,~~ identify what the software makes easy and [differentiate] what it makes (or allows to remain) difficult. To encourage block movement, identify word processors that make it simple. To encourage proofreading for spelling, identify word processors with spelling checkers. [Distinguish... motivation as well as execution while... challenge principle behaviors then make execution easy]

[INSERT] In adopting software, choose programs that ~~make~~ desirable composing behaviors ~~easy but still challenging~~ but make execution easy. This precept may dictate ~~so~~ [different software] at different grade or ability levels. For example, STORY MAKER helps elementary students combine already-written story segments. COMPUPOEM ~~prompts~~ [prompts...] Young writers who doubt their ability to produce coherent stories would benefit from STORY MAKER, or the guided haiku COMPUPOEM. But these might bore high school writers, to whom the leading questions of Hugh Burns' TOPOI offers more challenge and control (Shostak, 1983). [provides only a printout of user response]

But we must ~~not stop~~ at "editing" / "invention" or "prewriting" programs in general, just as we must not accept the myth of one Writing Process.

needed to go through and was impatient with himself only once. After draft four he wrote that he was "having trouble with the implications section. Want to lead up to something significant—a payoff. But don't want just a bromide. Or what doesn't follow from the main part of the paper." At this point he felt moderately angry, anxious, disgusted, and confused. Figure 9.2 shows that struggle. But satisfaction, relief, interest, and excitement were the only emotions to rise above moderate intensities from draft to draft. As the piece matured, even those feelings moderated. But his feelings of satisfaction resisted erosion.

All in all, of the four observation points examined, immediately before writing and writing in general seemed to be the more critical junctures affectively for these working writers. A greater number of differences among the three emotion clusters occurred just before writing and when the professionals reported their feelings about writing in general. Skill, self-sponsored writing experience, and emotionality correlated more highly with the state emotions before writing than with the state emotions during or after writing. In addition, the rank orders indicated a greater intermixing of positive, negative passive, and negative active emotions at those two observations.

Qualitatively, the results indicated that the experience of the writing process for the professionals was enlivening. Because the positive and negative active emotions were unaffected by skill level, self-sponsored writing experience, and the writing session itself, I do not mean to suggest that those emotions are superfluous to the process. On the contrary. Given the population, these results provide more evidence for the relevance not only of the positive emotions but the negative active emotions in writers' affective repertoires.

NOTE

1. The repeated measures analysis of variance performed on the first four State form sessions found no significant differences for the positive or negative active emotions before, during, or after writing. A significant decline in the negative passive emotions writing was found only before writing ($F(3.16) = 3.57, p < .05$). The negative passive emotions weakened from session one to session three but intensified slightly by session four.

10. *Study 4: English Teachers*

Emotional profiles have potential influence not only on written texts but also on the composing process itself. Emerging from the body of knowledge on the writing process is the relatively underdeveloped matter of writing style. Although, in actuality, writing styles are as multifaceted as the writers they belong to, at this point composing styles seem to crystallize around two poles. The free associative approach advocates a relaxed, intuitive style exemplified in the work of Elbow (1973) and Rico (1983). The structured/planning approach advocates conscious, goal-directed planning and is exemplified in the work of cognitivist Flower (1985).

Composing style may be linked conceptually to cognitive and learning styles, both characteristic modes of mental functioning. Messick (1976) refers to the construct of cognitive style as information processing regularities that develop in congenial ways around underlying personality trends. There are several basic cognitive styles, set once again at opposing poles: reflective versus impulsive, analytic versus global, and field independent versus dependent (Witkin & Goodenough, 1981). Sometimes likened to cognitive style, learning style refers to a consistency in organizing and processing information to be learned.

While the intellectual abilities that underlie both styles are cognitive, the corresponding personality characteristics are regarded as conative and affective. Both cognitive and learning styles explain human variation in processing information and differ from but are constrained by personality. Like baseline or trait emotions, cognitive manifestations of personality may be conceptualized as attitudes, preferences, and habitual ways of problem solving, remembering, and perceiving (for example, sensory mode preference can be kinesthetic, visual, or verbal).

Although the literature on composing styles is small, research indicates that, like cognitive style, composing styles have their counterpart in personality (Jensen & DiTiberio, 1984; Schiff, 1981) and, by extension, emotion. For example, "feeling" types would likely abandon an organizational plan in favor of the "flow" of their thoughts. "Thinking" types would use the outline or other formal organizing arrangements more successfully.

This fourth study asked first about the degree to which different composing styles influence individuals' emotions when they write in those styles. The two conceptually opposite—but in fact not mutually exclusive—composing styles were chosen for comparison: the free writing method and the structured/planning method of composing. The free writing method is akin to free associative thinking. It is characterized by spontaneous, relatively uncensored streams of thought, except that this material is set on paper rather than spoken. Structured techniques, on the other hand, are controlled approaches to composing. They set out particular rhetorical or procedural constraints within which text is generated. The composing style groups were expected to experience equivalent emotional intensities before writing, but those feelings were expected to diverge in intensity after writing. The direction of these differences was unspecified. This study also gathered information about the emotions of English teachers when writing, thus extending the three previous studies.

PROCEDURE

Participating in Study 4 was a subject sample of obvious importance to pedagogy. With varying visions of their own writing experience, English teachers make a penetrating impact on apprentice writers, and they represent part of us all—writers, scholars, practitioners, and learners. Twenty-two current and prospective English teachers and college instructors were enrolled in an upper-division English course on the teaching of writing. There were five males and seventeen females, and the median age was 40. Fourteen took the course for graduate credit.

The experiment took place during the first three sessions of class.

Session 1. On the first day of class, the teachers were introduced to the research project. They were assured that the feelings they experienced while participating in the project would have no impact on their course grade. They were also told that an in-class essay would be assigned the next week.

Session 2. At the beginning of class the group received the Glossary of the emotion items and completed the Before-writing page of the State form. They were then randomly assigned in equal numbers to one of two groups that met in separate but adjacent rooms. The participants were given envelopes containing instructions for the writing assignment and the

After-writing page of the State form to complete when they finished. They were told that they had as much time as they needed, although the exercise was not likely to take more than an hour. What was important was to follow the instructions and do a reasonably good job on the writing.

The Assignment. Both groups received the following prompt:

The goal of this exercise is to describe in detail an experience you routinely have, one about which you have no strong feelings. Think of an experience that is familiar but not boring, neither pleasant nor unpleasant (for example, getting dressed, taking a walk).

The essay should be 2 to 3 double-spaced pages long and written on only one side of the paper.

As soon as you have placed your written work (drafts as well as your finished product) in the envelope, complete the enclosed scale and also place it in the envelope. The graduate assistant will collect it as you leave.

Your essay will be graded according to two criteria:

1. How faithfully you follow the method given below.
2. How skillfully you describe the experience.

Group 1 used the following free-write method:

A. For the first draft, plunge right in. Brainstorm or find all the ideas you can about your experience as they come to you. You won't use every one of them in your completed paper, but don't worry about that now. Don't stop to consider whether an idea is silly, boring, or irrelevant. Don't bother with grammatically complete sentences. Don't write neat, carefully constructed paragraphs. Get the ideas down in columns, circles, or helter-skelter across the page—any way you want. Remember, this draft is not your finished product.
B. Look over the material you wrote in Step A above. Pick out the ideas that are worth keeping and begin to connect them with lines, arrows, or just other words. Gradually develop and organize them.
C. Write your final draft.

Group 2 used the following structured/planning method:

A. Plan the essay fully before you actually begin writing it. Keep your goal in mind as you plan. Prepare an outline, flow chart, or something similar to organize and sequence your topics and subtopics.
B. Expand key words and sentence fragments into complete sentences. Then expand those key sentences into the essay.
C. Start your actual essay by stating your purpose or goal. Then explain how your essay is organized. Finally, describe the experience.

Session 3. A Trait-When-Writing form and Demographic Data Sheet were administered.

Session 4. The teachers filled out an information sheet that asked about their preferred method of composing: the free associative method, the structured/planning method, or another method. They were also asked to check off their reason(s) for choosing that method from a list of nine items.

COMPOSING STYLE

The purpose of this study was to investigate the effects of two composing styles on the emotions of teachers of writing. It was expected that "randomly" assigning the free-write approach or the structured/planning composing approach would elicit distinctive emotions that would change differentially over the writing session. Neither occurred. The emotions did not differ between the two composing-style groups. Nor did the intensity ratings of the three emotion clusters shift differentially during the writing process, regardless of composing style.

The post hoc analysis of the preferred method of composing accounts for the first finding. It indicated that ten teachers preferred the free-write style of composing, nine preferred the structured/planning style, and three could use either method equally. In this design, preference for a writing style was not expected to influence emotion because "preference" was distributed equally between the groups. However, when the preferred composing styles and the assigned composing styles were compared, the reason became clear. Only 18% or four members of the group wrote against the grain. There was thus little cause for emotional differences between the two composing style groups. The teachers were apparently comfortable with the style to which they were assigned.

Concerning the second finding, what is curious in light of the earlier studies is the absence of significant changes in emotion during writing altogether, regardless of composing approach. Did these teachers behave emotionally like the professionals or like the students? Was this finding a function of the essay, the study itself, or some other ingredient?

Let me address the last possibilities first. The resistance to emotional change observed here may be explained in part by the relative bloodlessness of the assignment. Although the essays conveyed emotion, applying a particular composing style to a relatively innocuous personal experience may not have been profound enough to elicit a measurable emotional response. Members of the group were English teachers, who were taking the course not because they were familiar with contemporary principles and practices of teaching writing, but because they were not. In some ways they seemed to exhibit behaviors expected of novice college writers. They may not have totally understood the process they were undergoing. They may not have completely understood the style they were using. They were perhaps only dimly aware of their own. And so, when asked their preference, they made confused choices. They would therefore exhibit little emotional change because they didn't fully know what they were doing. What they didn't know, as the saying goes, wouldn't hurt them.

A rival interpretation invokes a kind of expectancy effect. Because the teachers were instructed to write about an emotionally neutral topic, they may have believed that their instructor wanted them to feel neutral and responded accordingly.

Emotional Experience and the Personal Essay

Dave. But even if the teachers did feel neutral, their essays were not. Only one essay was considered almost entirely free of emotional language, figurative or literal. Witness Dave's:

The purpose of this essay is to give the reader a basic understanding of how Dave Restare prepares himself for an average working day. First, I brainstormed and developed a topic. Second, I developed subtopics to support my main topic. After each subtopic, a list of at least short phrases details that subtopic. Lastly, I expanded each short phrase into complete sentences. Thus, this brings me to the point of the actual essay.

Startled, I quickly turn the buzzing alarm clock off. Picking the sleep from my eyes I see the bright lights through the half drawn window shade. Unwantingly, I kick the covers from my sweaty body. After struggling to the bathroom, I adjust the temperature of the shower water. Before stepping into the shower I slowly slide the underwear from my waist. The shower is now warm and inviting because of the steam that lays on the mirrors. Starting with my face, I lather the cloth and begin rubbing or scrubbing the dirt from my skin. After all scrubbing is completed I shampoo my hair. After thoroughly rinsing the soap from my body and hair I turn the water off. Quickly, I dry off because the clock says I have to leave in ten minutes.

Simultaneously, I spray Right Guard and step into my Levis. Knowing that I have to comb my hair and find a T-shirt, I do so: however, one should not run as I have done. Driving down Highway 55 I complete dressing by tying my shoe laces when traffic is halted because of an accident.

Dave was a preservice English teacher with seven years of experience writing on his own. Although his essay was stiff and undistinguished, the good feelings that Dave experienced after writing exceeded all other negative ones both in frequency and intensity. Before the writing episode Dave felt strongly positive and, at most, slightly negative. As his anxiety moved up a notch after writing, his excitement, happiness, and interest moved up even more. Dave no doubt believed that he satisfied the demands of the task. And, for all intents and purposes, he did. He succeeded in keeping his subjective self out of the introduction. He framed the action in the present and tried using the passive construction (as in "all scrubbing is completed").

Colleen. Most essays, however, were rich in feeling. An elementary school teacher, Colleen began her essay: "Sunday mornings are always a scheduled routine for me. Things just seem to flow and I'm always in a pleasant mood." But her opening sentences did not square with what followed. This particular morning was not routine or pleasant. Getting ready for church coincided with a veritable circus of mishaps: bath water overflowed; the cat walked on the stereo; her sisters needed scolding; her nylons ripped; she was running twenty minutes behind schedule when she tripped on the stairs, and so on. Her feelings before writing reflected that frustrating scenario. After writing, except for anxiety and shame, her negative feelings weakened and her positive feelings intensified overwhelmingly. That Colleen's emotions moved in the expected direction is not surprising, given the hair-raising quality of her narrative.

It is also possible that, because the subject matter was meant to be routine, the study and the class itself might have become objects of the groups' feelings. Like any students in the first days of a course, the teachers may have felt intimidated by the experiment. They knew they were participating in one. They knew their writing was going to be evaluated; maybe their feelings would be, too. They would surely be unwilling to express unpleasant emotions if they believed those feelings would be judged, despite being told otherwise. The impact of the procedure might have overshadowed any effect that would have occurred under less threatening conditions.

Katie. An anecdote illustrates the difficulty in identifying and expressing negative feelings. One of the researchers was outside the rooms in which the experiment was conducted when Katie finished. The researcher casually asked how it [the experiment] went. Her brow furrowed and she exclaimed, "It was boring! You don't ask students to write that way. That's not the way you teach writing!" The investigator answered, "You said it was boring. But you don't sound bored." Katie admitted that the experience was frustrating and that, although she was previously unaware of her anger, she was in fact angry—at the instructor and the class—which made for a fairly uninspired effort:

My life—even the routine moments—is never free from emotion; however, I suppose choosing what to wear this particular morning was as close to an emotion-free experience as I can describe.

Katie enumerates her decisions about dressing (like Dave, even trying to objectify her feelings, as in "The emotions" rather than "My emotions"), concluding:

The emotions, however, get stronger when I can't fit into some clothes or something needs mending or cleaning and I don't discover that before putting it on.

Katie's response is interesting for two reasons. First, she immediately recognized the limitations of the assignment. Second, while she began writing blandly enough, feelings seeped into her text which were crowned by her outburst after the session itself. In fact, Katie reported that she was a fairly emotional person. When writing, she routinely felt anger and anxiety which were counterbalanced by adventure, interest, and satisfaction. However, before the exercise she reported feeling nothing more than slight feelings of any kind. During the writing, virtually every negative active emotion intensified along with boredom, the strongest. Relief and satisfaction played no role at all in her emotional profile. She walked out of the room greatly aroused, from which followed her telling comments.

It is not difficult to see why Katie was upset. As the coordinator of writing in an academic development center of a university and the only doctoral candidate in the group, she was conversant in composition theory and research before she began the course. Although Katie had acquired only six years of self-sponsored writing experience and considered herself an average writer, she was appalled to see the instructor defy the very process pedagogy that should have informed the course and the first writing exercise required in it. On top of what she considered an unchallenging assignment, she was also asked to write against the grain, a subject which I take up later in the chapter.

Sharon. Many pieces were openly emotional. In others, emotion surfaced by intimation. From its very opening questions, Sharon's piece carried the subtle tone of nostalgia, even resignation:

How many times had I repeated those actions? ... How many times had I planned a menu, shopped for food and then prepared a meal for my family? And why was it so often the same meal? I remembered a time when the children were younger when I enjoyed trying new recipes. Of course their reaction was always the same: "Yuk! What's that?" Now that I am a student our meals are anything but interesting and creative. ...

I guess women have always tried to please their families by serving favorite foods. ...

I felt grateful that my husband would be doing the dishes after we ate—and I could go upstairs to study.

Even though Sharon did well in her expository writing courses, she almost always felt anxious when writing and very often felt frustrated, too. Sharon's facility with the casual but limited expressive form was confirmed in her trait profile. Moderately emotional, she had been keeping a personal journal for ten years and stated that it was "therapeutic." It stands to reason that personal writing would be the only form of writing she was comfortable with. Yet, her general feelings of anxiety and frustration with academic writing failed to register before or after the session. Immediately before writing Sharon felt calm and a little bored. Afterward, her feelings were still flat except for interest, happiness, and satisfaction. Although Sharon was not terribly pleased with her essay, the shallow quality of her feelings may represent the inherent irony in writing personal pieces in an academic setting.

Ron. Chair of a high school English department, Ron wrote the most disciplined and professional essay of the group. The goal of his paper was to introduce beginning English teachers to methods of preparing and giving final exams. But even at that, Ron's feelings showed through when he started sharing his own rationale and procedures half way down the first page:

I determined that my students should be prepared well for my Tenth Grade English course, but at the same time, I did not want to make it difficult on myself.

The reason that I started two weeks ahead of time was to guide my students toward the most important highlights of the semester and to make sure that the exam was quite clear. However, I got a bit lazy and failed to proofread it, and sure enough, I found several typographical errors after [the students] started taking it. . . .

I felt more relaxed about tying up loose ends and closing out the semester. . . .

Today was the first day of exams, and I can honestly say they went successfully. . . . I waited for them to arrive. After everyone was seated, I took on a serious demeanor in order to let them know the [seriousness] of the test. I maintained this attitude throughout the period; as a result, the test was a success.

Ron rated himself as moderately emotional. However, his trait profile indicated fewer emotional experiences when writing in general than his state profile indicated. Before the writing exercise, he described himself as contemplative, confused, and depressed which outranked his negative active feelings twofold. After writing, he still felt contemplative but his anxiety, frustration, and shyness trebled. The relationship between Ron's feelings, his disclosures about himself in the writing, and its quality is suggestive. If writing helps students "discover" what they really mean and should tell instructors things instructors do not already know, such a romantic view may produce better writing; but it also may produce discomfort—as it did for Ron.

Holly. Holly framed two thesis statements to introduce a routine morning. As had Dave and Katie, Holly activated certain rhetorical devices in an effort to neutralize her essay. She tried using the passive voice, referred to herself in the third person, and generalized from her husband to "persons" available to help with chores:

There are many responsibilities that have to be completed in order for members of the Miller family to leave the house at 6:30 A.M. headed toward work, school, or nursery. These responsibilities are completed in time segments during which one or two persons are responsible for certain things being completed.

The morning begins around 4:45 with mother awakening. She gets about 20 minutes to get herself together. . . . This time is so precious because everyone is asleep.

An elaborate four-page schedule ensues: having a bath, dressing, taking rollers out, awakening one child, taking him to the bathroom, dressing him, remembering to make "dressing a positive, learning experience." The younger child is "grabbed next—the easy one." He is dressed and washed. They are all brought down to breakfast for oatmeal and chocolate milk. She makes their lunches while they "practice the alphabet, count to ten, or just talk." Then they are back to the bathroom for teeth brushing and hair combing. It is 6:15. One youngster leaves out the back door. The other "leaves for nursery school with the mother out the front door." The routine completed, Holly concludes:

The interesting thing about this description of a typical morning at the Miller house is that Daddy was never mentioned. Daddy is there, but does not help to get the responsibilities completed. He takes the easy way out by reading the paper and playing or talking with Keith and Kevin.

Holly could no longer sustain her composure or objectivity. And her trait emotions confirmed that tendency. When writing in general, the only emotions she seemingly never experienced were, oddly enough, anger and shyness. This did not quite hold up during the session. Before writing, only Holly's inhibitory and depressive emotions were conspicuous by their absence. What she did experience was strong interest, frustration, and being "closed in." After writing she reported *expressing* strong anxiety in her work. But she did not report feeling anxious. Instead, she felt moderately afraid but strongly positive and comfortable, a nod perhaps to the releasing effects of the exercise.

Delores. Delores was direct. No sooner did she enter her text than she registered boredom:

Grocery shopping, while it can be many things, exciting isn't one of them. . . . It actually comes close to being tedious. . . .
 To better explain why I feel this way, let me recall a typical shopping trip. . . .

Delores proceeds down the first aisle, becoming "upset" by the cost of things. She collides with a display at an intersection and must "pick up and reassemble [it]." As usual she has forgotten her list, which delays her, so that she must hurry toward an empty check-out lane, and stands in line

wondering why a few more registers weren't in operation. As I stood, not so patiently. . . . Again, a very familiar feeling came over me, the feeling of frustration. . . .
 I never seem to stay within our budget when it comes to grocery shopping but it still bothers me when I don't.

She is late picking up her daughter but leaves the store "smiling that . . . my tedious, weekly chore . . . was finished for another week."

A junior high school teacher, Delores had been writing on her own for twenty years. Like Katie, Delores acknowledged her emotionality and reported as much negative active feeling when writing as she did positive. She named frustration as the single most prevalent emotion when she wrote in general which, during the actual writing session, she experienced at an even higher corresponding intensity. Despite her expression of boredom, before she wrote, she felt more interested than anything else. It was after writing that her emotions moderated—except, as might be predicted, interest and frustration. Any emotion connected with that last "smile" went unrecorded.

It seems that, like Delores, some members of the group may have *expressed* more emotion in their text than they reported *experiencing*, if the preliminary studies provide any guidance. But I am more inclined to believe that, as affectively uncontaminated as an assignment may be intended, and as under control as the Katies and Rons try to be, the idea of a neutral personal experience is a contradiction in terms.

Emotional Consistency and Other Correlates of Composing Style

As a whole, the teachers' feelings about writing in general were only in small ways related to the emotions they experienced before or after the session. The positive feelings about writing in general predicted positive feelings after writing. There was some evidence that the teachers' negative passive and negative active feelings about writing in general undermined their positive feelings as they entered the writing process. But not enough evidence was obtained about the contribution of the negative trait emotions to the state outcome emotions, that is, how writers felt after they wrote. This supports an interpretation presented in Study 2. The trait emotions may in fact be more labile than the construct indicates, at least for novice writers.

Indeed, the trait emotions appeared to be an unreliable predictor of the state emotions. This finding became important when the data were divided by preferred composing approaches. An analysis of composing styles revealed no significant relationships between the trait and state emotions for the group favoring the free-write method of composing. However, links between the trait and state emotions and composing style were evident for those favoring the structured approach to composing. This subgroup experienced emotions when writing in general that were compatible with those surrounding the actual writing session. When the teachers preferring the structured/planning method experienced negative passive emotions more often, they also felt more intense negative passive state emotions and less intense positive emotions before writing. At the same time that those teachers felt negative active more often when writing in general, they also felt more negative passive and less positive before writing. Last, when they felt positive about writing in general, they also experienced more intense positive emotions after writing.

What is called to our attention here is not what the subgroup felt so much as the consistency with which they felt it. The writers with fewer emotional fluctuations seem to be attracted to the structured style. The structured approach is relatively formal, sequential, and purposive. It works on controlled and intentional planning, avoiding errant thoughts which the free-associative method capitalizes on. The free-write composing style is informal—intuitive, fluid, and immediate. With its allowance for divergent thinking, the free-writing approach is apt to move writers toward unexpected ideas with emotional states to match. As a result, for writers gravitating to the free-writing approach, the trait emotions would be less predictive of the state emotions during actual writing sessions.

Equally instructive was the information obtained about the teachers' preferred approaches to composing. Given their age, background, and years in education, the group was expected to favor the structured composing style, the more traditional of the two approaches. This was not the case. The teachers, likely weaned on the structured composing style, were not necessarily committed to it. Half preferred the nontraditional free-write method. But their reasons were traditional. Eighty percent of the teachers favoring the structured method chose that method because the topic suggested that approach and the writing was required, whereas only 44% of the teachers favoring the free-write method chose free writing for the same reasons. Ten percent of the teachers from the structured group chose the structured style when the writing was self-initiated. Seventy percent from the free-write group chose free writing when the writing was self-initiated. Seventy percent of the teachers from the structured group chose the structured approach when the writing was completed in class. Forty-four percent of the free-writing group reported choosing the free-writing approach when the writing was completed in class. Twenty percent favoring the structured method chose that approach for writing completed at home without restrictions in time. Fifty-five percent favoring the free-write method chose it for writing done at home and when they had a lot of time.

In short, the structured/planning composing style was associated with required writing, in-class writing, limited time, and topics that suggested that style. The free-write composing style was associated with unrestricted time and self-initiated writing completed outside the school setting. This matter is taken up again in Chapters 11 and 12.

Figures 10.1 through 10.5 reify the two composing approaches. For example, Dave favored the structured/planning composing style. When assigned it, he used it to advantage to explain his morning shower routine. Figure 10.1 shows Dave's version of that approach. Ron stated his

Figure 10.1
Dave's Version of the Structured/Planning Composing Style

<u>OUTLINE</u>   1

I. GET READY FOR THE WORKING DAY

    A. WAKE UP
        1. Turn alarm off
        2. Wipe sleep from eyes
        3. Pull off covers

    B. SHOWER
        1. Turn on shower
        2. Adjust Temperature
        3. Take off clothes
        4. Climb in
        5. Wash
        6. Shampoo
        7. Rinse
        8. Turn off shower
        9. Dry off

    C. Dress
        1. Put on underwear
        2. Deodorant
        3. Pants
        4. Shirt
        5. Tuck in shirt
        6. Socks
        7. Shoes
        8. Belt

2

<u>Sentences or Fragments Expanded</u>

    When waking I turn to that buzzing alarm and gently push to off.

    Quickly I pick the sleep from my eyes in order to see the sun through the half-drawn window shade.

    As I adjust the temperature in the shower with my right hand my left hand is taking off my underwear.

    After climbing in the warm, steaming shower I wash. First starting with my face then moving down to my feet.

    After I rinse and dry off I decide on the clothing I will wear.

    Putting on clothes is an art most of us have not achieved. Some will never.

    After dressing completely you are now ready for the working world.

Figure 10.2
Ron's Composing Style Guided by Subject Matter

Getting Ready for the First Day of Finals.

I. <u>How</u> — There are several steps which one should take in preparing to administer a final exam.

II. <u>Why</u> — The purpose of pre-planning is to avoid trouble for yourself and to avoid confusion for your students.

III. <u>When</u> — One should begin preparing for finals at least two weeks in advance of the final day.

IV. <u>The First Day</u> — The first day sets the tone for the teacher's entire week, and it will determine whether or not it will be a total success.

<u>THE ESSAY</u>: (pre-written first ¶)

The goal of this paper is to introduce the beginning teacher to the proper methods of preparing for final exams, no matter what subject he may teach. One may ask the following questions as he begins to ponder the last few days of a semester: (1) how am I going to prepare my students, (2) why I need so much preparation, (3) when should I begin preparing, and how should I act on the first day.

    I. How — A. Type of Test B. Length of time
    II. Why — B. Proofread B. Student understanding
    III. When — A. Two weeks B. Purpose for time.
    IV. 1st Day A. Discipline B. Room Prep.

Figure 10.3
Delores' "Limited Structured" Draft Work

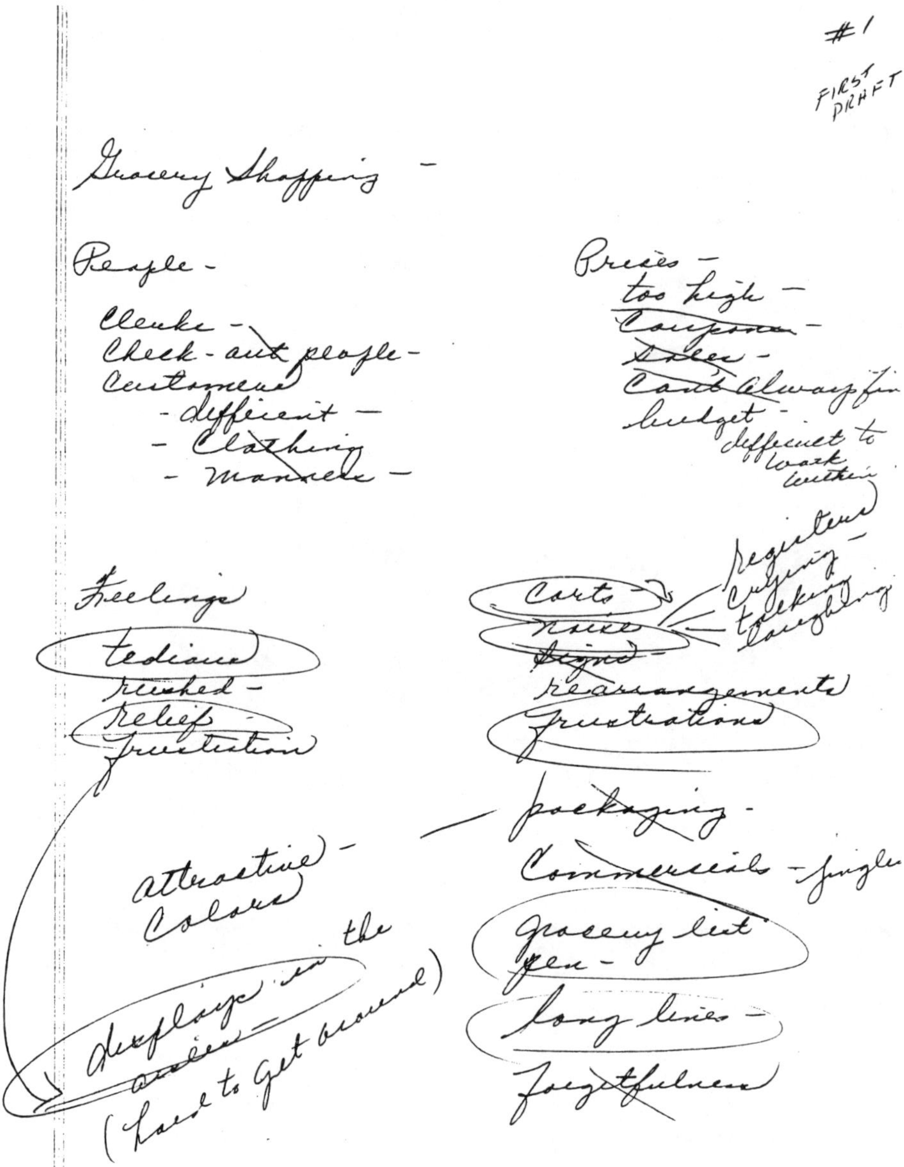

#2
FIRST DRAFT

Introduction
    Necessity in life –
        not exciting – tedious –

Development: (description of shopping)
                (step-by-step)

1) Arrival –
    – parking
    – enter store   – (Rushed –
    – familiar faces, sounds etc.
    – Cart
    – list, pen

2) Aisle by aisle –
    – products –
    – displays
        – some in the aisles – frustration)
    – people –
        friendly, polite
        obnoxious

    – Sounds –
        carts –
        baby crying
        registers
        talking, laughing etc.

Figure 10.4
Katie's Planning Against the Grain

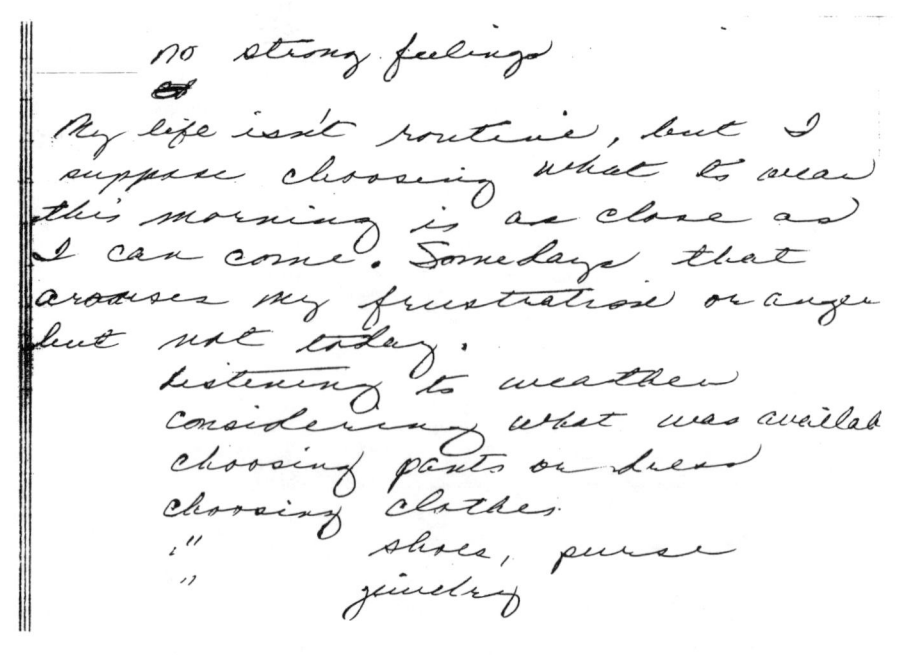

[handwritten notes:]

no strong feelings

My life isn't routine, but I suppose choosing what to wear this morning is as close as I can come. Somedays that arouses my frustration or anger but not today.

listening to weather
considering what was available
choosing pants or dress
choosing clothes
" shoes, purse
" jewelry

preference for a combined free-write and structured method so as "not to squelch creativity but to prevent meandering." While he admitted to difficulties in organizing his papers, it is clear from Figure 10.2 that he took to the structured approach with finesse and exactitude—an instance of subject matter guiding composing style. So, if composing styles are grounded in the trait emotions and the quality of Dave's and Ron's work reflects their composing styles, the levels of dispassion with which they executed their writing tasks may be responsible for the quality of their prose.

Many teachers gravitated to the structured approach, even when they reported preferring the free-write composing style and were assigned it. Delores was a prime example. On the first page of her prewriting, she lapsed into something shown in Figure 10.3 that she called a "limited structured approach." By the second page Delores could not have been more traditional. Katie was an inveterate free writer. When restricted to the structured/planning approach, she had difficulty putting it into practice. Figure 10.4 shows the extent of her prewriting activities before she moved into the full essay. Given her academic background, she was undoubtedly more unwilling than unable to produce anything but the most primitive and commonplace of plans.

Dorothy was a free-spirited, expansive individual. It therefore seemed natural for her to gravitate to the free associative style to which she was assigned. Perhaps her relaxed personal style and thirty years of self-sponsored writing enabled her to turn out the only draft work that did not look like a forced version of the familiar cluster motif. Dorothy's first page is shown in Figure 10.5 (see pp. 166 and 167).

ENGLISH TEACHERS AS WRITING STUDENTS

If the findings from Study 2 are any indication of what writing personal and descriptive essays do affectively, these results represent a marked reversal. A glance back at Study 2 shows that the descriptive essay of the advanced expository group tied with the personal affective essays for the highest number of significant emotional changes it elicited. The descriptive essay also produced the most emotional change, regardless of valence. Moreover, the description was the only essay out of nine to produce significantly weaker negative active emotions.

Nothing like that occurred in this study. The most compelling explanation for the immobility of the emotion clusters may be found in connection with the individual items themselves. The rank orders of the individual emotions for the trait and state observations are listed in Table 10.1. As I had come to anticipate, the positive items dominated the negative active and negative passive emotions during writing. The positive item relief rose to the highest rank by the end of the writing session. Positive items interest and satisfaction remained high. The negative passive items shame and boredom remained at low ranks across all observations. The negative emotions maintaining moderate to high ranks throughout the session were anxiety, frustration, confusion, and fear. But it was the negative active items of anxiety and frustration that made the deepest inroads into the positive ranks after writing of any group in the research.

Despite the intensifying of relief in this study and the stability of high ranking emotions like interest and satisfaction, this group did not feel in any way better about their writing experience once it was over. Even the recalcitrance of the negative emotion clusters of the college and advanced expository group did not prevent those groups from experiencing intensified positive emotions while writing. The teachers were the only *student* group under study, including the poets still to be considered in Chapter 11, whose positive emotions failed to intensify within the writing session itself.

The inflexible, almost frozen quality of the teachers' emotions, on the one hand, might be considered similar to the emotional experiences of the advanced expository writers across the semester. But while a practice effect could account for the progressively blunted emotions of the

Figure 10.5
Dorothy's Personal Style Reflected in her Composing Style

①

getting to work this morning — more narrative
teaching a class today
* listing North Drive

① Time Phone — → Dinner over, shed clothes, phone again, dress & go out → Office and compute
   Thurs — immediate

② Jim & Becky — old clients
                    Globe
landscaping ④ Description of house, sc p, bay window LR CapeCod, Centerhall, f.p.
patio S/P   blues —
          ⑥ Sold immed — charm & area
          ⑤ many showings

③ pleasure of — W office situation

The It was Thurs right. One more day of classes
lesson plans, one more til the weekend.
After dinner I ~~threw~~ slipped ~~hastily~~ quickly
out of the red suit, & stretched $\frac{cozily}{out on}$ into a housecoat,
the bed.

Oh, the luxury for tired feet & mind.
Buzz, buzz. The phone began ringing
insistently. After a conversation punctuated

166

*****, – "that's great", "I'm happy to help", I took the somewhat wrinkled red suit jacket & skirt out of the closet, dressed, & headed out to the car (a Mercedes) & up to my office. Tomorrow's lesson plans would have to wait.

Punching a program into the computer, I sat back & watched it spew forth detailed info, line after line of information.

Shirley

A pink highlighter came next as I selected bits of detail relevant to analyze & compare the variety of homes on the list. With this information I felt confident as I drove to Warson Woods. It was a good feeling. I was also surprised that Becky & Jim had trusted me. While he was in limbo, Jim had made the his job as an editorial writer close

Table 10.1
Rank Order of Means for the Individual Emotions of the English Teachers across One Trait Observation and One Writing Session

Trait Emotions		State Emotions			
		Before Writing		After Writing	
Interested	3.64	Interested	3.27	Relieved	3.18
Happy	3.14	Happy	2.95	Interested	2.54
Satisfied	3.13	Affectionate	2.54	Satisfied	2.53
Excited	3.04	Satisfied	2.53	Anxious	2.46
Inspired	3.03	Adventurous	2.41	Happy	2.45
Adventurous	2.95	Anxious	2.36	Frustrated	2.32
Relieved	2.91	Inspired	2.27	Affectionate	2.27
Affectionate	2.77	Frustrated	2.23	Inspired	2.23
Anxious	2.72	Excited	2.18	Excited	2.09
Frustrated	2.32	Confused	2.09	Adventurous	2.00
Surprised	2.31	Shy	2.00	Confused	1.95
Confused	2.18	Relieved	1.86	Afraid	1.64
Afraid	2.04	Afraid	1.82	Lonely	1.54
Disgusted	1.81	Depressed	1.73	Shy	1.50
Angry	1.73	Lonely	1.68	Depressed	1.45
Depressed	1.72	Angry	1.64	Surprised	1.43
Bored	1.68	Disgusted	1.59	Ashamed	1.36
Shy	1.50	Bored	1.27	Disgusted	1.35
Lonely	1.48	Surprised	1.26	Angry	1.18
Ashamed	1.36	Ashamed	1.18	Bored	1.14

Note: n = 22.

advanced expository group, it was not likely operating here because the BESW was administered over only one writing session. Moreover, during the debriefing immediately following the experiment, many teachers expressed excitement about the experience and were interested in the results. The only thing left that the teachers and the advanced expository writers might have shared was their inexperience. But the comparison ends there.

Taken together and item for item the emotions of the teachers more closely resembled the practicing professionals. The teachers and professionals shared an overall stability of the emotion clusters through the writing process. The positive emotions failed to intensify and the negative emotions failed to weaken over the course of their respective writing sessions. In addition, several individual emotions had common paths. The ranks and corresponding values of confusion, surprise, and boredom of the teachers most closely resembled those of the professionals. Both the professionals and teachers felt more confused than bored. Confusion remained entrenched in the middle of both distributions. Surprise and boredom, holding unusually low ranks, did not seem particularly pertinent to writing for either group. And, apart from any data, the teachers and professionals shared perhaps the single most important yet elusive characteristic: maturity.

But the teachers stood apart from both the expository writing students and the practicing writers in striking ways. For the traditional student and professional groups, satisfaction showed dramatic increases in rank and intensity. Here, the teachers experienced moderately high intensities of satisfaction before writing. However, they enjoyed no greater increases in satisfaction in either rank or intensity by the end of writing. Inspiration showed a similar pattern. In all other groups inspiration ranked relatively high and tended to rise during writing. The teachers experienced moderate inspiration which actually declined slightly in rank during writing. In the earlier studies, shyness ranked so consistently low in relation to writing in general and during the sessions that it hardly seemed relevant. Here, shyness ranked equally low in relation to writing in general. But before writing, it rose to the middle of the rank order distribution and only dropped off after writing. In the previous studies, anxiety dropped in rank, if not in intensity, during writing. Although anxiety ranked 9 in relation to writing in general—the middle of the distribution—it rose conspicuously to rank 6 before writing and rose still higher after.

In sum, the teachers shared their inexperience with students and their maturity with the professionals. Their feelings surrounding the writing episode were as stable as the professionals' but not nearly as positive. The teachers were less inspired and satisfied and more shy and anxious. On balance, they were more tentative about their work than the other writers—each in his or her own way more practiced: students as beneficiaries of previous writing classes; professionals as beneficiaries of on-the-job experience.

ADDITIONAL DESCRIPTIVE DIMENSIONS

Other analyses conducted on the group as a whole and linking several subject variables helped profile these special writers.

Self-Sponsored Writing

The teachers' estimates of their emotional predispositions created a normal curve. Five members of the group reported themselves to be generally placid, twelve were moderately emotional, and five were intensely emotional. The median number of years that the teachers wrote on their own was twenty. Levels of emotionality and self-sponsored writing experience were inversely related. The more years that the English teachers engaged in self-sponsored writing and the younger they started, the more placid they perceived themselves to be, lending credence to the salutary effects of writing that were also observed in Studies 1 and 3. The more formal education the teachers had completed, the more placid they considered themselves to be and the more satisfied they were with their writing in general—quite unlike the professional writers of Study 3.

Writing Skill

In Study 1 the self-rating of skill of the college writers was considered a more sensitive predictor of emotional response to writing than the instructor rating. Findings here revealed the opposite. Significant correlations occurred only on the analyses using the instructor ratings.

Again approximating a normal curve, the distribution indicated that two members of the group considered themselves less skilled in writing than their peers, two considered themselves more skilled than their peers, and the remaining eighteen considered themselves as skilled as their peers. However, the instructor awarded them higher proficiencies. Twelve teachers were rated as skilled writers and nine as unskilled. Nonetheless, the instructor-rated and self-rated skills were directly related ($r = .48$; $p < .034$), indicating that the teachers identified as skilled or unskilled by the instructor were likely to rate themselves similarly—surely evidence of like-mindedness.

The instructor ratings were directly associated with age and self-sponsored writing experience. Those teachers rated as skilled by the instructor were more accustomed to writing on their own than those rated as unskilled. Those teachers rated as skilled writers by the instructor were also older. These two findings are linked logically in that older teachers would simply have had more opportunity to engage in writing activities. And, because the instructor-rated skilled teachers had a longer history of self-initiated writing, it should come as no surprise that these very same writers felt significantly less positive after the writing session.

The nature of the group helps explain this result. Projecting themselves into their instructor's role, the teachers would be expected to share—that is, value and internalize—their instructor's assessment of skill. This stronger agreement between the instructor and the self-skill ratings than with earlier groups would most obviously suggest an accuracy in assessing abilities that the role of teacher affords. From this it could follow that the group's insights about effective writing reflected a negative assessment of their own. This interpretation, of course, does not categorically signal weak writing so much as a special sensitivity to writing in classrooms.

However, it is more complicated than that. Members of this group find themselves in the conflicting and unenviable position of being writing students, writing teachers, and mature adult learners. I have already addressed their role as writing students. As English teachers, the group could easily feel under more than the usual pressure to perform well. Standards would presumably be higher than those they set for their students, but their inexperience could cause doubts about their ability to live up to those standards.

To add to the predicament, by virtue of their maturity, this group is burdened with greater responsibilities than typical undergraduates, and that could complicate learning. Nontraditional learners are known to experience considerable trepidation about returning to school as well as writing anxiety (Thompson, 1981) to which these teachers would be especially vulnerable. Despite the statistical stability of the negative active emotions, it seems that evaluation apprehension intensified for the teachers, very unlike their younger and professional counterparts. Teachers are, after all, accustomed to having students, not being them.

11. Study 5: Student Poets

Nowhere in the annals of literature is emotional disturbance more visible than in writers of creative work. The emotional history of poets is especially notorious. In and out of public attention, one group constitutes the poet suicide: John Berryman, Robert Lowell, Charlotte Mew, Sylvia Plath, Theodore Roethke, Delmore Schwartz, Anne Sexton, and Dylan Thomas. Poets seem overrepresented on the rolls of the manic-depressives: Lord Byron, Samuel Taylor Coleridge, Hart Crane, Gerard Manley Hopkins, Edgar Allan Poe, Dante Gabriel Rossetti, John Ruskin, Percy Bysshe Shelley, Ezra Pound (alternately diagnosed as paranoid, "of unsound mind," or as simply insane), and again, John Berryman, Robert Lowell, Theodore Roethke, Sylvia Plath, Delmore Schwartz, and Anne Sexton.

A positive by-product of affective disorders is, of course, creativity. Its wavelike effect produces periods of fatigue, profound anguish, and despondency followed by periods of relief and rest, or excitability and exuberance, during which there is high productivity. Poets presumably benefit from mood changes more than other types of writers because the language of poetry is more akin to primitive thought processes and psychosis and because the nature of sustained work is probably different (Leo, 1984).

What is thus available about poets and writers to students of literature and psychologists, if not the wider public, is a monumental dislocation of feeling. Indeed, the interfering emotions that have occupied writing researchers seem to be the very ones that move leading literary figures to composing. In Chapter 2 the personal documents of literary luminaries confirm the transformation of both flight and fight tendencies into invitations to write. Incompatible emotions not only coexist, but may have more potential for stimulating and sustaining writing than predominantly negative or positive ones. Yet the professional writers described in Study 3 did not appear freighted by emotional extremes or distress. Rather, when writing, they seemed to enjoy internal experiences that were stable and enfranchising. The poets in that study were not much different affectively from their prose counterparts, with one striking footnote. They experienced stronger negative active impulses.

The anecdotal data are unwieldy, the clinical findings bleak, and these studies small. The purpose of Study 5 was not to determine if creative writing classes were a breeding ground for emotional disorder but to extend the general inquiry into a highly neglected subset of student writer, the poet.

PROCEDURE

Nineteen students in an introductory poetry writing course participated. Eleven had declared majors in the College of Arts and Sciences, nine of which were English or English education. Members of the group ranged in age from 19 to 60 with an average age of 24. Eleven students were females and eight were males.

Over a fifteen-week fall semester the group completed a Demographic Data Sheet and two Trait-When-Writing forms. They completed State forms immediately before and after seven required poetry writing assignments. The students also paused to complete a Very Moment page during the writing sessions. The writing schedule follows:

Week 1: Trait-When-Writing form
State form with a 20-minute *in-class* free write
Week 3: State form with an *at-home* draft of a poem
Week 5: State form with a 20-minute *in-class* free write
Week 7: Trait-When-Writing form
State form with an *in-class* structured exercise based on Hugo (1979, pp. 19–25)
Week 9: State form with an *at-home* draft of a poem
Week 11: State form with an *in-class* structured exercise adapted from Hugo (p. 30)
Week 15: State form with an *at-home* finished poem based on either Hugo exercise

CHANGES IN THE STATE AND TRAIT EMOTIONS

The single most incontrovertible finding throughout the studies has been the intensifying of the positive emotions during writing. The negative passive emotions weakened and the negative active emotions, on the whole, resisted change. This study was no exception on all three counts. However, the practice effect that may have been responsible for the progressively flattening emotions in the semester-long data collection in Study 2, did not seem to occur here. Nor did the intensities of the emotion clusters seem influenced by the position of the writing assignments in the course sequence. The students felt most positive during writing session 4, least negative active during session 5, and most negative passive during session 6.

Table 11.1 shows the rank order of means across the seven writing sessions. I will not retrace the paths followed by the individual emotions because the items reflect patterns established earlier. Some exceptions are noteworthy. Satisfaction rose only to rank 5, and relief did not quite make it to the top by the end of the writing sessions. Both frustration and anger held their ranks in the middle of the distribution, but both rose in rank and intensity at the pause in the writing. Whereas inspiration held its own or rose in rank in the previous studies, here, it fell in rank.

How the student poets felt about writing in general was measured twice during the semester. These trait emotions are ranked in Table 11.2. As I have noted, trait emotions should resist change and show a direct relationship to their corresponding states. Here, the frequency with which the students experienced the positive, negative passive, and negative active trait clusters, when writing in general, was related to the intensity with which the students experienced the corresponding states across the seven writing sessions. This also held true within the writing process itself. The more often students experienced the trait emotions, the stronger they experienced their corresponding states before, during, and after writing.

But consistent with the advanced expository writers of Study 2, the frequencies of individual emotions decreased between the two Trait-When-Writing observations, regardless of valence. The question remains as to whether the downward shift was a function of other changes or a function of a practice effect. Were a practice effect operating, my sense is that intensities might decrease but the order of the items would remain generally the same. If the traits anger and adventurousness, which rose either in rank or intensity, are temporarily excluded, the two Trait-When-Writing rank orders show remarkable consonance. In fact, that is what a comparison suggests: a practice effect controlling the values, but the actual arrangement of the trait emotions overall reflecting baseline affective priorities.

Table 11.1
Rank Order of Means for the Individual Emotions of the Student Poets across Seven Writing Sessions

Before Writing		At a Pause (State Emotions)		After Writing	
Adventurous	2.73	Adventurous	2.85	Adventurous	2.65
Interested	2.66	Interested	2.83	Relieved	2.53
Anxious	2.50	Excited	2.42	Interested	2.50
Excited	2.48	Anxious	2.36	Excited	2.46
Happy	2.20	Frustrated	2.34	Satisfied	2.32
Inspired	2.16	Inspired	2.25	Happy	2.28
Frustrated	2.12	Happy	2.10	Affectionate	2.26
Affectionate	2.07	Affectionate	2.09	Anxious	2.21
Confused	1.94	Angry	1.92	Inspired	2.18
Satisfied	1.72	Confused	1.92	Frustrated	2.08
Angry	1.71	Satisfied	1.87	Angry	1.80
Disgusted	1.65	Relieved	1.83	Afraid	1.71
Afraid	1.64	Disgusted	1.76	Disgusted	1.64
Lonely	1.61	Afraid	1.72	Confused	1.63
Bored	1.59	Depressed	1.69	Depressed	1.57
Depressed	1.54	Lonely	1.63	Lonely	1.57
Relieved	1.54	Surprised	1.48	Surprised	1.57
Surprised	1.38	Bored	1.42	Bored	1.41
Shy	1.34	Ashamed	1.34	Ashamed	1.33
Ashamed	1.30	Shy	1.22	Shy	1.25

Note: n = 19.

Table 11.2
Rank Order of Means for the Individual Emotions of the Student Poets across Two Trait Observations

Trait Emotions

1		2	
Interested	3.72	Interested	3.47
Inspired	3.56	Adventurous	3.42
Excited	3.50	Excited	3.10
Adventurous	3.06	Inspired	3.05
Anxious	2.94	Happy	2.95
Happy	2.89	Anxious	2.94
Frustrated	2.82	Affectionate	2.73
Affectionate	2.76	Angry	2.63
Lonely	2.67	Frustrated	2.37
Confused	2.65	Lonely	2.37
Satisfied	2.58	Relieved	2.26
Depressed	2.44	Depressed	2.21
Angry	2.41	Disgusted	2.21
Surprised	2.41	Confused	2.16
Relieved	2.23	Satisfied	2.15
Disgusted	2.17	Afraid	2.00
Afraid	2.12	Surprised	1.78
Bored	1.76	Bored	1.52
Shy	1.76	Shy	1.37
Ashamed	1.70	Ashamed	1.31

Note: n = 19.

WRITING SKILL

The skill variable produced some anticipated and some curious results. Three levels of instructor and student ratings were used in this study. At the beginning of the semester, of the sixteen students answering this question, ten rated themselves about as skilled in writing as their peers, four rated themselves more skilled than their peers, and two rated themselves less skilled than their peers. At the end of the semester the instructor rated two students as highly skilled, nine students as moderately skilled, and eight as unskilled. The correlation between these two skill ratings was low and not significant, reflecting discrepant views of competence and, according to the instructor, an even split between high and low writing abilities.

The instructor ratings of skill were found to be a significant predictor of emotional change. Those student poets whom the instructor rated as *highly skilled* felt more positive than their *unskilled* counterparts. When it came to negative passive emotional change, the instructor-rated *highly skilled* poets felt less depressed and inhibited than their *unskilled* counterparts, and the poets whom the instructor rated as *unskilled* or *moderately skilled* felt more so. Despite the discrepancy in skill ratings, the students behaved in actuality as their instructor's evaluation would have predicted, perfect Pygmalions in the classroom. The weaker writers felt more confused, bored, depressed, or ashamed while composing. Poets performing above average work felt happier about the writing experience and were more interested in it.

Jim. One of two skilled poets in the group, Jim mirrored the working writers of Study 3. He was under control, and that pattern remained stable across the semester. Jim typically felt less negative and more positive when writing, particularly interested and satisfied. During the sessions, he felt especially adventurous. Apart from moderate anxiety and slight confusion, he was least stricken with nervous arousal. However, at no time did he feel unusually inspired or surprised or, for that matter, bored. Any retreating and inhibitory emotions were virtually nonexistent. His first free write reflected on the composing process:

What is most adventurous about writing is having nothing in mind, setting a course forward and reading the names of the streets passed. Sometimes street signs are blurred, not because of the great speed but because they are paths I know nothing about.

Writing was Jim's "calling." His poetry had already been anthologized, and he was working on a second novel. Prose seemed his strong suit as this later free write shows:

Up in the city, it's cold. The wind breaks the leaves on the trees like icicles, brittle green splattering on the grass. Gray skies swim. The birds are hiding in Texas and Mississippi. A mathematician is walking to class, measuring his quick steps in the cold. The physics of his strides, the gravity of his motion. He writes letters full of equations and idiosyncrasies. The letters come by mail to my desk. . . . Time goes quickly on Chicago streets. In the cafe at night black overcoats stroll in with cigars and brown clay faces like Edward G. Robinson say hello to the store owners. . . . At a table, the mathematician wants the number of people in the cafe. The woman with a ball of string for hair with her friend who smokes with a foot long cigarette holder lipstick like a bright invitation on the filter, the writer in the alcove, expresso in his teeth, pen in numbed hands, writing in frenzy, drawing word pictures of the cafe, newlyweds sharing breakfast in the window, shiny rings reflecting off their forks and glasses. They laugh quietly, gazing out the immense window. . . . The cook . . . pot belly pushing on his T-shirt calling out to the waitress across the room, the waitress deep in conversation with the clay mold who talks like Eddie Robinson in grunts of cigar sounds, who lets her deliver her food to the mathematician who had forgotten he was there to eat.

The outcome emotions in terms of self-rated skill were somewhat more surprising. Student poets seeing themselves as *more skilled* than their peers felt less positive. The student poets rating themselves *less skilled* or *as skilled* felt significantly more positive—which intensified steadily during writing. Furthermore, the self-rated *less skilled* student poets felt significantly more negative active across the seven sessions.

Mitch. Mitch is a good example. Writing on his own only one year, he considered himself less able than his classmates but highly emotional. This would account for the way he approached writing, as his first free write makes plain:

I am so pissed I woke up late and it wouldn't happen if I didn't stay up late. I am so hungry right now I feel like an empty vat never being filled. Now is today going to go slow, fast, is it going to be boring or exciting I wish I could leave right now I can't wait till Thursday when my girlfriend . . . gets here I wish I'd quit sneezing Coming to the university sucks. My foot hurts Here come the sniffles I feel like I'm not even awake Can't think, Can't think Hell I never know what to write I am the shittiest writer and this class scares me Give me a pillow I'm tired Crack my knuckles and my hand is getting tired writing this bull shit about nothing I don't understand what this is all about.

He came away from the exercise as anxious and afraid as he felt excited and relieved. For the remainder of the semester, his anxiety and anger and his excitement and adventurousness stayed within close intensities of one another, regardless of the assignment and level of satisfaction—for example, the following poem with which he was pleased:

Stuck
My eyes ready to fall out
Lids slipping and repelling
The highway jammed, a confetti of colors

I glare at the fire engine. . . .
I reach back a night
Instead I journey into nothingness
Trying to focus, there is only a blur
Clouds of cotton candy whirl at my feet
The heavens colored like the Mediterranean
I approach the illuminated door to reality
. . . .
I tumble down towards hell
The hosts of evil taunt and torture me
No means of escape is evident. . . .

To repeat, the self-rated less-skilled poets felt less positive about writing but that feeling intensified during writing. One way to understand this result is to look at the positive emotions satisfaction and relief, which again made the most dramatic shifts. In keeping with an idea raised in Study 2, given the perception of their skill, unskilled writers in general—and that would include poets—would likely have low standards for their work, experience considerable relief when it was done, and be easily satisfied with it, regardless of its actual quality. As Eastman put it: Untrained writers are often handicapped by premature assurance. They equate their own natural pride in completing the first draft with the probable applause of the audience. Why endanger the happy harmony of the piece by tinkering with it? It seems that, if student poets go so far as to rate themselves more proficient than their classmates, they may indeed be less frivolous, more serious about their work. They have higher expectations for themselves and, for example, like Jim, experience relief and satisfaction at levels tempered by those expectations.

Then there were the negative active emotions. The students perceiving themselves as less skilled than their classmates also felt more intense nervous arousal. Part of the explanation may lie with the students' perception of their temperament. Two out of the sixteen students answering this question rated themselves as easy-going, eight students rated themselves as moderately emotional, and six rated themselves as highly emotional. With a decided tilt toward greater emotionality, the highly emotional poets equated their temperament with negative active feelings. What makes this particular set of findings interesting is that the relatively easy-going poets also associated themselves with negative active impulses.

Louise. Louise best represents this latter group. She saw herself as less skilled than her classmates but also placid. For Louise it was "easier to write than to speak." However, except for shyness, the negative passive feelings were conspicuous by their absence. Instead, her poetry was accompanied by strong negative active feelings. After she completed the following poem, she wrote, "I feel like ... maybe I do not show emotion enough by crying," a complicated message that remained unrealized in the poem itself:

> From a tiny duct
> moisture rolls
> Without a limit
> reflections in the light
> wrinkles appearing
> streaks upon the mirror
> the tissue
> holds the treasure
> tears, so many
> but so few
> drop like rain
> on the desert
> the sharing
> of the relief of misery
> oval in shape
> moving slowly
> to the edge
> almost transparent
> as the morning dew

It is not unreasonable for the so-called quiet and composed student poets to nurse strong negative active feelings. Without entering into a full-blown discussion on the psychology of passive aggression, I expect that such supposedly conflicting subjective states are not conflicting at all. Rather, they are spread with some democracy among the larger public. What may distinguish poets emotionally from other individuals, if not writers, is that, though one type of poet may *express* negative active feelings more easily than the other, the *experience* of those emotions is less repressible. Poets at both emotional poles have found their form.

Given the affective history of poets, I was not startled by the link of poetry to the negative active emotions so much as by the link between the groups under study themselves. For, oddly enough, these *self-rated less skilled poets* felt similar when writing not merely to another group of poets but to the group of *experienced poets* sampled in Study 3. The groups, of course, had virtually nothing in common with one another beyond the writing of poetry and their strong negative active feelings, so that the result may be anomalous. But I wish to suspend that possibility temporarily in order to explore the implications of this finding.

I arrived at two equally plausible explanations: The emotions making up the negative active cluster meant different things; or similar emotions were experienced for different reasons. First, the difference between these groups may rest with the way the negative active impulses were interpreted. Unskilled writers may interpret negative arousal as debilitating, while skilled writers may interpret it as a cue to write (McLeod, 1987). Negative agitation may also shift in meaning during writing. Before writing, it may represent physiological tension and anticipation. At the end it may come to mean evaluation apprehension. But it must be underscored that anxiety ranked high among the positive emotions. From this vantage it seems to have a good deal of utility and may even be considered positive.

Second, although causality was not a priority in this research, contemporary psychology views emotion as an epiphenomenon. Something in the internal or external environment triggers feelings which, in turn, triggers composing. The participation of emotion in composing is apt to arise in response to a wide range of phenomena: the sponsor of the writing, the precipitating event, the subject matter of the text, the adequacy of the self to perform the task, the composing process, the developing text, or the written product. Because the professional poets were skilled and were engaged in a self-selected activity that is expected to come relatively easily to them, negative active emotions would less likely follow from the sponsor, the ability to perform the task, the composing process, or the written product (even though, like the rest of us, experienced writers do generate their share of weak material). This leaves the precipitating event itself or the subject matter responsible for the negative active feelings.

For the unskilled student poets like Louise and Mitch who recognize themselves as such, a more pervasive range of reasons may account for their negative active feelings. Apart from the precipitating event or subject matter, these emotions could just as easily refer to their developing text or written product as to the writing process, the sponsoring agent (their instructor), and/or themselves. Self-rated unskilled student poets are likely to be angry, anxious, disgusted, and/or frustrated—even afraid. After all, on top of the ups and downs of everyday life, they *elected* a course that *requires* writing tasks at which they *realize* they are performing poorly.

SELF-SPONSORED WRITING AND ADOLESCENCE

Regardless of descriptive variables, the studies showed that the positive and negative passive emotions followed opposite courses during writing. Students feeling high levels of excitement, interest, adventurousness, and happiness tended to experience low levels of boredom, loneliness, shyness, and depression. Some negative active emotions dropped in rank, but others strengthened slightly to the pause, before weakening by the end of the session. The net result was that the positive emotions intensified during writing, the negative passive emotions dropped off, and, as usual, the negative active emotions remained intractable.

This pattern failed to hold up when the self-sponsored writing experience of the student poets was analyzed in terms of the state emotions. The positive and negative emotions tended to follow parallel courses both across and within the writing sessions. Ranging between one and twenty years with an average of seven years, self-sponsored writing experience made an unmistakable impact on the emotions of this group.

For students having up to seven years of self-sponsored writing experience, the positive emotions were relatively intense. From eight years on, these values were weaker. Then they intensified slightly after twenty years of self-sponsored writing experience. A similar dip in intensity reappeared for the negative active emotions. Those students acquiring up to four years of self-sponsored writing experience felt stronger negative active impulses across the sessions than their peers. For those students reporting between five and fifteen years of self-sponsored writing, their negative active emotions weakened. Those emotions again intensified slightly for student poets writing on their own for twenty years or over. Although the start and end points varied, the negative passive emotions followed an equivalent path.

Results derived from the actual writing sessions elaborated on this pattern developmentally. Taken together, the demographic data helped establish that students *unaccustomed* to writing on their own had acquired up to seven years of self-sponsored writing. This would set its beginning during late adolescence. Students acquiring more than seven years of self-sponsored writing experience were considered *accustomed* to writing on their own, implicating early adolescence.

Study 3 results indicated that the negative active emotions were as obvious in the emotional landscapes of the professionals as they were in the student poets. However, given the parameters above, those student poets *accustomed* to writing on their own felt less positive and negative active during the writing sessions.[1] Students *unaccustomed* to writing on their own felt more positive, but also more negative active by the end of the sessions (which also tended to peak during the writing). The negative passive emotions again followed a similar pattern but fluctuated more actively.

The age that the students began writing on their own created a third set of emotional peaks and valleys. The age that students began self-sponsored writing ranged from 5 to 25 or older, with the modal age between 15 and 18, or late adolescence. Those student poets beginning self-sponsored writing during that modal period, or late adolescence, felt less positive across the poetry writing sessions than those poets beginning later. Students beginning self-sponsored writing between the ages of 10 and 14, or early adolescence, felt most negative active. Those beginning it after 25 years of age felt, again, least negative active. When it came to the negative passive emotions, poets unaccustomed to self-sponsored writing felt less negative passive. Those accustomed to self-sponsored writing felt more negative passive.

What this comes down to is this: Students unaccustomed to writing on their own felt more intensely positive, negative passive, and negative active. Students accustomed to writing on their own felt less so. At the same time, weak positive and negative passive feelings showed links to writing begun during late adolescence. Strong negative active and negative passive feelings showed links to self-sponsored writing begun during early adolescence.

Diane. In her twenties, Diane claimed fifteen years of poetry writing experience, and her affective profile showed the distinct sag predicted by the statistical results. She remained underaroused throughout the writing sessions, her emotions flat, regardless of valence. Her first free write barely generated confusion, anxiety, frustration, or excitement. At the pause, she felt satisfied and happy. By the end, she felt nothing but relief:

I've never done a free-write before and I have no idea what to write about. Although when you really stop to think of it every poem is a free-write. Maybe not a spontaneous one but if you pick a subject and just start writing about it that's a free-write isn't it?

I don't like poems that don't rhyme. All of my poems have four stanzas and the first two lines and the last two lines always rhyme.

I love Robert Louis Stevenson. I memorized a poem of his in third grade. I still know it.

I have a great dog. Her name's Sandy and she's almost a year and a half. I taught her to sit, give her paw and play dead before she was four months old. A few months ago I taught her to roll over. Isn't she smart?

I wish I would see John again. I'd like to tell him to take a flying leap. I doubt that I would ever be able to say anything like that to him though no matter how much I might want to. I'd probably get tongue-tied like I used to be when I would see him more often.

I wonder if Kathy's met him yet. She's taking a lab with him, a TA, this semester. She'll probably say what did Diane ever see in this guy.

I'm running out of things to write.

Friends considered her good at poetry and recommended a course. But, if her fifteen years of experience was accompanied by growth, it was not of the right kind. Diane was bound by antiquated poetic sensibilities. Moreover, her work showed little improvement over the semester. A later poem described a picnic that was rained out. Initially Diane felt slightly adventurous, anxious, and bored. All too soon, the piece, and her feelings, became as washed out as the picnic.

Still later came a tired poem about spring:

Clouds kiss the sky
The sun warms the earth
Rain cleanses the land
and brings new life to trees and flowers
Withering after the long, hot summer.
All seems right with the world.

Then the snow comes
Placing a blanket of pure white
Over the rejuvenated land.
The trees and flowers that had been given
a second chance will die now
To be reborn in Spring.

Spring brings new life
Squirrels scurry to gather nuts
Trees are once again clothed
After standing naked through the winter
Birds chirp happily outside my window
And all is right with the world.

Where she evidenced potential was in her free writing. One episode speculated on the death of a relative and the recent death of a friend's father. But even at that, Diane began writing feeling only slightly adventurous, anxious, and confused. These feelings gave way to slight loneliness, anxiety, and satisfaction, which ended up as slight loneliness, frustration, and depression. These emotions are clearly consonant with the subject matter, but perhaps less than adequate, given Diane's relationship to her aunt:

I hope Aunt Wanda's going to be o.k. First it was lung cancer, they got rid of that. Then it went to the brain. They thought they got rid of that but it looks like it's back. Bruce's father just died of cancer 2 weeks ago. He didn't have to. The chemotherapy was working. He was in remission. Then they messed up his hands and had to stop. The cancer came back and he died. His eyes lit up like a Christmas tree when Bruce told him about the casket he picked. It was solid wood which was appropriate since Mr. Delkers always loved to work with wood until the cancer took away the use of his hands. If he hadn't had cancer he wouldn't have had to have chemotherapy and lose his hands. He couldn't do much for himself either. Bruce had to carry him from place to place, this man who had once been so full of life and was now reduced to little more than dead. He was also hallucinating.

This sounds dangerously close to Aunt Wanda's condition now. She is unable to walk of her own volition and is seeing double. I'm going to see her tonight and I'm scared. Hospitals scare me with their antiseptic smell and cold, impersonal colors. What scares me the most is the thought that people go there to get better and some don't. One of those people could turn out to be Aunt Wanda. She's such a good lady, never hurt anyone. Why do bad things always happen to good people and never to bad? That's the way it's always been. People that spend their lives being good and helping people always seem to be the ones who get incurable diseases or are mugged, murdered, beaten, or raped.

Diane wanted "to be creative and had stories in me that I want to get out." What she produced poetically was not unusual, but deeply adolescent in outlook—in a word, immature.

Marilyn. Marilyn, also in her twenties, represented the other extreme. Marilyn experienced all three clusters of emotions frequently and intensely. She had been writing on her own for five years. But in that time, she had come to use it to "sort out my feelings and clean my head of thoughts, problems."

She felt slightly bored and moderately contented and satisfied before her sensuous free write on rain. Intense negative active feelings punctuated the pause. By the end of the session, Marilyn's emotions moderated except for frustration, affection, and happiness:

I stuck my arm out the window, the wind blowing the hair on my arm neatly back. The wind pushed my skin through my finger bones. My hand looked like a skeleton with a piece of leather sticking to it. Then it rained. My arm still out, it felt like millions of tacks were hitting my arm, each raindrop would explode splash and sting me. . . .

I walked across campus in the rain one day. It was cold and slick. . . . The rain formed dew drops on my hairy arms and clung to each strand. My shirt felt not wet, but dampened and it clung to my breast which was dampened skin. My hair took the worst beating. The hairspray matted my bangs after the mist blew on them. The wisps at my neck and ear lobes felt sticky and wet. . . . My jeans felt moist and snugging to my thighs. My book bag was changing colors, dripping drops of water off onto my tennis shoes, then bouncing off my heels, disappearing on the crowded concrete that drinks raindrops.

Rain feels clean and warm and can send shivers across my shoulders down my arms to the tips of my fingers. I close my eyes and let them splash on my eyelashes, anticipating but never prepared and always blinking. Lick the wetness from my shoulder, suck up the water from my hand and wipe your arms on my back. Feel the rain, the wetness of the rain. The cool touch, the slick surface of your skin. . . . I turn my face upwards stretching my arms and legs, hands out, palms up, offering me, thanking him for the rain, letting me feel wet. I can drink rainwater and wash myself out completely. Let the rain hit me all over. Don't cover my eyes or carry an umbrella. Let my hair down let every strand fill up with water let my fingernails become soft from soaking in the rain. My mouth is dry so I open up and drink, filling me up inside. . . .

Rain can feel so good. So slick and sliding, makes me sweat. And even if you try to dry off the rain keeps coming down. Steady. Wipe off your chest, young man, and wipe off again, and again and still again, and still you'll be behind. Rub it into your skin, it will clean you so much better.

Marilyn's vehicle, rain, representing the sexual experience, points equally to the religious experience—sin, confession, and redemption. It crystallized in another poem suggested by the starter sentence—A few people attend church and the sermons are boring:

> Msgr. Meyer high on the pulpit
> Instead of smoke
> Preaches
> To the lights above
> Or else he coughs in his
> Hand and plays with
> His phlegm.
> He abuses the altar boys
> Splashing water into their eyes
> The boys cringe and turn red
> But keep their holy positions.*

Before the session Marilyn felt good. At the pause marked by the asterisk, Marilyn reported feeling sharply negative active which, she wrote, caused her to "stray from the topic." But not far:

> . . . .
> Wooden kneelers
> Bow to the cross
> . . . .
> Growling stomachs
> Droning songs
> Sitting properly
> Kneeling properly
> Stand up straight, Miss Marilyn
> . . . .
> Don't laugh
> Don't talk
> Don't look at your neighbor
> Don't touch your neighbor
> You will be a good little Christian girl
> If we make you hate it.
> Well you did. . . .

In the narrative after the writing she explained that she "got off the track and began to remember my grade school days of attending church and how much I hated it. I began to brainstorm for ideas because I felt stuck and this is what came out."

Her ability to resist the rational was no more apparent than with a later iteration of this theme. This poem incorporated the first stanzas of an earlier one and was accompanied by similar intensities of positive and negative arousal:

The thick, sweet, burning smoke
Makes it harder to keep my eyes open
And so I drift up with it.
. . . .
He comes after me . . .
With his hands
Outstretched, fingers . . .
Clawing at my hair.
I can't seem to run fast
I slip on the holy green floor of the altar.
. . . .
He pins me down.
Behind him, the dark dusty crucifix
Glares at him, not me.
But he didn't see
. . . .
I screamed.
Msgr. told me that wasn't the proper
Response for the prayer
. . . .
The sweat dripping from his brow
Becomes my tears
And I still couldn't breathe.

The candles drip milky wax
Into his eyes and now he knows
. . . .
I can breathe better so I start to laugh
Suddenly I am stronger. . . .

In fact, so virulent was the material that Marilyn's feelings were largely unaffected by the setting, type of exercise, or number of permutations it had undergone. Her anxiety, interest, and inspiration remained moderate throughout the session. But by the time the session was over, her excitement, interest, and frustration rose and her anger doubled. Again, her reason for writing was "to express my anger at the Catholic religion for what it did to me. I wanted to make it look foolish and cruel. But I don't think I succeeded"—though from her ending one could argue resolution, at least symbolically.

Several things may be learned here. Most incontrovertible is the similarity in direction of all three emotion clusters. Experiencing strong positive emotions did not preclude experiencing strong negative emotions. Nor the converse. Feeling strongly negative did not preclude feeling strongly positive. The earlier studies indicated that the longer the self-sponsored writing experience, the more stable the emotions. There was agreement here. The self-sponsored writing experience had a moderating effect on how the student poets felt while writing. Emotional predispositions and subject matter notwithstanding, those students *unaccustomed* to writing on their own were affectively *more* sensitive when writing poetry. The student poets *accustomed* to writing on their own were generally *less* sensitive: less negative active, negative passive, and positive. Somewhere along the self-sponsored writing continuum, an emotional dip—or fizzle effect—occurs which seems to work its way out after twenty years of experience with it. Whenever the dip occurs chronologically, the negative passive and negative active emotions are suppressed, but so are the positive.

Of course, this effect is confused by the rhetorical and subject variables, but a point should be made here. Students who began writing on their own during adolescence seemed more vulnerable emotionally, at least when writing poetry. Apparently, neither the self-sponsored writers with little experience nor those with considerable experience were spared the pronounced affective response. Moreover, self-sponsored writing begun during adolescence seemed to make a lasting impact on feelings of this group of writers, even well after adolescence.

Whether the adolescent period is early or late, it is the traditional developmental stage of psychological inhibition and withdrawal and/or high emotional turbulence. Candor is not fully masked by socialization. Or the socializing process is rendered temporarily irrelevant. Indeed, many teenagers keep journals and/or write poetry or letters during this highly impressionable period when they develop a heightened awareness of their feelings (see Brand, 1980; Kagle, cited in Huyghe, 1985). Personal writing at home is an especially appropriate route for expressing feelings unacceptable in academic discourse, thus making the connection between emotion and poetry all the more powerful. The entire phase would hardly matter, one might suppose, were adolescents not at the same time compelled to attend school. But of course they are. These emotions enter the discursive equation via forms like poetry, and resonate in all writing—expository as well as imaginative.

FREE WRITING AND STRUCTURED EXERCISES

The writing activities were divided into three types: Free writes (Sessions 1 and 3); Intermediary drafts of poems (Sessions 2 and 5); and Structured exercises (Sessions 4, 6, and 7). My inquiry extended to the free writes and structured poetry exercises. The free-writing method of composing is marked by the absence of an imposed structure. It is meant to capture continuous, relatively unedited thoughts. Structured writing assignments are exercises that guide responses by laying out particular rhetorical constraints.

Overall, type of assignment had little impact on the positive, negative passive, or negative active emotion clusters, and the rank orders showed the familiar patterns (see Appendixes A.9 and A.10). Students' feelings of inspiration remained stable at moderately high ranks. Their shyness and shame remained stable at the lowest ranks. Relief rose in rank during writing for both types. Boredom held low moderate ranks for both types of assignments before writing and dropped discernibly after writing, placing among the lowest of all the studies. However, unlike all other studies, satisfaction during both the free associative or structured exercises remained low.

The differences between the two assignment types are informative. Relief rose from rank 16 to rank 4 for the free writes, but from rank 17 to only rank 7 for the structured exercises. Surprise dropped from rank 15 to rank 18 during the free writes, but rose from rank 18 to rank 13 during the structured exercises. During the free writing, confusion remained stable at a moderate rank of 11. During the structured exercises, confusion dropped dramatically from rank 8 to rank 18. The negative active emotion anxiety stood out. Anxiety remained uniformly intense at rank 2 across the free-writing observations, the highest rank and intensity of all five studies. But for students engaged in the structured exercises, anxiety dropped from rank 5 to rank 9. In sum, students felt less surprised and more anxious, confused, and relieved when engaged in free writing than when engaged in the structured writing.

Jim. Jim's responses to the in-class structured exercises substantiates some of those differences. A glance back at the discussion of Jim's free writing indicates that he felt moderately anxious, slightly confused, but not at all surprised during those sessions. Jim also felt no surprise before undertaking the structured exercises. However, afterwards he felt moderately surprised by his effort. Although his sense of relief was equivalent for the two assignment types, completing the structured exercise also elicited virtually no confusion and less anxiety than his free writes did.

From the sentence starter: "There is one prisoner in jail, always the same prisoner. No one is certain why he is there. He doesn't want to get out," Jim produced:

The Town Prisoner

Children throw food through the window
faces solemn with ritual
fingers stiff with mystery.
The prisoner knows the town by the food they throw.
. . .
The jailer was gone when the prisoner came
He searched the desk below the dust to find the skeleton key
He locked the door behind himself and threw the key in the street
A young boy picked it up. . . .

> The prisoner remembers the little boy sometimes at dusk
> when the sun hides its head and the summer heat fades
> Years ago he heard the boy holding up banks,
> shooting friends in the back.
> but no one plays cops and robbers anymore,
> someone lost the key
> and all the prisoners ... lay in the
> shadows of the rotting jail.

Mac. However dissimilar Jim and Mac were in background and writing skill, the two assignment types produced in them somewhat analogous emotional profiles. Mac was an unskilled writer with considerable but informal experience writing on his own. Like Jim, Mac felt only modestly confused during the free writing. Like Jim (and the group as a whole), Mac's anxiety remained extraordinarily high. While Mac's feelings of surprise did not remain stable like Jim's, his feelings of surprise diminished during the free writing like those of the group. However, unlike the group, Mac felt only minimally relieved after the free writing. Given the nature of his material, these shifts make eminent sense. As a veteran of Vietnam and a railroad worker, there were a lot of things he wanted to do. One early free write rambled about his wanting to return to school, to write, and to recover from a "bitter" childhood that left him with a crippled sense of himself and his ability to be a parent:

What holds me prisoner still—me who is the only one who can restrain me—me. The anxiety of thinking of my sad child sitting in her chair—writing. Perhaps fear of her condemnation for my lack of parenting—the guilt rises again—I had no choice damn it.

Mac's emotional experience during the structured assignments also conformed to the group results. A dolorous piece about the "Only Whore in Town" did not get very far in a first draft, as is clear from Figure 11.1. Mac felt very frustrated. He experienced greater surprise during the structured exercises than he did during the free writing. His sense of confusion was low during the structured writing. But it was also stable like the group results for the free writing. And he felt equally modest relief here as he did after the free writes. At the same time Mac's interest, adventurousness, and excitement mounted steadily. The structured exercises engaged him. In a later draft the poem coalesced at five lines and, except for anxiety, was accompanied by a similar but more modulated emotional profile.

Craig. A fairly emotional student, Craig reported one year of writing experience. In comparison to his free writing, the structured exercises elicited in Craig less relief but also less anxiety and more surprise. Of the structured activities, generating a poem from three lists of unrelated words

Figure 11.1
A Seductive Topic Aroused Mac's Frustration yet Interest

The only whore in town rejected a proposal of marriage years ago. The man left town & later became ~~famous~~ wealthy and famous in New York

She lies alone now
on her stained sheets

Age ~~has~~ stolen her passport

~~[illegible] Mirrors [illegible] ([illegible])~~ *

~~Bitterness [illegible] wallowing in bitterness~~

Once her friend,
Mirrors ~~[illegible]~~ mock her image

Once her friend,
Mirrors mock her image.
Age stole her passport.
She lies alone now
on stained sheets
dampened by the sadness of her life.

(life's irony)

(italicized in the poem below) would certainly be expected to prompt confusion for any writer. It had a dramatic effect on Craig.

Confusion was the most prevalent component of Craig's trait profile. Theoretically, the more often writers feel confused about writing in general, the more intensely they would feel confused when actually writing. This rang true for Craig. His confusion remained strong and intransigent throughout the course and peaked during this exercise. It is easy to see why:

> A beech tree dancing
> between different weather fronts.
> *Swinging* in a Tony Bennett fashion
> to a serenading breeze.
> The others join in belief of the
> power and pleasure of movement.
>
> *Soft* dormant *mud* is important
> in an indirect way.
> A *cool*, foundation
> for the warmth of life.
> A lazy *frog* no doubt ignores
> the tender bugs in the soil.
>
> I say *leather* lasts forever.
> Its texture *curves* around mine
> and moves with me
> Its collar turns my *throat*
> *red* with abrasion.
> It *bruises* me with its power.

Craig was serenely underaroused by the end of this poem and most unimpressed by it. Even after exposure to instruction and to contemporary poetry, he may have felt that his work still failed to resemble his vision of poetry. He followed the instructions. He performed the task. In fact this was his best effort. He just didn't know why.

EFFECTS OF SETTING

Whether the writing was undertaken out of class (Sessions 2, 5, and 7) or at school (Sessions 1, 3, 4, and 6) produced essentially no statistical effect on the three emotion clusters. A cross section of the emotional intensities by locale indicated stability (see Appendixes A.11 and A.12). However, differences between the individual emotion items were more pronounced when setting was considered than when type of assignment was. Relief catapulted to rank 1 at home, but only reached rank 6 in class. Satisfaction increased to rank 4 at home, but to only rank 8 in class. Inspiration held its own at home at a moderately high rank of 6, but dropped from rank 6 to rank 9 in class. At home surprise rose from rank 20 to rank 15 while writing. In class surprise made no appreciable gains from its low rank. Anxiety dropped to rank 10 at home, but dropped only to rank 7 in class. Confusion plummeted to rank 17 at home, but in class resisted change from its rank of 9.

Jim. There was little distinction in the intensity of Jim's negative feelings between the home or in-class settings. However, at home Jim felt substantially more positive. Even the poem about the town prisoner that evoked in Jim "loneliness and mystery," liberated several positive feelings when he completed the final draft at home. Still other poems written at home confirmed that, despite the content, Jim's confusion and anxiety diminished. At home he felt more adventurous and inspired. He also experienced greatest relief and satisfaction there.

Moonlighting

1

I'm not a carpenter, but I cut wood today
. . . with a power saw, formica board
propped up on 2 × 4s and old curtains.
I'm not a carpenter, but I glued the boards
to the bathroom wall. It wasn't perfect
but I'm not a carpenter. A little caulk will
cover my mistakes. . . .

2

They came to see the apartment today. . . .
I was painting the window sill in the front room.
Donnie was eight, in parachute pants
his dad was short and round. . . .
They talked about the rooms and what needed
fixing and where they could put the dinette set.
. . . .
They left in whiffs of sunglasses and
cotton melting on hot down-home skin.
I dipped my brush back in the can,
Jungle Moss Light and Autumn Grain.

Kevin. Written at home, Kevin's extended metaphor about a bee sting had a profound effect on him. His strong anxiety disappeared by the end of the session. More important, the poem provided him with the greatest inspiration, relief, and satisfaction of the entire semester, demonstrating again that quality of text and impact can operate independently:

Victims of Honor

The noble guard with hanging thorn
draws life a gallant sword
light, swift-dashes evading the wind
or purging, extracting earth's friendly blossoms
perched atop, bouncing on leaning stems
then hovering flat rounded limbs
vibrating quietly armored black
and yellow stripes bold, proud colors
ugly faces unhidden below black helmets
mounted protection for sporadic flight
the Queen's delight then unknown giant
intruder calmly trespassing
with man's scent swift sudden stab
the victim's surging pain, gasping for life's breath
the heart's pounding rhythm interrupted—changed
by a piercing sword allergic—stained
still he reared forth
but the knight though honor gained
lost venom, weapon and life, shakened victim escaped
in pain caped with unsheathed spite
found a near-by haven tended upon by payment
or else certain plight
the Queen remained silent on her throne
the knight entombed peaceful—protection shown.

This swashbuckler—forced, bloated, and overwritten—was awash with problems that characterize untrained poets. Kevin's in-class efforts stood in sharp contrast. From the sentence: The water tower is gray and the paint is peeling, he generated this zero-level draft:

A dog in the alley is on his hind legs, pawing at the broken crates then growls and stomps on to the next alley. A white-haired man straddles the walkway, clicking his cane in steady beats. He was late for the town meeting. He was not invited and does not notice the water tower. ... Randy's Spirits is closed where late nights start early. And he is thirsty and knows his rights. So the town meeting has another issue because a young mother spotted a dog in the alley. She doesn't want loose animals wandering the streets. ... Now everyone is at the town meeting. ... Even the dog, his hungry face staring in the side window.

Except in one instance, Kevin's in-class work yielded less but more stable inspiration, less relief, and less confusion than his at-home work, regardless of its position in the course sequence. He also felt less satisfied with his in-class material. John Ciardi once said: Show me a student who writes a piddling little poem in September and who still admires it in June and I will show you a case of no hope. Kevin was a graduating senior with barely three years of self-sponsored writing experience. Poems like

"Victims of Honor" typify a stage that novice writers pass through on the way to a mature style. However, there was hope for Kevin. Not only was Kevin's in-class work more familiar, natural, and sensitive, but it was also stout with poetic possibilities.

Another interesting finding was that the rank order for the emotions experienced after writing at home produced the most homogeneous distribution of emotion items; by that I mean the extent to which the individual items grouped together by cluster in almost categorical fashion. Throughout the studies, the items in any one rank order approached such homogeneity in varying degrees. When the poetry was written at home, except for surprise, all the positive emotions ranked the highest, all the negative active items ranked together in the middle of the distribution, and all the negative passive items ranked together at the low end of the distribution. If the rank order approximates subjective experience, what may be concluded is that the two writing climates are distinguished by the affective "purity" they elicit.

From sets of primary or "pure" emotions, both Izard and Plutchik conceptualize the entire spectrum of subjective experience. From ten primary emotions, Izard claimed, could be traced the subtle or more complex emotions that rang truer to life. However, these mixed emotions often included a so-called pure emotion. In anxiety, it was fear. In depression, it was distress. In love, it was joy. Plutchik's mixed emotions were formed from nearby primary or "pure" emotions and became increasingly sophisticated the further they got from the primary feeling. A graphic representation in a color wheel allowed Plutchik to postulate about conflicting emotions. Just as opposite colors when mixed in equal intensity produced gray, opposite emotions, when occurring concurrently and with equal strength, neutralized or inhibited each other. What is important for writing is that clashing emotions, as opposed to mixtures of adjacent emotions, could result in greater immobility during the process as well as in truncated or distorted written products.

Perhaps this hypothesis places too much responsibility for the quality of composing and the composition on the psychological fallout from writing in the two environments. But, it gives us pause. Demands at home are substantially different from those at school. Stimuli are typically fewer at home, more predictable, and more capable of being controlled. At home, students' internal experiences would be less contaminated by distractions and intrusions that could elicit renegade feelings, thwart concentration and the writing process, and subvert the product. Put another way, if certain forms of writing depend on particular levels of emotional "purity," settings other than classrooms may be more perfect writing environments.

The rank orders continue to underscore the emotional implications of composing from two assignment types and in two settings. As prescriptive alternatives to the free associative style, structured techniques in creative writing impose constraints on poetic messages that can alter—if not suppress—emotion, and distance writers from personal renderings of the material. (And that is fine, so long as practitioners know this is what they want.) The rank orders here indicated that, when the student poets were engaged in structured exercises, they experienced less confusion, less satisfaction, and less relief. Moreover, they felt less anxious. In fact, the rank for negative active emotion, anxiety, proved to be the most startling.

Although the activity of a whole cluster cannot be assessed from only one of its constituents, anxiety ranked higher and was considerably more stubborn in the free writes than in the structured exercises, a finding evidenced in the literature (Cheshire, 1984). Of the four conditions (the two assignment types and two settings), only when the students engaged in free writing did satisfaction and relief *fail* to dislodge that powerful emotion. Anxiety maintained its position as second highest in the distribution before, during, and even after the poets engaged in free writing. It also ranked higher here than in all other studies. Despite the fact that the assignments in other studies were more academic, this held true for the self-sponsored college writers of Study 1. In that study, students engaged in self-sponsored writing at home experienced stronger negative active emotions than they did when they engaged in required writing in class.

Just what the links are between free writing, at-home writing, self-sponsored writing, and the negative active emotions is far from clear or certain. What is known is that they overlapped conceptually and empirically. Free writing, self-sponsored writing, and at-home writing were directly related for the teacher group. The emotions linked to poetry written at home were more mutable than those linked to in-class writing. The negative active emotion anxiety seemed to be a by-product of free associative forms of invention and writing at home. However, at home the student poets felt better all around. They made greater net gains in inspiration, surprise, relief, and satisfaction. There were greater improvements in the levels of anxiety and confusion when the student poets wrote at home.

The negative active emotions cluster was also linked to self-sponsored writing here and in Study 1. The self-sponsored writing experience seemed to make the student poets particularly liable to affective variation, but the direction and quality of this variation depended on the amount of that experience. It seems, therefore, that the richer, more essential subjective experiences students have when writing imaginatively have little place in school-sponsored writing.

Writing sponsorship is a particularly important variable because it is related conceptually to motivation, the conundrum of learning. *Choosing* to write as professionals do rather than being *required* to write as students may make an important affective difference. Self-sponsored writing simply does not occur in writing classes, and the acting out impulses inherent in negative active feelings are soundly discouraged. All the more reason for writers to experience them in risk-free settings like home.

These findings strengthen our intuitions about writing in schools. Once again, classrooms are places where emotional expression is circumscribed by tacit but strict and pervasive rules. If the stronger increases in the positive emotions and stronger decreases in the negative ones, observed in the safer, less judgmental environment of the home, are associated with the free-writing method of invention, then the free writing assigned in academic settings may unintentionally pose a dilemma for student writers. Free writing bespeaks self-disclosure, intimacy, and safety, while in-class writing bespeaks restraint, formality, and caution. To put the two together is to invite conflict.

NOTE

1. An inconsistency occurs in the direction of change of the emotion clusters during the adolescent period. This is largely because Question 6 on the Demographic Data Sheet allowed respondents to name the exact years of their self-sponsored writing experience whereas Question 7 confined responses to five age intervals (see Appendix A.3).

12. Conclusion

With this first look at the participation of emotion in composing, this research tries to broaden the knowledge of how human minds operate on written language. In this chapter my intentions are several: to carry forward the most important empirical findings, to propose opportunities for research, and to suggest its utility for pedagogy.

What then can be concluded?

This work demonstrates that individuals' emotions change discernibly when they write. In the studies that spanned several writing sessions, writers' emotions tended to flatten, particularly the negative passive ones.

During the writing sessions, their positive emotions intensified, their negative passive emotions weakened, and their negative active emotions resisted change. Individuals felt consistently more relieved and satisfied after writing. Happiness, inspiration, excitement, and interest were also unvarying priorities in the affective landscape.

Relief preempted satisfaction for all groups except the college students. Satisfaction contained a negative element in the way writers meant the term and so reflected a complex psychological condition for learners engaged in academic writing. However, considering relief and satisfaction the prevailing positive emotions when writing would be a misstatement. Writers experienced unflagging positive arousal. The fact that excitement and interest resisted change, and satisfaction and relief intensified is evidence of their strength and autonomy. To be sure, high interest is not necessarily linked to quality essays. Nor is minimal relief symptomatic of weak ones. Feelings of relief undoubtedly function independently of effective work, as does satisfaction. One characteristic of unskilled writers is that satisfaction with their writing is reached all too quickly.

Writers felt the negative passive emotions loneliness, depression, shame, and shyness rarely and weakly. They felt more confused than bored when composing.

The patterns associated with confusion and fly-in-the-academic-ointment boredom are worthy of note. Before writing students felt moderately confused, while their boredom fluctuated between middle and low intensities. During composing confusion remained stable or declined. Boredom followed that pattern at a lower level. Indeed, the literature links boredom with high levels of low activity and moderate moving away behavior. The studies bear that out. Confusion is a more common correlate of writing than boredom, a finding that also resonates in accounts from writers.

The negative active emotions remained moderately strong and intransigent. The professional and student poets alike felt more negative active during composing than other writers.

If any patterns for the negative active cluster are apparent, the negative active items that tended to increase were offset by others that tended to decrease and, thus, neutralized change. Or the pattern was curvilinear. Individuals' negative active feelings rose until the pause in writing, then fell off by the end of the session.

One of the difficulties in studying the negative active emotions falls to their antisocial connotations. Confounding any study of emotion are the social issues. Emotional displays are deeply and pervasively controlled, particularly the striking-out ones. The implications of marking at extreme ends of an emotions scale would be expected to level certain responses. Negative active feelings may well hover at moderate intensity because they are highly reprehensible. But this does not reduce their salience in writing.

Anxiety was the highest ranking negative emotion for all writer groups and generally weakened after writing. Only the teachers experienced stronger anxiety and frustration and no greater relief or satisfaction after writing.

It is with the item anxiety that the findings depart from the prevailing theoretical position. An approximation of anxiety, writer's apprehension has been linked to unskilled writers. This emphasis on inadequacy is consistent with the apprehension literature and would make sense for student writers. A hybrid of traditional student and mature adult, English teachers would be expected to identify with the instructor and therefore be unusually hard on themselves.

But the inadequacy model would not square with similar levels of anxiety experienced by the practicing writers. The anxiety of the professional writers ranked as high among the positive or "approach" emotions that are expected to enhance writing as it did among the untrained writers. Furthermore, factor analysis indicated that writers marked anxiety with other negative emotions *only* as a postwriting state. As Bloom (1984) has pointed out, anxiety is not exclusive to unskilled writers. Nor is it necessarily bad. True, unskilled writers are likely to feel anxious because they are performing a task about which they have a sense of inadequacy. But skilled writers may experience anxiety because of their high expectations. Anxiety may also reflect a rhetorical tension stimulated by a topic. Insofar as it resembles the disequilibrium involved in creative activity, a certain amount of anxiety is undoubtedly a necessary adjunct to composing (Rothenberg, 1979; Sommers, 1980).

In short, the negative active emotions are powerful and essential. Anxiety seems to mean different things to different writers. And it is not inexorably negative.

Skilled student writers felt generally more positive and less negative passive than their unskilled counterparts, regardless of rater. After writing, the positive feelings of the unskilled writers intensified to the level of the skilled writers, thereby producing more overall positive emotional change for the unskilled writers.

The instructor-rated skilled English teachers felt less positive after writing than their unskilled counterparts did. The instructor-rated skilled advanced expository writers felt more negative after writing than their self-rated counterparts.

The self-rated skilled college writers felt less negative passive when writing than their unskilled counterparts. The more skilled the professionals rated themselves, the less often they felt negative passive. The self-rated skilled advanced expository writers felt more negative passive, but only during the research writing. Last, the self-rated skilled poets felt less negative active when writing.

When raters of writing skill were distinguished, the findings were not so amenable to generalization. And those associated with self-rating of skill were still less receptive to it. My sense, at the outset, is that writing instructors value the assignments they require and communicate it. It stands to reason that they would rate as skilled, students who perform well on them. These students would, in turn, feel good about themselves.

However, given the findings associated with the self-rating of skill, what learners think about themselves as writers—accurate or not—may not only be a more sensitive predictor of affective response to academic writing than instructor ratings, but may also be more meaningful to them. There is some support for this in the literature. Csikszentmihalyi and Larson (1984) have proposed that, irrespective of ability, students get better grades in classes they enjoy. McCarthy, Meier, and Rinderer (1985) have found that students with strong efficacy expectations demonstrate improved writing performance. In other words, belief in the ability to write makes a difference in the quality of the product. Apparently, no matter how well individuals write, if they enjoy it and feel they will do well, actual capabilities matter less.

A corollary to this concerns the negative emotions. As much as I would like to conclude otherwise, the negative emotions probably tell us more about the emotional profiles of writers than do the positive ones. Writing appeared to make all the respondents feel better. But the writers did not uniformly experience changes in their negative feelings. Because such emotional change occurred for only select subgroups, the negative emotions seem to be the more discriminating affective variable.

Writers with considerable self-sponsored writing experience felt better about writing in general and tended to perform better. The more years of self-sponsored writing, the more under control the writers felt.

Students engaged in self-sponsored writing reported more negative active feelings than when engaged in required writing.

Self-sponsored writing not only enhanced the positive emotions but also liberated some negative ones. Perhaps two interpretations are justified. Again, identifying our feelings and expressing them in school is, at best, risky. It is as if students retain from childhood the lesson that emotional displays are indecent. Certainly there are good reasons not to express emotions. There are strong demand characteristics associated with the examination of feelings in academic settings and pressures to respond in certain ways. Education rewards students who conform to, if not strengthen, the social order. Boredom, confusion, shame, even anxiety are simply not as disruptive as other negative active emotions—in school or in society. Student writers seem better able to express nervous arousal and lashing out impulses, not only in poetry, but also when writing on their own rather than in school where passivity is prized.

Students may also feel more comfortable with classroom assignments in which the rhetorical parameters are spelled out for them. Giving instructors what they want may not be very challenging, but it is safe. Another benefit of disciplining the emotions is that learners can approach writing in a motivated yet business-like manner. The drawback is that, because evaluation so dominates academic writing, they would be less likely to experience the intensity or kind of emotions—unpleasant or pleasant—that some professionals find useful in composing.

When the emotions of the student poets were examined in light of their self-sponsored writing experience, intensified negative emotions were accompanied by equivalent intensities of positive emotions.

Overall, positive and negative feelings during writing followed opposite courses. Increases in pleasant feelings were associated with decreases in unpleasant ones. A special relationship between the emotion clusters was observed for the apprentice poets when they began writing on their own during adolescence. Their feelings followed parallel patterns.

While motivation, concentration, and activation have been found lower for teenagers than for adults, adolescents have been found to experience more extreme and varied emotions than adults, particularly the negative (Brand, 1980; Csikszentmihalyi & Larson, 1984). Although the student poets were chronologically past adolescence, their emotional experiences when writing may well be a by-product of self-sponsored writing begun during that time. These writers found in poetry a particularly congenial form.

The emotional states of the professional writers in this study were modulated and positive. They tended to feel less satisfied with their work. This was particularly true of those with more formal education.

The emotional experience of the practicing writers when writing was pleasant—notably, interesting, enjoyable, and satisfying—in comparison to those making literary headlines. To be sure, making money from writing does not eliminate emotion but may rearrange its intensities. But for every emotionally dysfunctional poet or writer, there are probably hundreds more leading emotionally appropriate lives. Even while feeling negative active, the practicing poets appeared emotionally enabled. All in all, whereas sponsorship of writing seemed to make a difference affectively to untrained writers, it had little impact on the quality of emotions experienced by the professionals. The professional writers loved what they did, no matter who told them to do it.

The teachers showing congruence between their trait and state emotions gravitated to the methodical, structured approach to composing.

The English teachers were emotionally unaffected by the free-writing and structured approach to composing—ideological and heuristic opposites—even when their preferences were taken into account. The data did, however, reveal a consistency between the trait and state emotions for those preferring the more methodical composing style. Without inferring too far beyond the data, this suggests that good writers are not necessarily distinguished from weak writers by their loyalty to a particular composing approach. Rather, personality guides composing style, an idea visible in the literature, but scarcely penetrated. Thus, different composing styles may well have equal utility for different individuals.

Compared to writing in class, at home the student poets felt more anxious and frustrated, but they also experienced deeper decreases in those emotions. In addition, they felt dramatically more relieved and less confused when writing at home. While at home their inspiration remained stable, the student poets felt more surprised and satisfied.

It should come as no surprise that situational variables mediate emotional quality and intensity. In their now-classic study, Schachter and Singer essentially demonstrated that people experience different feelings because they define them on the basis of the situations in which they occur. If the responses of the teachers and student poets are any indication of people's sensibilities about where they write, setting is potentially important in the composing process. It bears repeating: Writing cannot be removed from its context without altering it. If writers write differently when put in different settings, it may well be because they feel different.

Free writing was associated with unrestricted time and self-initiated and informal writing that was completed at home. The structured/planning method of composing was associated with timed, required writing that was completed in class.

The student poets felt similarly confused before both types of exercises, but less anxious before the structured than before the free-writing exercises. After the structured exercises they felt less relieved, but they also felt less confused and anxious. The student poets also experienced more surprise after the structured writing.

Of course, as modes of invention, each method has its virtues. Free writing aims for root meaning. It speaks to an ordinary, idiomatic reality grounded in natural if not homely truths. If free associative writing produced more anxiety than the structured exercises, it is probably because it is also more essential. The free writing so suited to poetry may well do likewise because it is apt to touch sensitive material. It is true that the intellectual demands made by structured exercises can engender their own emotional fluctuations. However, because structured methods are more formal and directive, learners might lose some control over content, but they would also risk less. Thus, structured methods would benefit shy or weak writers. They would also give reluctant writers a head start as well as challenge creative thinkers (Reed, Burton, & Kelly, 1985).

The positive emotions of the more advanced expository writers intensified during more of the affectively toned and descriptive assignments than they did during the other two assignment types. However modest the findings, the traditional essays seemed equally capable of eliciting decreases in the negative passive emotions. The advanced expository writers tended to experience more intense negative emotions before the affectively toned and descriptive essays. Although the order of the assignments confounds this result, those feelings diminished equivalently after both assignment types. The advanced expository writers also felt more positive after completing the research draft but no less negative after either research exercise.

When the emotion items were taken individually, the advanced expository writers felt more confused and afraid during the affective personal writing than during the other two assignment types. But they felt no more interested, excited, inspired, and adventurous before or after the traditional and research essays than they did before or after the emotionally toned personal essays. They also felt the greatest relief and satisfaction after the traditional essays.

The impact on emotion of type of assignment merits attention. The personal experience paper as an essay form has been of recent pedagogical relevance as well as debate—the hard-liners versus those still soft on Dartmouth. One question arises as to the quality of engagement of the personal essay as opposed to other expository forms. Rose (1984a), for example, does not categorically dismiss the motivational potential of personal experience topics. Personal subjects undoubtedly call forth highly complex cognitive and affective responses. What he questions is the assumption that the closer the topic is to students' personal experience the more it will capture their interests—engage or hook them.

The closest analogues to the personal experience paper in these studies are the affectively toned personal essays completed by the advanced expository group. If by engagement during writing is meant magnitude of positive change, it is possible to say that the emotionally toned essays produced the most positive increases. But because the activity of relief and satisfaction blurs other changes in the positive cluster, there is another, possibly more fruitful way to look at emotional engagement.

If by engagement is meant the motivational and anticipatory emotions, the key items could include adventurousness, excitement, inspiration, and interest, which psychologists are just beginning to study. The apprentice writers felt these emotions more intensely before writing the traditional papers. It seems, however, that the capacity to hook students at prewriting is only part of what engagement means. The other, and perhaps more crucial part, is the sustaining of that engagement. In that case, what should be observed during writing are higher ranks and/or higher intensities for any or all of these four emotions from some assignments but not from others. What I found instead was that the ranks and outcome intensities of these four emotions were similar, particularly for the affectively toned and traditional assignment types. Moreover, based on these emotions, the research writing was numerically less engaging despite the fact that students felt more positive after writing the research draft. It seems, therefore, that the more academically challenging the assignment, the more tenacious the emotions. The adequacy of these findings is still to be tested.

And, as for writing assignments, however neutral they may be intended, few are emotion-free. Students are more likely to reckon with provocative topics like child abuse or police brutality that Hillocks speaks so well of, than an analysis of the game of Bingo. One way or another academic writing engages the emotions. For instance, the neutral topics for writing narratives, suggested in *The Bedford Reader*, number three while the negative topics number nine. Another assignment in Eastman's fine text on style points up just what we think of when we think about emotion. It asks students to write about an experience that has changed their lives. The prompt includes the following recommendations: an auto accident, rejection by a lover or employer, betrayal by a friend, or loss of a loved one. And the data here confirm it. When we think of benchmarks in our lives, we bracket them with emotion, and that emotion is negative.

I do not advocate abolishing writing about issues any more than I would abolish reading about them. Individuals need to locate themselves with respect to social realities. But psychologists and discourse specialists have suffered from tunnel vision. The pejorations associated with emotion not only govern the way writing prompts are designed and the topics suggested to learners, but also the pedagogical outlook. Integrative emotional states have been hypothesized as a narrow band within which mental activity flows. If we miss that narrow footing, as I am sure most of us continually do, are we forever besieged by boredom or anxiety? I think not. I have pointed out the problems with easy dualisms. I have argued that emotions may be ultimately traceable to good or bad. But writers' emotional environments are infinitely richer than that. However complicated the affective phenomena and modest these findings, the studies clearly show that it is unwarranted to make generalizations about emotion from a single strand as if it constituted the whole domain. Language specialists and cognitive psychologists need to educate their attitudes about emotion in general, and broaden their inquiries into it beyond apprehension and blocking.

RESEARCH OPPORTUNITIES

What can be learned about the role of emotion in composing represents an effort to complete the description of writers in the act of writing. Even though this early work asks more questions than it answers, its research potential is extraordinary because there is little precedence for it. While knowledge on composing is accruing so fast that it is difficult to chart a research course of any stability, I would like to define several avenues of inquiry.

Writing Skill

Because writing skill was found to mediate the relationship between writing and emotion, a more thorough investigation of the emotions of professionals and skilled learners should yield information about the emotions associated with quality texts. Are there emotional distinctions between professional writers, skilled student writers, and learners in general? Do novelists, journalists, and poets bring to the writing process different baseline feelings? Do professional writers experience the state emotions during actual composing with corresponding intensities? Do trait emotions guide choice of genre, or are emotions and genre independent? More generally, can a relationship be posited between affective sensitivity and intellectual ability? Can particular emotional states be used as measures of writing skill?

Writing Sponsorship

The reason that self-sponsored writing was examined in this work (when schools require writing) is similar, I suspect, to the reason that professional writers are studied in general. It is from published writers that researchers and practitioners uncover ideas about their process, and their work becomes exemplars of excellence. To the extent that professionals begin as self-sponsored writers and continue to write when they "don't have to," their emotional profiles should be understood. Little attention has also been paid to the emotional states that might be differentially induced by various sponsoring agents. How do emotional profiles change when writing is initiated by a boss, an editor, or the self? What impact does self-sponsored writing have on writers' perception of their skill?

Personality Traits

Theoretically, the stronger a trait emotion, the more probable that individuals will experience its corresponding emotional state, and the greater the probability that behaviors associated with that trait are characterized by high intensities (Spielberger, 1972). For example, adventurous individuals would be prone to taking risks on paper and less apt to follow traditional rhetorical models. By the same token, individuals strongly disposed to anger would be more readily "provoked" into writing by frustrating situations or by the thought of being frustrated. Under pleasant circumstances in which provoking stimuli were minimal, even individuals inclined to frustration might not feel or write so. What emotional proclivities are a poor fit for writing? What emotions are a good fit for it? And how may these be enlisted for effective writing performance? How might emotional versatility help expand writers' discursive repertoires?

Composing Style

Contemporary writing theory assumes that ineffective writing results from ineffective processes. Changing the way learners compose is thus an implicit outcome of writing courses (Faigley et al., 1985; Selzer, 1984). However, if composing styles and personality are linked, educators have underestimated the emotional value of imposing specific writing approaches on learners. Training in particular composing styles intervenes in the natural response process, and, as both Irmscher and Selzer have observed, may represent an intrusion. Jensen and DiTiberio suggest that such teaching should be resisted until students have had a chance to develop their preferred approaches. What are the emotional correlates of particular composing styles once they are established? What happens emotionally when writers are taught to become conscious of their composing style and then asked to alter it? What happens emotionally when they compose in preferred and nonpreferred styles? Are writers stymied by too much planning or not enough? How is this reflected in texts?

Motivation and Engagement

The relationship between motivation and school achievement is generally regarded as curvilinear, a particularization of the Yerkes-Dodson law. Low levels of motivation generally result in low levels of achievement. Moderate levels of motivation result in higher levels of achievement. But very high levels of motivation again result in low levels of achievement. A similar pattern would be expected for engagement in writing, a form of sustained motivation and a construct particularly useful to composition specialists.

Both engagement and motivation have been assumed in learners. Students are imagined as having an innate urge to write, or some lofty motivation to discover through writing, when, at best, more than half the students comprising composition courses are barely motivated—even extrinsically (Williams & Alden, 1983). How does the impulse to write arise? How is it sustained? What, if any, are the differences between the emotional profiles of intrinsically and extrinsically motivated writers?

Even when motivation and engagement are high, determining the quality of a writing task and the ability of oneself to engage successfully in it guide immediate performance. When the match between motivation, skill, and task is good, presumably the appraisal of the writing situation is positive, and individuals approach it. Positive emotions indicate that the relevant goals are within reach. It comes down to saying, "This writing task is easy or hard, good or bad, and I can do it." When the match between motivation, skill, and task is off, individuals feel confused, ashamed, angry, anxious, bored—in short, bad. It comes down to saying, "This writing task is easy or hard, good or bad. But I can't or I don't want to do it."

Recognizing one's discursive limitations is not, in and of itself, an unpleasant thought. There are intellectual tasks outside our capabilities, and we are none the worse for it. Appraising a writing situation becomes a problem if, for example, we do not want to do what we are capable of, or we want to do what we are incapable of. In either case, such negative emotional states mean that negative feedback has been received and individuals realize they have failed to meet the relevant goals. The writing task is then avoided or "attacked" in some unproductive way. What are the situational, temporal, and textual variables that enhance motivation for, or engagement in, writing? Do the demands and constraints of certain writing tasks outweigh individuals' motivation? Their skills?

Emotional Arousal

Similar to the relationship between motivation and achievement, the Yerkes-Dodson law provides an effective way of summarizing the relationship between affective arousal and task difficulty. Intermediate levels of emotional arousal yield high performance—in other words, the best written products. Low levels of arousal would be inadequate to influence or even produce text. But the very highest levels of emotional arousal would be so tyrannical as to distort or limit text.

Modern variants may be found in reading (see also Reading/Writing Relationships) and testing research. When arousal stimulated by reading in various journalistic styles is high, emotional change is only slightly negative. However, when arousal is low, emotional change is more negative. In testing, least anxious students have been found to do best on hard tests, whereas moderately anxious students do best on easy tests. The most anxious students do poorly on both (Rocklin & Thompson, 1985). In composing, Flower and Hayes point out that when arousal is high, writers cannot juggle as many constraints. Thus, moderate arousal should be optimal for quality writing. What is the nature of the emotional states of individuals when they operate under high information loads? Can we identify optimal ranges of affective arousal for writing to occur successfully?

As a corollary, arousal and emotions are different but overlapping orders of response. I have been treating individual emotions with the valences that tradition has assigned them. Interest is good. Anger is bad. This research demonstrates that emotions can coexist with their so-called opposites. Unpleasant feelings may be neutral or positive, just as pleasant feelings may be neutral or any shade of negative. In Chapter 4 I referred to Mandler's position in which emotions are theorized as valence-free, only physiologically arousing until that arousal is submitted to cognitive interpretation. This hypothesis replaces emotions as warring opposites with a unitary construct. Accordingly, emotions result from shifts in arousal and the meaning attached to those shifts. Arousal provides the physiological cues. But through meaning analyses, skilled and unskilled writers receive different messages from their physiology. How do affective meanings change during writing? Can weak writers learn to interpret emotional arousal in helpful ways, as a stimulant for writing, not as an impediment?

Reading/Writing Relationships

In reader-response theory, readers enter into a transactional relationship with an author's text (Rosenblatt, 1938/1976). They build meaning and interpretation as they read. But their first encounter with a book is emotional (Bleich, 1975; Holland, 1975; Purves & Beach, 1972), a theme rarely disputed. If discourse specialists and literary critics subscribe to this theory, important parallels between writers and readers may be drawn. How similar to reading the writing of others are emotional encounters with our own texts? Would the psychological states that writers experience as readers of their own texts be equivalent—ongoing and cumulative—as they move along as creators, revisors, editors, and rereaders of their own work?

In recent research by Hidi and Baird, emotion was implicated insofar as interest and importance were found to vary with the recall of narratives and exposition. Within genres, the narrative style of news stories has been shown to increase reader arousal, and the traditional journalistic style to decrease arousal (Donohew, 1981). Does a similar thing happen when we write in these styles? It has been hypothesized that reading "takes in," deriving from a need to be stimulated; and writing "gives out," deriving from a need for tension reduction. Arousal is reported to be a strong predictor of decisions to continue or stop reading. Apart from relief and satisfaction, are there other emotions that slow writing down or bring it to closure?

The Writing Process

The psychological chemistry between the trait and prewriting state emotions sets up certain dispositions to think and act as writers move through composing. Excluding for a moment affective and cognitive memory, at the first instant of writing the prewriting emotional states can only anticipate the task because no writing has yet occurred. The "before" emotions get writing going and so are instigators or motivators. Once the process is underway, writers' psychological states are continuously in flux—reinforcing, reversing, or replacing the states they started with. The "after" emotions are the outcome emotions with which writers end writing and feed forward to the next session. Certain emotions may even arise during the process but "disappear" before it is over, leaving no apparent trace of them.

To increase information about the "during" emotions, the composing process itself needs to be penetrated. If a stage model of writing is envisioned, what is the role of emotion during prewriting, writing, revising, and editing? If a recursive, information-processing model is envisioned, how do emotions and cognition collaborate in getting writers from one point in the process to another? At what points in text production do the emotions shift and why? Which emotions are linked to particular subprocesses? Which emotions are linked to interruptions in them? How do writers envision lexical choices? How do their emotional states vary with audience, purpose, topic, and time restrictions?

Related to this question is the matter of causality, an issue raised several times in this work. In its present form, the BESW identifies emotions but does not investigate their sources. What exactly are emotions responses to at particular points in writing? The sponsor? The situation or context? The subject matter? The process? The developing text? The product? The self? What measures can best capture this information?

Instrumentation and Research Design

The BESW appears to be an internally consistent instrument with the usual time to time and test to test fluctuations as well as practice and fatigue effects. At times, the scale appeared too subtle for the untrained writers but not subtle enough for the professionals; it seemed less able to rise to the complexity suggested by their texts or their anecdotal material.

In addition, as it stands, the BESW was not designed to measure emotions continuously during a writing session. Because tracking emotions during writing presents the quintessential challenge, discourse studies would profit from a collaboration by researchers of both the cognitive and affective persuasions. Pilot efforts have been explored using a case study, think-aloud protocol with college-level expository writers (Fitzgerald, 1986). Time-sampling methods have been attempted with secondary school students, using an abbreviated BESW in both whole group and case study designs (Brand, 1986b).

Clearly, the state emotions are profoundly complex, fleeting, and highly delimited by social propriety. To gain a full and accurate understanding of emotion, there must be greater methodological precision. Future inquiries would undoubtedly benefit from alternating between laboratory methods to test critical variables and real life situations in which a few variables interact on several levels. Is it possible to track unobtrusively and accurately the course that particular emotions travel during a writing session? If researchers want to zoom in on one emotion, can a trustworthy subscale of the BESW be constructed to track it through the composing process? What modifications in the BESW would enable it to follow the more subtle emotions? Can protocol analysis be incorporated into such research designs?

PRACTICAL IMPLICATIONS

Any new knowledge about emotion will not simplify our understanding of the higher mental function of writing. Emotions are complicated and often invisible. They are processed in ways we know very little about. But such processes take place. Emotions are important and can be made useful to psychologists and composition specialists as well as to writers themselves.

As Murray has suggested for internal revision, writers should become familiar with the emotional as well as intellectual cues that tell them they are ready to write, ready to stop, and ready to do a number of things in between. These task constraints invariably involve motivation and preference, both affective in origin. Writers' long-term affective and cognitive memory informs them about their previous encounters with writing and about their skills. It tells writers what their motivations are or should be, whether the writing session is relevant, and how congruent they are with the stimulus event—the very basis of their psychological states. Affective and cognitive memory shapes every choice during actual writing sessions and prepares writers psychologically for their next attempt.

We know that the trait emotions and personality overlap conceptually and empirically. We are just now recognizing that personality governs discursive style just as discursive style influences personality. We need to recognize the multiple cognitive and affective styles that writing requires. This research should help us understand the extent to which certain types of persons and approaches are successful in some writing situations but not in others.

Applebee (1987) has maintained that educational research (much like this, I assume) need not be justified by immediate translation into curricula. However, this line of inquiry can help writing instructors teach students who do not write easily. As the utility of certain emotions becomes clear at critical points in the process, novice writers may enjoy new opportunities to improve at a range of writing tasks by mobilizing those feelings. For how those feelings work during composing may be part of what distinguishes skilled from unskilled writers.

Whatever answers result from research on the emotions should ultimately be handled by a comprehensive model of writing. It is certainly too early to attempt a conceptual fit between the data and a model of the various ways emotion and cognition interact. Almost all the information is missing. With this research, a description of emotion has basically begun at two points: before and after writing. I have pointed out that the "during writing" emotions are the most complicated interval to study. A model should show the continual exchange between the information processing elements and the affective strands that go with them—that is, the properties of value or sign, intensity, direction, and degree of change.

Emotions are involved in mobilizing for writing and sustaining it. They are also involved as we commit information to paper. I am referring to choice. Emotions perform a selective function. Every time we pick a sentence order or contemplate a modifier, we are prompted by our feelings. Every time we choose a unit of content or determine a paragraph break, we are acting from a basic affective bipolarity of good or bad—which is a very different order of emotion from the arousing ones. However simplistic this view, even coarse discriminations about what writers like or don't like in simple lexical decisions are emotional phenomena. Of course, in reality things are rarely that clear cut. Emotions are not typically found in their pure forms. They mix, blend, become richer in meaning, occur simultaneously, and at times even appear paradoxical. Emotions operate along a continuum from the most elemental to hair-splitting levels of sophistication and subtlety. And like real numbers, emotions can be subdivided into finer and finer entities. However ambitious, a comprehensive model should finally be sensitive enough to depict both ends.

Steinman (cited in Nystrand, 1982) has stated that a process should not be studied without knowing why individuals enter into it. By describing the major influences of thought and emotion on writing, a model should account for the causal links. Not enough is known to argue causality in either direction. Two themes are clear. First, although in a broad sense human emotion depends on symbolic capacities, the emotional aspects of writing cannot be defined out of existence, treated as unalterably postcognitive, or reduced to a cognitive auxiliary. Emotions arise effortlessly and inescapably. Their unique freedom from attentive control, their speed, the range and depth of writing that results suggest something special about their influence on language. Neisser has stated that, as a discipline, cognitive psychology is sufficiently healthy that it can afford to pay attention to the ways in which social and emotional phenomena provide the substructure for more cognitive learning.

Second, affect and cognition cannot truly be uncoupled, although I have taken heuristic advantage of the distinction in this book. What is wonderful about studying emotion is that there is a greater democracy of affective structures than intellectual ones. To be emotionally competent is not the prerogative of the privileged. To be emotionally deprived is not exclusive to the poor. Emotions do not discriminate on the basis of social class or race. You don't have to go to private school or an Ivy League college to feel. (On the contrary, education in America is notorious for teaching us how to unfeel.)

Finally, we are reminded that emotions are markers. They lend significance to situations. Emotions organize. Emotions are instructive. Words are interpretive, but emotions empower them. The whole history of written discourse indicates that writers are very much influenced by their feelings. Evidence points, at least, to the reciprocity between cognitive and affective processes that makes the role of emotion in writing inapposite to ignore. Indeed, to study the emotional as well as the cognitive content of composing is to acknowledge their true interpenetration.

Appendixes

A.1	Cluster Scores in Descending Order of Emphasis for Select Emotion Items	218
A.2	BESW Glossary	220
A.3	Demographic Data Sheet	221
A.4	Means and Standard Deviations for the Three Emotion Clusters of the Advanced Expository Writers across Three Trait Observations and Nine Writing Sessions	222
A.5	Rank Order of Means for the Individual Emotions of the Advanced Expository Writers across Sessions 1, 4, and 6: Affectively Toned Personal Essays	224
A.6	Rank Order of Means for the Individual Emotions of the Advanced Expository Writers across Sessions 2, 3, 7, and 8: Traditional Expository Essays	225
A.7	Rank Order of Means for the Individual Emotions of the Advanced Expository Writers across Sessions 5 and 9: Research Assignments	226
A.8	Means and Standard Deviations for the Three Emotion Clusters of the Professionals Before, At a Pause, and After Writing	227
A.9	Rank Order of Means for the Individual Emotions of the Student Poets across Sessions 1 and 3: Free Writes	228
A.10	Rank Order of Means for the Individual Emotions of the Student Poets across Sessions 4, 6, and 7: Structured Exercises	229
A.11	Rank Order of Means for the Individual Emotions of the Student Poets across In-class Sessions 1, 3, 4, and 6	230
A.12	Rank Order of Means for the Individual Emotions of the Student Poets across At-home Sessions 2, 5, and 7	231

Appendix 1
Cluster Scores in Descending Order of Emphasis for Select Emotion Items

Emotion			Cluster		
Adventurous[a]	Hyperactive Moving Toward 47.0	Enhancement Comfort 22.4	Tension Activation 15.4	Moving Toward Enhancement 4.0	
Affectionate	Inadequacy 45.4	Hyperactivation 44.6	Tension 26.0	Moving Away 5.4	Incompetence/ Dissatisfaction 4.8
Afraid (Fear)	Hyperactivation 53.0	Moving Against 46.0	Tension 19.0	Inadequacy 16.8	
Angry	Inadequate 20.0	Tension 18.2	Moving Against 8.0	Discomfort 7.2	
Anxious	Incompetence/ Dissatisfaction 47.6	Moving Away 5.8	Inadequacy 5.2	Hypoactivation 3.4	Incompetence/ Dissatisfaction 4.2
Ashamed (Shame)	Hypoactivation 51.2	Moving Away 28.0	Incompetence/ Dissatisfaction 12.0	Tension 9.0	
Bored	Inadequacy	Incompetence/ Dissatisfaction	Tension	Hypoactivation	
Confused[a]	Hypoactivation 48.6	Discomfort 41.8	Moving Away 38.0	Inadequacy 35.2	Incompetence/ Dissatisfaction 19.0
Depressed	Tension 9.8	Hyperactivation 5.4	Inadequacy 5.4	Hypoactivation 3.4	
Disgusted	Hyperactivation 31.4	Activation 28.6	Inadequacy 11.8	Comfort 5.8	Tension 5.0
Excited	Tension 45.6	Inadequacy 21.8	Incompetence/ Dissatisfaction 12.8	Moving Against 7.2	Hyperactivation 4.8
Frustrated					Hypoactivation 4.6 Discomfort 3.8

Happy	Activation 56.6		Comfort 42.8	Enhancement 26.8	Hyperactivation 5.8	Moving Toward 3.6
Inspired	Enhancement 36.8	Activation 23.0	Enhancement	Hyperactivation 11.4	Comfort 10.8	Inadequacy 10.2
Interested[a]	Activation	Enhancement	Hyperactivation	Moving Toward	
Lonely[a]	Moving Away	Incompetence/ Dissatisfaction	Hypoactivation	Inadequacy	Discomfort
Relieved	Comfort 28.8	Activation 10.4	Enhancement 3.4		
Satisfied[a] (Contentment) (Serenity)	Comfort 51.0 42.0	Enhancement 13.6 7.4	Activation 6.8	Moving Toward 5.0	
Shy[a] (antonym of Friendly)	Discomfort 27.6	Moving Away 25.8	Hypoactivation 13.0	Inadequacy 10.8	Hypoactivation 3.6
Surprised	Hyperactivation 28.2	Activation 11.4	Hypoactivation 23.0	Comfort 4.2	

Source: Adapted from Davitz, J. R. (1969). *The language of emotion* (pp. 117–119). New York: Academic Press.

Note: Cluster scores (indicating the relative emphasis of a cluster in the particular definition of an emotion) were computed as a product of the proportion of items in a cluster appearing in a definition and the mean percentage of subjects who checked each item in the cluster (p. 115). There was no absolute upper limit for the cluster scores.

[a]Because Davitz does not assess emotional states *Adventurous*, *Confused*, *Interested*, *Lonely*, *Satisfied*, or *Shy*, clusters and relative emphases were interpolated. Davitz's emotion terms *Contentment* and *Serenity* served as approximations of *Satisfied*. The clusters obtained for *Contentment* and *Serenity* along with their corresponding scores were considered, in general, what *Satisfied* would yield had it been scored directly. Although bipolarity was not generally assumed among the terms, in order to estimate scores for *Shy*, *Friendly* was taken as its antonym. By using the data derived for *Friendly*, the clusters, relative emphases, and scores for *Shy* were obtained. For the remaining four terms—*Adventurous*, *Confused*, *Interested*, and *Lonely*—clusters and orders of emphases were assigned by analyzing the content of the item bank from which the clusters were originally derived (pp. 110–113). The descriptions, composed of content that appeared in them with greatest frequency, were read for themes that referred to the emotion item in question. These descriptions were then ordered by the frequency with which they recurred within the content making up the cluster. Scores were not assigned. For example, although Davitz did not define *Lonely* directly, the *Moving Away* cluster referred to "a sense of aloneness, being cut off, completely by myself; a feeling of a certain distance from others; everyone seems far away" (p. 111). On this basis, the *Moving Away* cluster was ranked along with clusters *Incompetence/Dissatisfaction*, *Hypoactivation*, and so on. There is the danger that this improvised procedure derived meanings beyond what could be supported by the data, or that it reflected more my projection than the meaning embodied in the term. Recognizing these possibilities, I tried to be cautious, and my procedures were verified by the consultant panel.

Appendix 2
BESW Glossary

ADVENTUROUS:	willing or open to taking chances or risks, trying something new, exploring the unknown
AFFECTIONATE:	loving, showing warmth, having fond or tender feelings for
AFRAID:	scared, fearful, apprehensive
ANGRY:	annoyed, furious, mad
ANXIOUS:	tense, nervous, worried
ASHAMED:	embarrassed, disgusted with yourself, guilty
BORED:	uninterested, apathetic, listless, indifferent
CONFUSED:	jumbled up, bewildered, muddled, disorganized
DEPRESSED:	sad, unhappy, dejected, low
DISGUSTED:	repelled by something, fed up, feeling that something offends or revolts you
EXCITED:	stimulated, stirred to action, aroused
FRUSTRATED:	prevented from accomplishing something or fulfilling a desire, thwarted, defeated
HAPPY:	cheerful, joyful, elated
INSPIRED:	exalted, uplifted, feeling a calm surge of power
INTERESTED:	attentive, alert, curious, fully engaged
LONELY:	isolated, solitary, alone
RELIEVED:	eased from discomfort, pent-up feelings lessened
SATISFIED:	contented, at ease, as if needing little or nothing at this moment, gratified
SHY:	timid, bashful
SURPRISED:	amazed, astonished, feeling that something unexpected has happened

Appendix 3
Demographic Data Sheet

```
                                              For Office Use Only
                                              U/S _____

                                              Name _____
                                              Code No. _____

                                              Date _____
```

1. ____ Age

2. ____ 1. Female
   ____ 2. Male

3. Current Educational Status:

   ____ 1. Not currently attending school
   ____ 2. Part-time student
   ____ 3. Full-time student

4. Highest Level of Education Completed:

   ____ 1. High school
   ____ 2. One year of college
   ____ 3. Two years of college
   ____ 4. Three years of college
   ____ 5. Bachelor's Degree
   ____ 6. College beyond the Bachelor's Degree
   ____ 7. Master's Degree
   ____ 8. Doctoral Degree

5. How long have you been writing on your own? _____ years

6. I began writing on my own at age:

   ____ 5. 25 or older
   ____ 4. 19 - 24
   ____ 3. 15 - 18
   ____ 2. 10 - 14
   ____ 1. 5 - 9

7. Indicate how you would describe your skill as a writer:

   ____ 3. More skilled than most of my peers
   ____ 2. About as skilled as most of my peers
   ____ 1. Less skilled than most of my peers

8. Indicate how you would describe your emotional self (check one):

   ____ 3. Intensely emotional
   ____ 2. Moderately emotional
   ____ 1. Easy-going or unemotional

Appendix 4
Means and Standard Deviations for the Three Emotion Clusters of the Advanced Expository Writers across Three Trait Observations and Nine Writing Sessions

	n	Positive M (SD)	Negative Passive M (SD)	Negative Active M (SD)
Trait Observations				
First	24	26.3 (5.1)	12.0 (4.3)	12.3 (3.5)
Second	21	22.8 (6.1)	10.0 (2.5)	10.6 (2.8)
Third	19	20.5 (5.5)	9.8 (2.1)	10.2 (3.0)
Writing Sessions				
Confused Before	23	21.2 (5.5)	9.9 (2.9)	9.7 (3.9)
Confused After	23	26.0 (7.4)	9.7 (4.3)	9.8 (5.2)
Description Before	20	19.0 (6.3)	9.4 (3.2)	9.2 (3.4)
Description After	20	24.6 (6.7)	7.6 (2.0)	6.9 (2.0)

Analysis Before	20	18.3	(6.2)	8.0	(1.5)	8.1 (2.8)
Analysis After	20	21.8	(7.2)	7.9	(2.0)	7.6 (3.7)
Adventure Before	18	15.8	(6.5)	8.7	(2.8)	7.5 (1.9)
At a Pause	18	19.5	(7.5)	7.5	(2.7)	7.8 (2.8)
Adventure After	18	21.8	(6.9)	7.3	(2.4)	6.8 (2.3)
Research Draft Before	19	16.8	(5.9)	8.1	(1.8)	7.8 (3.4)
Research Draft After	19	20.8	(8.1)	7.6	(2.0)	7.9 (4.3)
Boring Before	16	14.3	(4.4)	8.4	(1.9)	6.8 (1.6)
At a Pause	16	14.1	(4.4)	8.3	(2.0)	7.5 (2.6)
Boring After	16	15.2	(5.8)	8.9	(2.7)	6.7 (1.9)
Comp/Cont Before	18	17.1	(7.0)	7.6	(1.3)	7.3 (1.9)
Comp/Cont After	18	20.0	(6.7)	6.9	(1.2)	7.4 (4.0)
Real Before	18	16.0	(4.8)	7.4	(1.8)	7.1 (2.1)
At a Pause	18	19.8	(7.1)	7.4	(2.3)	7.6 (2.6)
Real After	18	20.6	(7.9)	7.2	(1.8)	7.5 (3.3)
Research Final Before	16	16.0	(6.3)	7.7	(1.3)	7.6 (2.0)
Research Final After	16	20.4	(9.1)	7.4	(1.8)	7.1 (2.9)

Appendix 5
Rank Order of Means for the Individual Emotions of the Advanced Expository Writers across Sessions 1, 4, and 6: Affectively Toned Personal Essays

State Emotions

Before Writing		After Writing	
Interested	2.56	Relieved	2.88
Happy	2.37	Interested	2.69
Adventurous	2.22	Happy	2.64
Anxious	2.17	Satisfied	2.59
Confused	2.05	Adventurous	2.47
Excited	2.03	Inspired	2.28
Inspired	2.02	Excited	2.26
Satisfied	1.85	Anxious	1.95
Afraid	1.78	Affectionate	1.85
Bored	1.66	Surprised	1.78
Affectionate	1.64	Frustrated	1.66
Frustrated	1.64	Confused	1.58
Shy	1.54	Bored	1.54
Relieved	1.49	Lonely	1.51
Surprised	1.36	Disgusted	1.49
Depressed	1.34	Afraid	1.46
Disgusted	1.34	Depressed	1.44
Lonely	1.24	Angry	1.37
Angry	1.22	Ashamed	1.36
Ashamed	1.20	Shy	1.31

Note: n = 23 to 16.

Appendix 6
Rank Order of Means for the Individual Emotions of the Advanced Expository Writers across Sessions 2, 3, 7, and 8: Traditional Expository Essays

State Emotions

	Before Writing		After Writing
Interested	2.65	Relieved	3.21
Adventurous	2.27	Satisfied	2.83
Happy	2.21	Happy	2.69
Excited	2.12	Interested	2.69
Inspired	2.04	Inspired	2.31
Anxious	2.01	Excited	2.26
Satisfied	1.83	Adventurous	2.21
Affectionate	1.82	Affectionate	2.04
Frustrated	1.71	Anxious	1.88
Confused	1.60	Frustrated	1.62
Relieved	1.48	Surprised	1.58
Depressed	1.47	Angry	1.36
Bored	1.45	Confused	1.35
Disgusted	1.44	Depressed	1.35
Angry	1.43	Disgusted	1.34
Afraid	1.41	Lonely	1.27
Lonely	1.30	Bored	1.22
Surprised	1.26	Afraid	1.17
Shy	1.26	Ashamed	1.17
Ashamed	1.12	Shy	1.13

Note: n = 20 to 18.

Appendix 7
Rank Order of Means for the Individual Emotions of the Advanced Expository Writers across Sessions 5 and 9: Research Assignments

State Emotions

Before Writing		After Writing	
Interested	2.33	Relieved	2.85
Happy	2.12	Satisfied	2.70
Adventurous	2.00	Interested	2.55
Excited	2.00	Happy	2.53
Inspired	1.87	Excited	2.36
Anxious	1.91	Adventurous	2.09
Confused	1.73	Inspired	2.09
Frustrated	1.65	Affectionate	1.88
Satisfied	1.65	Anxious	1.85
Relieved	1.62	Surprised	1.67
Affectionate	1.59	Frustrated	1.61
Bored	1.50	Angry	1.58
Disgusted	1.47	Depressed	1.52
Angry	1.40	Disgusted	1.41
Depressed	1.38	Confused	1.39
Afraid	1.35	Ashamed	1.18
Surprised	1.32	Bored	1.18
Lonely	1.24	Afraid	1.15
Shy	1.09	Lonely	1.15
Ashamed	1.03	Shy	1.12

Note: n = 19 to 16.

Appendix 8
Means and Standard Deviations for the Three Emotion Clusters of the Professionals Before, At a Pause, and After Writing

Emotion Clusters	Writing Sessions		
	Before Writing	*At a Pause*	*After Writing*
Positive			
M	2.20	2.45	2.70
SD	.77	1.00	1.03
Negative Active			
M	1.65	1.70	1.55
SD	.75	.80	.89
Negative Passive			
M	1.65	1.50	1.40
SD	.59	.61	.60

Note: $n = 24$.

Appendix 9
Rank Order of Means for the Individual Emotions of the Student Poets across Sessions 1 and 3: Free Writes

State Emotions

Before Writing		At a Pause		After Writing	
Interested	2.81	Interested	2.96	Adventurous	2.87
Anxious	2.67	Anxious	2.78	Anxious	2.67
Adventurous	2.57	Adventurous	2.72	Excited	2.63
Excited	2.51	Excited	2.56	Relieved	2.62
Frustrated	2.26	Frustrated	2.45	Interested	2.49
Happy	2.23	Happy	2.33	Affectionate	2.42
Inspired	2.14	Inspired	2.22	Happy	2.41
Affectionate	2.09	Affectionate	2.19	Frustrated	2.33
Confused	2.00	Angry	2.03	Satisfied	2.26
Afraid	1.85	Relieved	2.03	Inspired	2.23
Angry	1.77	Confused	1.97	Confused	1.98
Disgusted	1.66	Satisfied	1.92	Angry	1.85
Satisfied	1.66	Disgusted	1.81	Afraid	1.77
Bored	1.64	Afraid	1.75	Disgusted	1.69
Surprised	1.58	Depressed	1.75	Depressed	1.55
Relieved	1.53	Surprised	1.53	Lonely	1.53
Depressed	1.46	Lonely	1.50	Ashamed	1.41
Lonely	1.46	Bored	1.36	Surprised	1.37
Shy	1.46	Shy	1.28	Shy	1.36
Ashamed	1.36	Ashamed	1.25	Bored	1.28

Note: $n = 19$.

Appendix 10
Rank Order of Means for the Individual Emotions of the Student Poets across Sessions 4, 6, and 7: Structured Exercises

Before Writing		State Emotions At a Pause		After Writing	
Adventurous	2.72	Adventurous	2.84	Adventurous	2.61
Interested	2.57	Interested	2.63	Excited	2.47
Excited	2.37	Frustrated	2.33	Interested	2.44
Happy	2.33	Excited	2.27	Affectionate	2.35
Anxious	2.26	Inspired	2.19	Happy	2.34
Inspired	2.20	Affectionate	2.17	Inspired	2.24
Affectionate	2.19	Happy	2.07	Relieved	2.19
Confused	1.93	Anxious	2.07	Satisfied	2.11
Frustrated	1.93	Confused	1.98	Anxious	2.07
Satisfied	1.70	Angry	1.85	Frustrated	1.93
Disgusted	1.64	Disgusted	1.77	Angry	1.73
Angry	1.63	Lonely	1.75	Afraid	1.69
Bored	1.63	Satisfied	1.74	Surprised	1.69
Lonely	1.63	Depressed	1.71	Depressed	1.64
Depressed	1.59	Afraid	1.68	Disgusted	1.58
Afraid	1.54	Relieved	1.66	Lonely	1.56
Relieved	1.54	Ashamed	1.46	Bored	1.51
Surprised	1.37	Surprised	1.45	Confused	1.49
Shy	1.30	Bored	1.44	Ashamed	1.27
Ashamed	1.24	Shy	1.19	Shy	1.17

Note: n = 19.

Appendix 11
Rank Order of Means for the Individual Emotions of the Student Poets across In-class Sessions 1, 3, 4, and 6

Before Writing		State Emotions At a Pause		After Writing	
Interested	2.71	Interested	2.80	Adventurous	2.76
Adventurous	2.67	Adventurous	2.79	Excited	2.51
Excited	2.45	Anxious	2.47	Interested	2.43
Anxious	2.41	Excited	2.43	Affectionate	2.42
Happy	2.35	Frustrated	2.39	Happy	2.42
Inspired	2.21	Affectionate	2.24	Relieved	2.39
Affectionate	2.20	Happy	2.22	Anxious	2.30
Frustrated	2.02	Inspired	2.21	Satisfied	2.21
Confused	1.97	Confused	1.96	Inspired	2.19
Afraid	1.70	Angry	1.92	Frustrated	2.11
Satisfied	1.69	Relieved	1.81	Confused	1.72
Bored	1.64	Disgusted	1.79	Afraid	1.71
Angry	1.62	Satisfied	1.79	Angry	1.70
Disgusted	1.61	Afraid	1.69	Disgusted	1.60
Relieved	1.57	Depressed	1.64	Depressed	1.58
Depressed	1.49	Lonely	1.64	Surprised	1.54
Surprised	1.49	Surprised	1.54	Lonely	1.53
Lonely	1.47	Bored	1.39	Bored	1.38
Shy	1.41	Ashamed	1.24	Ashamed	1.31
Ashamed	1.29	Shy	1.22	Shy	1.27

Note: $n = 19$.

Appendix 12
Rank Order of Means for the Individual Emotions of the Student Poets across At-home Sessions 2, 5, and 7

State Emotions

Before Writing		At a Pause		After Writing	
Adventurous	2.84	Adventurous	2.95	Relieved	2.79
Anxious	2.64	Interested	2.89	Interested	2.63
Interested	2.62	Excited	2.41	Adventurous	2.55
Excited	2.53	Inspired	2.35	Satisfied	2.54
Frustrated	2.29	Frustrated	2.25	Excited	2.34
Inspired	2.10	Anxious	2.18	Inspired	2.16
Happy	1.96	Satisfied	2.01	Happy	2.09
Affectionate	1.89	Angry	1.92	Affectionate	2.07
Confused	1.88	Happy	1.90	Frustrated	2.04
Angry	1.82	Relieved	1.87	Anxious	2.03
Lonely	1.82	Affectionate	1.86	Angry	1.91
Satisfied	1.77	Confused	1.85	Afraid	1.75
Disgusted	1.69	Afraid	1.78	Disgusted	1.66
Depressed	1.59	Depressed	1.75	Lonely	1.59
Afraid	1.56	Disgusted	1.67	Surprised	1.59
Bored	1.52	Lonely	1.58	Depressed	1.53
Relieved	1.52	Ashamed	1.51	Confused	1.49
Ashamed	1.33	Bored	1.49	Bored	1.45
Shy	1.28	Surprised	1.37	Ashamed	1.36
Surprised	1.22	Shy	1.21	Shy	1.24

Note: n = 19.

References

Abelson, R.P. (1963). Computer simulation of "hot cognitions." In S. Tomkins & S. Messick (Eds.), *Computer simulation of personality: Frontier of psychological theory* (pp. 277–323). New York: Wiley.

Amsel, A. (1962). Frustrative nonreward in partial reinforcement and discrimination learning: Some recent history and a theoretical extension. *Psychological Review, 69*, 306–328.

Anderson, J. (1979). *Confessions of a muckraker*. New York: Random House.

Anderson, J.R. (1976). *Language, memory, and thought*. Hillsdale, NJ: Lawrence Erlbaum.

Applebee, A.N. (1987). Musings . . . teachers and the process of research. *Research in the Teaching of English, 21* (1), 5–7.

Applebee, A.N., Langer, J.A., & Mullis, I.V.S. (n.d.). *Writing across the decade, 1974–84*. (Report No. 15–W–01). Princeton, NJ: Educational Testing Service. National Assessment of Educational Progress.

Arnold, M.B. (Ed.) (1970). *Feelings and emotions: The Loyola symposium*. New York: Academic Press.

Aronowitz, B.L. (1987). A comment on "collaborative learning in the classroom: A guide to evaluation." *College English, 49* (7), 831–833.

Averill, J.R. (1980a). A constructivist view of emotion. In R. Plutchik & H. Kellerman (Eds.), *Emotion: Theory, research, and experience. Volume 1. Theories of emotion* (pp. 305–339). New York: Academic Press.

Averill, J.R. (1980b). On the paucity of positive emotions. In K.R. Blankstein, P. Pliner, & J. Polivy (Eds.), *Assessment and modification of emotional behavior. Advances in the study of communication and affect* (Vol. 6, pp. 7–45). New York: Plenum Press.

Bain, A. (1875). *The emotions and the will* (3rd ed.). London: Longmans, Green.

Bartholomae, D. (1983). Writing assignments: Where writing begins. In P.L. Stock (Ed.), *fForum: Essays on theory and practice in the teaching of writing* (pp. 300–312). Upper Montclair, NJ: Boynton/Cook.

References

Barzun, J. (1971). *On writing, editing, and publishing*. Chicago: University of Chicago Press.
Beauvoir, S. de (1960). *The prime of life*. New York: Lancer Books.
Bellow, S. (1982, June). Quotes for writers. They say. ... In *The Writer*, p. 6.
Bentler, P.M. (1969). Semantic space is (approximately) bipolar. *Journal of Psychology, 71*, 33–40.
Bereiter, C., & Scardamalia, M. (1987). *The psychology of written composition*. Hillsdale, NJ: Lawrence Erlbaum.
Berger, J., & Berger, D. (Eds.) (1957). *Diary of America*. New York: Simon & Schuster.
Berkenkotter, C. (1981). Understanding a writer's awareness of audience. *College Composition and Communication, 32* (4), 388–399.
Berthoff, A.E. (1981). *The making of meaning: Metaphors, models and maxims for writing teachers*. Montclair, NJ: Boynton/Cook.
Birnbaum, J.C. (1982). The reading and composing behavior of selected fourth- and seventh-grade students. *Research in the Teaching of English, 16* (3), 214–260.
Bizzell, P. (1979). Thomas Kuhn, scientism, and English studies. *College English, 40* (7), 764–771.
Blakeslee, T.R. (1980). *The right brain: A new understanding of the unconscious mind and its creative powers*. Garden City, NY: Anchor Press/Doubleday.
Blau, S. (1983). Invisible writing: Investigating cognitive processes in composition. *College Composition and Communication, 34* (3), 297–312.
Bleich, D.F. (1975). *Readings and feelings: An introduction to subjective criticism*. Urbana, IL: NCTE, Johns Hopkins University Press.
Bleich, D.F. (1976). Pedagogical directions in subjective criticism. *College English, 37* (5), 454–467.
Bloom, L.Z. (1980, March). *The composing processes of anxious and non-anxious writers*. Paper presented at the annual Conference on College Composition and Communication. Washington, DC.
Bloom, L.Z. (1984). Research on writing blocks, writing anxiety, and writing apprehension. In M.G. Moran & R.F. Lunsford (Eds.), *Research in composition and rhetoric. A bibliographic sourcebook* (pp. 71–92). Westport, CT: Greenwood Press.
Bloom, L.Z. (1985). Anxious writers in context: Graduate school and beyond. In M. Rose (Ed.), *When a writer can't write* (pp. 119–133). New York: Guilford Press.
Bower, G.H. (1981). Mood and memory. *American Psychologist, 36*, 129–148.
Bradburn, N.M. (1969). *The structure of psychological well-being*. Chicago: Aldine.
Bradbury, R. (1973). *Zen & the art of writing*. Santa Barbara, CA: Capra Press.
Braddock, R., Lloyd-Jones, R., & Schoer, L. (1963). *Research in written composition*. Champaign, IL: NCTE.
Brand, A.G. (1980). *Therapy in writing: A psycho-educational enterprise*. Lexington, MA: D.C. Heath.
Brand, A.G. (1985, March). *Toward a reconstruction of the cognitive model of writing*. Paper presented at the annual Conference on College Composition and Communication, Minneapolis, MN.

Brand, A.G. (1985–1986). Hot cognition: Emotions and writing behavior. *Journal of Advanced Composition, 6*, 5–15. (ERIC Document Reproduction Service No. ED 236 677).

Brand, A.G. (1986a, December). *Emotion in writing: Its place and potential.* Paper presented at the annual Convention of the Modern Language Association, New York.

Brand, A.G. (1986b). *Notes on adapting the BESW for secondary school writing students using whole class and case study research designs.* Unpublished manuscript, University of Missouri–St. Louis.

Brand, A.G. (1987). The why of cognition: Emotions and the writing process. *College Composition and Communication, 38* (4), 436–443.

Brand, A.G., & Chibnall, J. (1989). The emotions of apprentice poets. *Empirical Studies of the Arts, 7* (1), 45–49.

Brand, A.G., & Chibnall, J.T. (1988). Relationships between composing styles, other writer variables, and emotions of teachers of writing. *Journal of Humanistic Education and Development, 27* (1), 28–44.

Brand, A.G., & House, G. (1987). Relationships between types of assignments, writer variables, and emotions of college composition students. *The Alberta Journal of Educational Research, 33* (1), 21–32.

Brand, A.G., & Leckie, P.A. (1988). The affects of professional writers. *Journal of Psychology, 122* (5), 421–439.

Brand, A.G., & Powell, J.L. (1986). Emotions and the writing process: A description of apprentice writers. *Journal of Educational Research, 79* (5), 280–285.

Bransford, J.D. (1979). *Human cognition: Learning, understanding and remembering.* Belmont, CA: Wadsworth.

Britton, J., Burgess, T., Martin, N., McLeod, A., & Rosen, H. (1975). *The development of writing abilities. 11–18.* London: Macmillan Education.

Broadbent, D.E. (1977). The hidden preattentive processes. *American Psychologist, 32* (2), 109–118.

Brodkey, L. (1987). Modernism and the scene(s) of writing. *College English, 49* (4), 396–418.

Brossell, G. (1985, March). *Research on writing assessment.* Paper presented at the annual National Testing Network in Writing Conference on Writing Assessment, San Francisco, CA.

Bruffee, K. (1981). Comment & response. Collaborative learning. *College English, 43* (7), 745–747.

Bruffee, K. (1984). Collaborative learning and the "conversation of mankind." *College English, 46* (7), 635–652.

Bruffee, K. (1986). Social construction, language, and the authority of knowledge: A bibliographical essay. *College English, 48* (8), 773–790.

Bruner, J. (1968). *Toward a theory of instruction.* New York: W.W. Norton.

Cannon, W.B. (1927). The James-Lange theory of emotions: A critical examination and an alternative theory. *American Journal of Psychology, 39*, 106–124.

Cannon, W.B. (1953). *Bodily changes in pain, hunger, fear and rage: An account of recent researches into the function of emotional excitement* (2nd ed.). Boston: Charles T. Branford Company. (Original work published 1929)

Carkeet, D. (1976). How critics write and how students write. *College English, 37* (6), 599–604.

Cattell, R. (1966). The scree test for number of factors. *Multivariate Behavioral Research, 2*, 245–276.

Cattell, R. (1973). *Personality and mood by questionnaire: A handbook of interpretive theory, psychometrics, and practical procedures.* San Francisco: Jossey-Bass.

Cheshire, B.W. (1984, March). *The effects of writing apprehension on writing quality.* Paper presented at the Conference on College Composition and Communication. New York, NY. (ERIC Document Reproduction Service No. ED 250 264)

Cicchetti, D., & Hesse, P. (1983). Affect and intellect: Piaget's contributions to the study of infant emotional development. In R. Plutchik & H. Kellerman (Eds.), *Emotion: Theory, research, and experience* (Vol. 2, pp. 115–170). New York: Academic Press.

Clark, M.S., & Isen, A.M. (1982). Toward understanding the relationship between feeling states and social behavior. In A.H. Hastorf & A.M. Isen (Eds.), *Cognitive social psychology* (pp. 73–108). New York: Elsevier/North-Holland.

Coleridge, S.T. (1907). *Biographia literaria: Vol. II.* London: Oxford University Press.

Connors, R.J. (1983). Composition studies and science. *College English, 45* (1), 1–20.

Connors, R.J. (1987). Personal writing assignments. *College Composition and Communication, 38* (2), 166–183.

Cooper, M., & Holzman, M. (1983). Talking about protocols. *College Composition and Communication, 34* (2), 284–293.

Cowley, M. (Ed.) (1958). *Writers at work: The Paris Review interviews* (1st series). New York: Viking Press.

Crawshaw, M., & Ottaway, M. (1977). A contact-pencil for research on writing. *Quarterly Journal of Experimental Psychology, 29*, 345–346.

Crowhurst, M., & Piche, G. (1979). Audience and mode of discourse effects on syntactic complexity in writing at two grade levels. *Research in the Teaching of English, 13* (2), 101–109.

Csikszentmihalyi, M., & Larson, R. (1984). *Being adolescent: Conflict and growth in the teen-age years.* New York: Basic Books.

Daly, J.A. (1978). Writing apprehension and writing competency. *Journal of Educational Research 2*, 10–14.

Daly, J.A., & Miller, M.D. (1975). The empirical development of an instrument to measure writing apprehension. *Research in the Teaching of English, 9* (3), 242–249.

Daly, J.A., & Wilson, D.A. (1983). Writing apprehension, self-esteem, and personality. *Research in the Teaching of English, 17* (4), 327–341.

Darwin, C. (1894). *The expression of the emotions in man and animals.* New York: D. Appleton & Company.

Davitz, J.R. (1964). *Communication of emotional meaning.* New York: McGraw-Hill.

Davitz, J.R. (1969). *The language of emotion.* New York: Academic Press.

De Bono, E. (1970). *Lateral thinking*. New York: Harper Colophon.
Diesing, P. (1971). *Patterns of discovery in the social sciences*. Hawthorne, NY: Aldine.
Dittmer, A. (1986). Guidelines for writing assignments in the content areas. *English Journal, 75*, 59–63.
Dobrin, D.N. (1986). Protocols once more. *College English, 48* (7), 713–725.
Dollard, J., Doob, L.W., Miller, N.E., Mowrer, O.H., & Sears, R.R. (1939). *Frustration and aggression*. New Haven, CT: Yale University Press.
Donohew, L. (1981). Arousal and affective responses to writing style. *Journal of Applied Communications Research, 9* (2), 109–119.
Dreyfus, H.L. (1979). *What computers can't do: The limits of artificial intelligence*. New York: Harper & Row.
Dunaway, P., & Evans, M. (Eds.) (1957). *Treasury of the world's great diaries*. Garden City, NY: Doubleday.
Eastman, R.M. (1984). *Style* (3rd ed.). New York: Oxford University Press.
Ebel, R.L. (Ed.) (1969). *Encyclopedia of Educational Research* (4th ed.). Toronto: Macmillan Company.
Eckhardt, C.D., & Stewart, D.H. (1979). Toward a functional taxonomy of composition. *College Composition and Communication, 30* (4), 338–342.
Eiseley, L. (1975). *All the strange hours: The excavation of a life*. New York: Charles Scribner's Sons.
Ekman, P., Friesen, W., & Ancoli, S. (1980). Facial signs of emotional experience. *Journal of Personality and Social Psychology, 39*, 1125–1134.
Elbow, P. (1973). *Writing without teachers*. New York: Oxford University Press.
Elbow, P. (1986). *Embracing contraries: Explorations in learning and teaching*. New York: Oxford University Press.
Emig, J. (1971). *The composing process of twelfth graders*. Urbana, IL: NCTE.
Emig, J. (1978). Hand, eye, brain: Some basics in the writing process. In C.R. Cooper & L. Odell (Eds.), *Research on composing: Points of departure* (pp. 59–72). Urbana, IL: NCTE.
Emig, J. (1982). Inquiry paradigms and writing. *College Composition and Communication, 33* (1), 64–75.
Epstein, S. (1979). Emotions in humans. In P. Pliner, K.R. Blankstein, & I. Spigel (Eds.), *Perception of emotion in self and others: Advances in the study of communication and affect* (Vol. 5, pp. 47–83). New York: Plenum Press.
Ericsson, K.A., & Simon, H.A. (1984). *Protocol analysis: Verbal reports as data*. Cambridge, MA: MIT Press.
Erikson, E.H. (1968). *Identity: Youth and crisis*. New York: Norton.
Eysenck, H.J., Arnold, W.A., & Meili, R. (Eds.) (1972). *Encyclopedia of psychology* (Vol. 1). New York: Herder & Herder.
Fagan, W.T., Cooper, C.R., & Jensen, J.M. (1975). *Measures for research and evaluation in the English language arts*. Urbana, IL: NCTE.
Fagan, W.T., Jensen, J.M., & Cooper, C.R. (1985). *Measures for research and evaluation in the English language arts. Vol. 2*. Urbana, IL: NCTE.
Faigley, L., & Witte, S. (1981). Analyzing revision. *College Composition and Communication, 32* (4), 400–414.
Faigley, L., Cherry, R.D., Jolliffe, D.A., & Skinner, A.M. (1985). *Assessing writers' knowledge and processes of composing*. Norwood, NJ: Ablex.

Faigley, L., Daly, J.A., & Witte, S.P. (1981). The role of writing apprehension in writing performance and writing competence. *Journal of Educational Research, 75,* 16–21.

Festinger, L. (1957). *A theory of cognitive dissonance.* Stanford, CA: Stanford University Press.

Fish, S. (1980). *Is there a text in this class? The authority of interpretive communities.* Cambridge, MA: Harvard University Press.

Fiske, S.T. (1981). Social cognition and affect. In J.H. Harvey (Ed.), *Cognition, social behavior, and the environment* (pp. 227–264). Hillsdale, NJ: Lawrence Erlbaum.

Fiske, S.T., & Linville, P.W. (1980). What does the schema concept buy us? *Personality and Social Psychology Bulletin, 6* (4), 543–557.

Fitzgerald, S. (1986). *Emotions and the writing process: Three case studies.* Unpublished manuscript, University of Missouri–St. Louis.

Flammer, A., & Kintsch, W. (Eds.) (1982). *Discourse processing.* Amsterdam: North-Holland Publishing.

Flower, L. (1985). *Problem-solving strategies for writing* (2nd ed.). San Diego: Harcourt Brace Jovanovich.

Flower, L. (1988). The construction of purpose in writing and reading. *College English, 50* (5), 528–550.

Flower, L., & Hayes, J.R. (1980). The dynamics of composing: Making plans and juggling constraints. In L.W. Gregg & E.R. Steinberg (Eds.), *Cognitive processes in writing* (pp. 31–50). Hillsdale, NJ: Lawrence Erlbaum.

Flower, L., & Hayes, J.R. (1981a). A cognitive process theory of writing. *College Composition and Communication, 32* (4), 365–387.

Flower, L., & Hayes, J.R. (1981b). The pregnant pause: An inquiry into the nature of planning. *Research in the Teaching of English, 15* (3), 229–243.

Flower, L., & Hayes, J.R. (1984). Images, plans, and prose: The representation of meaning in writing. *Written Communication, 1* (1), 120–160.

Flower, L., Hayes, J.R., Carey, L., Schriver, K., & Stratman, J. (1986). Detection, diagnosis, and the strategies of revision. *College Composition and Communication, 37* (1), 16–55.

Fox, R.E. (1980). Treatment of writing apprehension and its effects on composition. *Research in the Teaching of English, 14* (1), 39–50.

Freud, S. (1908/1959). Creative writers and day-dreaming. In J. Strachey (Ed.), *Standard edition of the complete psychological works of Sigmund Freud* (pp. 143–153). London: Hogarth Press.

Freud, S. (1915/1925). The unconscious. *Collected Papers (Vol. 4).* London: Hogarth.

Freud, S. (1925). Formulations regarding the two principles in mental functioning. *Collected Papers (Vol. 4).* London: Hogarth.

Freud, S. (1936). *The problem of anxiety* (H.A. Bunker, Trans.). New York: Norton.

Gendlin, E. (1978). *Focusing.* New York: Everest House.

Ghiselin, B. (Ed.) (1952). *The creative process. A symposium.* New York: New American Library.

Gilligan, C. (1982). *In a different voice.* Cambridge, MA: Harvard University Press.

Gilligan, S.G., & Bower, G.H. (1984). Cognitive consequences of emotional

arousal. In C. Izard et al. (Eds.), *Emotions, cognitions, and behavior* (pp. 547–600). Cambridge, England: Cambridge University Press.
Glatthorn, A.A. (1981). *Writing in the schools*. Reston, VA: National Association of Secondary School Principals.
Godshalk, F.L., Swineford, F., & Coffman, W.E. (1966). *The measurement of writing ability*. New York: CEEB.
Goldberg, M. (1983). Recovering and discovering treasures of the mind. In J.N. Hays et al. (Eds.), *The writer's mind: Writing as a mode of thinking* (pp. 35–42). Urbana, IL: NCTE.
Gorsuch, R.L. (1983). *Factor analysis*. Hillsdale, NJ: Lawrence Erlbaum.
Gough, H.G., & Heilbrun, A.B. (1980). *The adjective check list manual*. Palo Alto, CA: Consulting Psychologists Press.
Griffin, J.H. (1981). *The hermitage journals: A diary kept while working on the biography of Thomas Merton*. New York: Andrews and McMeel.
Guba, E. (1978). *Toward a methodology of naturalistic inquiry in educational evaluation*. UCLA Monograph Series in Evaluation #8. Los Angeles, CA: Center for the Study of Evaluation.
Gunther, J. (1961). *A fragment of an autobiography: The fun of writing the "Inside" books*. New York: Harper and Row.
Hairston, M. (1986). *Contemporary composition* (4th ed.). Boston: Houghton Mifflin.
Hall, D. (1980). Goatfoot, milktongue, twinbird: The psychic origins of poetic form. In S. Friebert & D. Young (Eds.), *A field guide to contemporary poetry and poetics* (pp. 26–36). New York: Longman.
Hall, E. (1986, February). Conversation: Robert B. Zajonc. Mining new gold from old research. *Psychology Today*, pp. 46–51.
Harre, R., & Lamb, R. (Eds.) (1983). *The encyclopedia dictionary of psychology*. Cambridge, MA: MIT Press.
Hastorf, A.H., & Isen, A.M. (Eds.) (1982). *Cognitive social psychology*. New York: Elsevier/North-Holland.
Hayes, J.R., & Flower, L. (1980). Identifying the organization of writing processes. In L.W. Gregg & E.R. Steinberg (Eds.), *Cognitive processes in writing* (pp. 3–30). Hillsdale, NJ: Lawrence Erlbaum.
Heller, S. (1988, April 27). Growing field of composition research forges links to literature, psychology, and other disciplines. *The Chronicle of Higher Education*, pp. A4–A7.
Hidi, S., & Baird, W. (1986). Interestingness—A neglected variable in discourse processing. *Cognitive Science, 10*, 179–194.
Hillocks, G.J. (1982). Inquiry and the composing process: Theory and research. *College English, 44* (7), 659–673.
Hoffman, E. (1982, January 17). The poet of the Polish diaspora. *New York Times Magazine*, pp. 29, 31–33, 64, 66.
Holladay, S.A. (1981, November). *Writing anxiety: What research tells us*. Paper presented at the annual Convention of National Council of Teachers of English, Boston, MA. (ERIC Document Reproduction Service No. ED 216 393).
Holland, N.N. (1975). *The dynamics of literary response*. New York: W.W. Norton.
Holland, N.N. (1985). *The I*. New Haven, CT: Yale University Press.

Hugo, R. (1979). *The triggering town.* New York: Norton.
Hunt, M. (1982, January 24). How the mind works. *New York Times Magazine,* pp. 29–33, 47, 50, 52, 64, 68.
Husserl, E. (1962). *Ideas.* New York: Collier. (Original work published 1913)
Huyghe, P. (1985, September). Voices, glances, flashbacks: Our first memories. *Psychology Today,* pp. 48–52.
Inhelder, B., & Piaget, J. (1958). *The growth of logical thinking from childhood to adolescence* (A. Parsons & S. Milgram, Trans.). New York: Basic Books.
Irmscher, W.F. (1984). Review—*The writer's mind: Writing as a mode of thinking. College Composition and Communication, 35* (3), 368–369.
Isen, A.M., & Hastorf, A.H. (1982). Some perspectives on cognitive social psychology. In A.H. Hastorf & A.M. Isen (Eds.), *Cognitive social psychology* (pp. 1–32). New York: Elsevier/North-Holland.
Iser, W. (1978). *The act of reading: A theory of aesthetic response.* Baltimore: Johns Hopkins University Press.
Izard, C.E. (1971). *The face of emotion.* New York: Appleton-Century-Crofts.
Izard, C.E. (1977). *Human emotions.* New York: Plenum Press.
Izard, C.E., Dougherty, F.E., Bloxom, B.M., & Kotsch, W.E. (1974). *The differential emotions scale: A method of measuring the subjective experience of discrete emotions.* Unpublished manuscript, Vanderbilt University, Nashville, TN.
James, W. (1884). What is an emotion? *Mind, 9,* 188–205.
Jensen, G.H., & DiTiberio, J.K. (1984). Personality and individual writing processes. *College Composition and Communication, 35* (3), 285–300.
John-Steiner, V. (1985). *Notebooks of the mind: Explorations of thinking.* Albuquerque, NM: University of New Mexico Press.
Kagan, J. (1984). The idea of emotion in human development. In C.E. Izard, J. Kagan, & R.B. Zajonc (Eds.), *Emotions, cognition, and behavior* (pp. 38–72). Cambridge, England: Cambridge University Press.
Kantor, K.J. (1984). Classroom contexts and the development of writing intuitions: An ethnographic case study. In R. Beach & L.S. Bridwell (Eds.), *New directions in composition research* (pp. 72–94). New York: Guilford Press.
Kelly, G. (1963). *A theory of personality: The psychology of personal constructs.* New York: W.W. Norton.
Kiniry, M., & Strenski, E. (1985). Sequencing expository writing: A recursive approach. *College Composition and Communication, 36* (2), 191–202.
Kinneavy, J.E. (1971). *A theory of discourse: The aims of discourse.* New York: W.W. Norton.
Klatsky, R.L. (1980). *Human memory: Structures and processes* (2nd ed.). San Francisco: W.H. Freeman.
Koestler, A. (1976). *The act of creation* (2nd ed.). London: Hutchinson.
Kohlberg, L. (1975, June). The cognitive-developmental approach to moral education. *Phi Delta Kappan,* pp. 670–677.
Krathwohl, D.R., Bloom, B.S., & Masia, B.B. (1964). *Taxonomy of educational objectives; The classification of educational goals. Handbook 2: Affective domain.* New York: David McKay.
Kubie, L. (1958). *Neurotic distortion of the creative process.* Lawrence, KA: University of Kansas Press.

Langer, S.K. (1957). *Philosophy in a new key* (3rd ed.). Cambridge, MA: Harvard University Press.
Langer, S.K. (1967). *Mind: An essay on human feeling* (Vol. 1). Baltimore, MD: The Johns Hopkins University Press.
Langer, S.K. (1972). *Mind: An essay on human feeling* (Vol. 2). Baltimore, MD: The Johns Hopkins University Press.
Larson, R. (1981). Teaching before we judge: Planning assignments in composition. In G. Tate & E.P.J. Corbett (Eds.), *The Writing Teachers' Sourcebook* (pp. 208–219). New York: Oxford University Press.
Larson, R. (1984, May). *Emotional scenarios in the writing process. An examination of young writers' affective experiences*. Paper presented at the 1984 Institute on Writing, Meaning and Higher Order Reasoning, Chicago, IL.
Lazarus, R.S. (1984). On the primacy of cognition. *American Psychologist, 39* (2), 124–129.
Lazarus, R.S., Averill, J.R., & Opton, E.M., Jr. (1970). Towards a cognitive theory of emotion. In M.B. Arnold (Ed.), *Feelings and emotions: The Loyola symposium* (pp. 207–232). New York: Academic Press.
Lazarus, R.S., Kanner, A.D., & Folkman, S. (1980). Emotions: A cognitive-phenomenological analysis. In R. Plutchik & H. Kellerman (Eds.), *Emotions: Theory, research, and experience.* Volume 1. *Theories of emotion* (pp. 189–218). New York: Academic Press.
Lazarus, R.S., Spiesman, J.C., Mordkoff, A.M., & Davison, L.A. (1962). A laboratory study of psychological stress produced by a motion picture film. *Psychological Monographs: General and Applied, 76* (34). (Whole No. 553).
Leeper, R.W. (1948). A motivational theory of emotion to replace emotion as a disorganized response. *Psychological Review, 55,* 5–21.
LeFevre, K.B., & Dickerson, M.J. (1981). *Until I see what I say: Teaching writing in all the disciplines.* Burlington, VT: IDC Publications.
Leo, J. (1984, October 4). The ups and downs of creativity. Genius and emotional disturbance are linked in a new study. *Time,* p. 76.
Lindemann, E. (1986/1987). Response. *The CEA Forum, 16–17* (4, 1), 18–19.
Lindemann, E. (1987). *A rhetoric for writing teachers* (2nd ed.). New York: Oxford University Press.
Lloyd-Jones, R. (1977). Primary trait scoring. In C.R. Cooper & L. Odell (Eds.), *Evaluating writing: Describing, measuring, judging* (pp. 33–66). Urbana, IL: NCTE.
Lubin, B. (1966). Fourteen brief depression adjective check lists. *Archives of General Psychiatry, 15* (2), 205–208.
Ludlum, R. (1982, September). *The Boston Globe Magazine.* In R. Charm, They say ... Quotes for writers, *The Writer,* p. 5.
Macrorie, K. (1976). *Telling writing* (2nd ed.). Rochelle Park, NJ: Hayden.
Mandel, B.J. (1978). Losing one's mind: Learning to write and edit. *College Composition and Communication, 29* (4), 362–368.
Mandel, B.J. (1980). The writer writing is not at home. *College Composition and Communication, 31* (4), 370–377.
Mandler, G. (1975). *Mind and emotion.* New York: Wiley.

Mandler, G. (1984). *Mind and body: The psychology of emotion and stress*. New York: W.W. Norton.

Matsuhashi, A., & Cooper, C. (1978, March). *A video time-monitored observational study: The transcribing behavior and composing processes of a competent school writer*. Paper presented at the annual meeting of the American Educational Research Association, Toronto, Canada. (ERIC Document Reproduction Service No. ED 155 701)

McCaffery, L., & Gregory, S. (Eds.) (1987). *Alive and writing: Interviews with American authors of the 1980s*. Urbana, IL: University of Illinois Press.

McCarthy, P., Meier, S., & Rinderer, R. (1985). Self-efficacy and writing: A different view of self-evaluation. *College Composition and Communication, 36* (4), 465–471.

McDougall, W. (1928). Emotion and feelings distinguished. In M.L. Reymert (Ed.), *Feelings and emotions: The Wittenburg symposium*. Worcester, MA: Clark University Press.

McLeod, S. (1987). Some thoughts about feelings: The affective domain and the writing process. *College Composition and Communication, 38* (4), 426–435.

McNair, D.M., Lorr, M., & Droppleman, L.F. (1971/1981). *EdiTS manual for the profile of mood states*. San Diego, CA: Educational and Industrial Testing Service.

Meckel, H.C. (1963). Research on teaching composition and literature. In N.C. Gage (Ed.), *Handbook of research on teaching* (pp. 966–1006). Chicago: Rand McNally.

Mehrabian, A. (1980). *Basic dimensions of a general psychological theory*. Cambridge, MA: Oelgeschlager, Gunn, & Hain.

Meichenbaum, D., & Butler, L. (1980). Cognitive ethology: Assessing the streams of cognition and emotion. In K.R. Blankstein, P. Pliner, & J. Polivy (Eds.), *Assessment and modification of emotional behavior. Advances in the study of communication and affect* (Vol. 6, pp. 139–164). New York: Plenum Press.

Messick, S. (1976). Personality consistencies in cognition and creativity. In S. Messick (Ed.), *Individuality in learning: Implications of cognitive styles and creativity for human development* (pp. 4–22). San Francisco: Jossey-Bass.

Miller, G.A. (1956). The magical number seven, plus or minus two: Some limits on our capacity for processing information. *The Psychological Review, 63* (2), 81–97.

Miller, N.E. (1951). Learnable drives and rewards. In S.S. Stevens (Ed.), *Handbook of experimental psychology* (pp. 435–472). New York: Wiley.

Miller, S. (1983). What does it mean to be able to write? The question of writing in the discourses of literature and composition. *College English, 45* (3), 219–235.

Mischel, W. (1981). A cognitive-social learning approach to assessment. In T. Merluzzi, C. Glass, & M. Genest (Eds.), *Cognitive assessment* (pp. 479–502). New York: Guilford Press.

Mitford, J. (1979). *Poison penmanship*. New York: Alfred Knopf.

Moers, E. (1976). *Literary women*. Garden City, NY: Doubleday.

Moffat, M.J., & Painter, C. (Eds.) (1974). *Revelations: Diaries of women*. New York: Random House.

Moffett, J. (1968). *Teaching the universe of discourse*. Boston: Houghton Mifflin.
Moffett, J. (1982). Writing, inner speech, and meditation. *College English, 44* (3), 231–246.
Mowrer, O.H. (1960). *Learning theory and behavior*. New York: Wiley.
Murphy, G. (1947). *A bisocial approach to origins and structure*. New York: Harper and Brothers.
Murray, D.M. (1968). *A writer teaches writing: A practical method of teaching composition*. Boston: Houghton Mifflin.
Murray, D.M. (1978). Internal revision: A process of discovery. In C. Cooper & L. Odell (Eds.), *Research on Composing: Points of Departure* (pp. 85–103). Urbana, IL: NCTE.
Neisser, U. (1967). *Cognitive psychology*. Englewood Cliffs, NJ: Prentice-Hall.
Neisser, U. (1980). The limits of cognition. In P.W. Jusczyk & R.M. Klein (Eds.), *The nature of thought. Essays in honor of D.O. Hebb* (pp. 115–132). Hillsdale, NJ: Lawrence Erlbaum.
Neisser, U. (1982, May). Psychology today: The state of the science. *Psychology Today*, pp. 44–48.
Newell, A., & Simon, H.A. (1972). *Human problem solving*. Englewood Cliffs, NJ: Prentice-Hall.
Nin, A. (1975). In E.J. Hinz (Ed.), *A woman speaks: The lectures, seminars, and interviews of Anais Nin*. Chicago: The Swallow Press.
Nisbett, R.E., & Wilson, T.D. (1977). Telling more than we can know: Verbal reports on mental processes. *Psychological Review, 84* (3), 231–259.
Norton, J.A. (1985, March). *Statistical studies on the emotions surrounding writing*. Paper presented at the annual Conference on College Composition and Communication, Minneapolis, MN.
Nowlis, V. (1965). Research with the mood adjective check list. In S.S. Tomkins & C.E. Izard (Eds.), *Affect, cognition and personality* (pp. 352–389). New York: Springer.
Nystrand, M. (Ed.) (1982). *What writers know: The language, process, and structure of written discourse*. New York: Academic Press.
Osgood, C.E., Suci, G.J., & Tannenbaum, P.H. (1957/1975). *The measurement of meaning*. Urbana, IL: University of Illinois Press.
Perry, W., Jr. (1970). *Forms of intellectual and ethical development in the college years*. New York: Holt, Rinehart & Winston.
Petrosky, A.R. (1983). Review—*Problem-solving strategies for writing*. *College Composition and Communication, 34* (2), 233–235.
Piaget, J. (1956). *The moral judgment of the child* (M. Gaubain, Trans.). New York: Free Press.
Piaget, J. (1973). The affective unconscious and the cognitive unconscious. *Journal of the American Psychoanalytic Association, 21*, 249–261.
Piaget, J., & Inhelder, B. (1969). *The psychology of the child* (H. Weaver, Trans.). New York: Basic Books.
Plimpton, G. (Ed.) (1963–1986). *Writers at work: The Paris Review interviews* (2nd to 7th series). New York: Viking Penguin.
Plutchik, R. (1962). *The emotions: Facts, theories, and a new model*. New York: Random House.

Plutchik, R. (1970). Emotions, evolution, and adaptive processes. In M.B. Arnold (Ed.), *Feelings and emotions: The Loyola symposium* (pp. 3–24). New York: Academic Press.

Plutchik, R. (1980). *Emotion: A psychoevolutionary synthesis*. New York: Harper & Row.

Plutchik, R., & Kellerman, H. (1974). *Emotions profile index: Manual*. Los Angeles: Western Psychological Services.

Polanyi, M. (1958). *Personal knowledge: Towards a post-critical philosophy*. Chicago: University of Chicago Press.

Polanyi, M. (1967). *The tacit dimension*. Garden City, NY: Doubleday.

Polivy, J. (1980). Measuring and modifying moods: An introduction. In K.R. Blankstein, P. Pliner, & J. Polivy (Eds.), *Assessment and modification of emotional behavior: Vol. 6. Advances in the study of communication and affect* (pp. 1–6). New York: Plenum Press.

Ponsonby, A. (1923). *English diaries*. London: Methuen & Co.

Posner, M.I., & Snyder, C.R. (1975). Attention and cognitive control. In R.L. Solso (Ed.), *Information processing and cognition: The Loyola symposium* (pp. 55–86). Hillsdale, NJ: Lawrence Erlbaum.

Powell, J.L., & Brand, A.G. (1987). The development of an emotions scale for writers. *Educational and Psychological Measurement, 47* (2), 329–338. (ERIC Document Reproduction Service No. ED 268 152)

Powers, W.G., Cook, J.A., & Meyer, R. (1979). The effect of compulsory writing on writing apprehension. *Research in the Teaching of English, 13* (3), 225–230.

Purves, A.C., & Beach, R. (1972). *Literature and the reader: Research in response to literature, reading interests, and the teaching of literature*. Urbana, IL: NCTE.

Purves, A.C., & Purves, W.C. (1986). Viewpoints: Cultures, text models, and the activity of writing. *Research in the Teaching of English, 20* (2), 174–197.

Rafoth, B.A., & Rubin, D.L. (Eds.) (1987). *The social construction of written communication*. Norwood, NJ: Ablex.

Raimes, A. (1980). Writing and learning across the curriculum: The experience of a faculty seminar. *College English, 41* (7), 797–801.

Ransom, J.C. (1941). *The new criticism*. Norfolk, CT: New Directions.

Reed, W.M., Burton, J.K., & Kelly, P.P. (1985). The effects of writing ability and mode of discourse on cognitive capacity engagement. *Research in the Teaching of English, 19* (3), 283–297.

Rico, G. (1983). *Writing the natural way*. Los Angeles: J.P. Tarcher.

Rocklin, T., & Thompson, J.M. (1985). Interactive effects of test anxiety, test difficulty, and feedback. *Journal of Educational Psychology, 3*, 368–372.

Rohman, D.G., & Wlecke, A.O. (1964). *Prewriting: The construction and application of models for concept formation in writing* (U.S.O.E. Cooperative Research Project No. 2174). East Lansing, MI: Michigan State University.

Rose, M. (1984a). Comment and response. *College English, 46* (3), 304–306.

Rose, M. (1984b). *Writer's block: The cognitive dimension*. Carbondale, IL: Southern Illinois University Press. (ERIC Document Reproduction Service No. ED 236 652)

Rosenblatt, L.M. (1938/1976). *Literature as exploration* (3rd ed.). New York: Noble and Noble.
Rothenberg, A. (1979, January). Creative contradictions. *Psychology Today*, pp. 55–56, 59–61.
Sartre, J.P. (1966). *The words*. Greenwich, CT: Fawcett.
Schachter, S., & Singer, J.E. (1962). Cognitive, social, and physiological determinants of emotional state. *Psychological Review, 69* (5), 379–399.
Schiff, P.M. (1981, March). *Writing styles and teaching styles*. Paper presented at the Conference on English Education, Anaheim, CA.
Schlosberg, H. (1954). Three dimensions of emotions. *Psychological Review, 61* (2), 81–88.
Searle, J. (1984). *Minds, brains, and science*. Cambridge, MA: Harvard University Press.
Selzer, J. (1984). Exploring options in composing. *College Composition and Communication, 35* (3), 276–284.
Sherwin, J.S. (1969). *Four problems in teaching English: A critique of research*. Scranton, PA: International Textbook Company.
Shrodes, C., Van Gundy, J., & Husband, W. (Eds.) (1943). *Psychology through literature: An anthology*. New York: Oxford University Press.
Singular, S. (1981, October 4). Master diarist Max Frisch. *New York Times Magazine*, pp. 94–96, 100–102, 106–107.
Smith, L.Z. (1984). Composing composition courses. *College English, 46* (5), 460–469.
Smith, M.W. (1984). *Reducing writing apprehension*. Urbana, IL: NCTE.
Smith, W.L., Hull, G.A., Land, R.E., Jr., Moore, M.T., Ball, C., Dunham, D.E., Hickey, L.S., & Ruzich, C.W. (1985). Some effects of varying the structure of a topic on college students' writing. *Written Communication, 2* (1), 73–89.
Sommers, N. (1980). Revision strategies of student writers and experienced adult writers. *College Composition and Communication, 31* (4), 378–388.
Spielberger, C.D. (1972). Anxiety as an emotional state. In C.D. Spielberger (Ed.), *Anxiety: Current trends and research* (Vol. 1, pp. 24–49). New York: Academic Press.
Spielberger, C.D. (1979). *Preliminary manual for the state-trait personality inventory (STPI)*. Unpublished manuscript, University of South Florida, Tampa.
Stallard, C. (1974). Analysis of the writing behavior of good student writers. *Research in the Teaching of English, 8*, 208–218.
Strouse, J. (1981, March 30). Toni Morrison's black magic. *Newsweek*, pp. 51–58.
Taylor, I.A., & Getzels, J.W. (Eds.) (1975). *Perspectives in creativity*. Chicago: Aldine.
Tchudi, S.N. (1986). *Teaching writing in the content areas: College level*. Washington, DC: NEA.
Thompson, M.O. (1981, October). *The returning student: Writing anxiety and general anxiety*. Paper presented at the annual Northeast Regional Conference on English in the Two-Year College, Baltimore, MD. (ERIC Document Reproduction Service No. ED 214 558)
Todd, J. (Ed.) (1983). *Women writers talking*. New York: Holmes & Meier.

Tomkins, S.S. (1962). *Affect, imagery, consciousness: The positive affects* (Vol. 1). New York: Springer.
Tomkins, S.S. (1963). *Affect, imagery, consciousness: The negative affects* (Vol. 2). New York: Springer.
Tomkins, S.S. (1981). The quest for primary motives: Biography and autobiography of an idea. *Journal of Personality and Social Psychology, 41* (2), 306–329.
Turner, A. (Ed.) (1977). *Fifty contemporary poets: The creative process.* New York: Longman.
Turner, A. (Ed.) (1985). *Forty-five contemporary poets: The creative process.* New York: Longman.
Vygotsky, L.S.(1962). *Thought and language* (E. Hanfmann & G. Vakav, Eds. and Trans.). New York, London, and Cambridge, MA: MIT Press and Wiley.
Warnock, J. (1984). The writing process. In M.G. Moran & R.F. Lunsford (Eds.), *Research in composition and rhetoric: A bibliographic sourcebook* (pp. 3–26). Westport, CT: Greenwood Press.
Wason, P.C. (1980). Specific thoughts on the writing process. In L.W. Gregg & E.R. Steinberg (Eds.), *Cognitive processes in writing* (pp. 129–138). Hillsdale, NJ: Lawrence Erlbaum.
Watson, J.B. (1929). *Psychology from the standpoint of a behaviorist* (3rd rev. ed.). Philadelphia: J.B. Lippincott.
West, M. (1980). Comment & response. *College English, 42* (4), 408–419.
White, E.M. (1985). *Teaching and assessing writing.* San Francisco: Jossey-Bass.
Wilkinson, A.G., Barnsley, G., Hanna, P., & Swan, M. (1980). *Assessing language development.* Oxford, England: Oxford University Press.
Williams, J.D., & Alden, S.D. (1983). Motivation in the composition classroom. *Research in the Teaching of English, 17* (2), 101–111.
Williams, W.C. (1958). *I wanted to write a poem: The autobiography of the works of a poet.* Boston: Beacon Press.
Wilson, A. (1965). *The wild garden, or, speaking of writing.* Berkeley, CA: University of California Press.
Wilson, W.R. (1979). Feeling more than we can know: Exposure effects without learning. *Journal of Personality and Social Psychology, 37* (6), 811–821.
Wimsatt, W.K., & Beardsley, M.C. (1954). *The verbal icon; studies in the meaning of poetry.* Lexington, KY: University of Kentucky Press.
Winter, D.G., McClelland, D.C., & Stewart, A.J. (1981). *A new case for the liberal arts.* San Francisco: Jossey-Bass.
Witkin, H.A., & Goodenough, D.R. (1981). *Cognitive styles: Essence and origins. Field dependence and field independence.* New York: International Universities Press.
Witte, S.P. (1980). Toward a model for research in written composition. *Research in the Teaching of English, 14* (1), 73–81.
Woodson, L. (1982). *From cases to composition.* Glenview, IL: Scott, Foresman.
Wordsworth, W. (1965). Preface to the 2nd edition. In R.L. Brett & A.R. Jones (Eds.), *Lyrical ballads. Wordsworth and Coleridge* (pp. 314–318). London: Methuen. (Original work published 1800)
Writer's quotation book. (1980). Yonkers, NY: Pushcart Press.

Wundt, W. (1907). *Outlines of psychology*. Leipzig: Wilhelm Englemann. (Original work published 1896)
Yarrow, L.J. (1979). Emotional development. *American Psychologist, 34* (10), 951–957.
Yerkes, R.M., & Dodson, J.D. (1908). The relation of strength of stimulus to rapidity of habit-formation. *Journal of Comparative Neurology and Psychology, 18* (1), 459–482.
Young, P.T. (1943). *Emotion in man and animals: Its nature and relation to attitude and motive*. New York: John Wiley & Sons.
Young, P.T. (1967). Affective arousal: Some implications. *American Psychologist, 22* (1), 32–40.
Young, R.W., Becker, A.L., & Pike, K.E. (1970). *Rhetoric: Discovery and change*. New York: Harcourt Brace and World.
Zajonc, R.B. (1980). Feeling and thinking: Preferences need no inferences. *American Psychologist, 35* (2), 151–175.
Zajonc, R.B. (1984). On the primacy of affect. *American Psychologist, 39* (2), 117–123.
Zoellner, R. (1969). Talk-write: A behavioral pedagogy for composition. *College English, 30* (4), 267–320.
Zuckerman, M. (1960). The development of an affect adjective check list for the measurement of anxiety. *Journal of Consulting Psychology, 24* (5), 457–462.
Zuckerman, M. (1977). Development of a situation-specific trait-state test for the prediction and measurement of affective responses. *Journal of Consulting and Clinical Psychology, 45* (4), 513–523.
Zuckerman, M., & Lubin, B. (1965). *Manual for the multiple affect adjective check list*. San Diego, CA: Educational and Industrial Testing Service.

Index

Abelson, Robert P., 1
Activation, 63–65, 96–97
Activation theories of emotion, 46–47
Adjective Check List, 77 n.9
"Adjustment" curricula, 19, 20
Adolescence, 336. *See also* Self-sponsored writing
Advanced expository writers, 103–124, 128, 130, 132, 201, 204
Adventurousness, 68; and factor analysis, 80; state, 99, 105, 175, 182, 204–205; trait, 110
Affection, 65; and cluster scores, 65; state, 80, 82
Affective experiential essays. *See* Affectively toned essays; Personal experience essays; Personal writing
Affective fallacy, 7
Affectively toned essays, 104–105, 112–114, 120–122, 204–205
Affective memory, 28–30, 210, 212
Affective primacy, 41, 54–55
Affective unconscious, 33. *See* Unconscious, the
Aggression. *See* Anger
Alden, Scott D., 208
Amsel, A., 44

Analytic essay, 104–105, 112, 120
Ancoli, S., 43
Anderson, Jack, 11, 12
Anderson, J.R., 1
Anger, 12, 14, 43–45, 65, 67; and cluster scores, 65, 98–99; and factor analysis, 80; state, 109, 113, 130, 175; trait, 110
Antithesis, emotional. *See* Disequilibrium
Anxiety, 43–44, 45, 65, 76 n.5, 171; and cluster scores, 65, 98; scales measuring, 76–77 nn.3, 5; theories of, 43–45. *See also* Writing anxiety
Applebee, Arthur N., 59, 61, 212
Appraisal, 49–50
Aristotle, *De Anima*, 40
Arnold, Magda B., 47, 52, 57, 80
Arnold, W.A., 61
Aronowitz, Beverly L., 4
Arousal, emotional, 10–11, 46, 49–51, 52, 80, 83, 86, 125, 133, 135, 208–209; negative, 143, 187; nervous, 178, 180, 182, 202; physiological, 46, 47, 50; positive, 187, 199; theories of, 46–47, 49–51
Assignments. *See* Writing assignments

250   *Index*

At-home writing, 174, 193–198, 203–204. *See also* Setting
Attending, 22, 38 n.10
"Automatic" processes, 24, 33, 38 n.10. *See also* Unconscious, the
Automatic writing, 20. *See also* Free writing
Averill, James R., 1, 48, 68

Bain, Alexander, 41
Baird, William, 30, 37, 38 n.13, 210
Ball, Carolyn, 103
Barbellion, W.N.P., 15
Bard, Phillip, 42
Barrett, Elizabeth, 9
Bartholomae, David, 103
Barzun, Jacques, 10
Baseline emotions. *See* Temperament
Basic education movement, 19, 20, 21
Basic Issues Conference, 19
Beach, Richard, 8, 209
Beardsley, Monroe C., 7
Becker, Alton L., 26, 103
Behaviorial theories of emotions, 47–48
Behaviorism, 43, 44, 45
Bellow, Saul, 11
Bentler, P.M., 82
Bereiter, Carl, 37 n.1
Berger, D., 10
Berger, J., 10
Berkenkotter, Carol, 61
Berthoff, Ann E., 26, 31, 37
Berryman, John, 173
BESW (Brand Emotions Scale for Writers), 68–75, 77 nn.9, 10, 94; administration of, 87–89, 94, 104, 126–128, 150–151, 174; scale development and design, 67–75, 77 n.9, 79–84, 89–91, 210–211. *See also* State form of BESW (S form); Trait-When-Writing form of BESW (TWW form); Very Moment (VM) page of BESW
Bibliotherapy, 8
Birnbaum, June C., 61
Bizzell, Patricia, 61
Blakeslee, Thomas R., 33
Blau, Sheridan, 61
Bleich, David F., 2, 3, 8, 30, 209

Bloom, Benjamin S., 31
Bloom, Lynn Z., 34, 62, 200
Bloxom, B.M., 47
Boredom, 67, 206; and cluster scores, 97; and factor analysis, 80, 82, 124 n.2; state, 105, 112, 114, 120, 122, 130–131, 165, 169, 178, 182, 190, 200, 202; trait, 110–112, 132, 141
Boring experience essay, 120–122
Boswell, James, 16
Bower, Gordon H., 1, 27, 28, 29, 38 nn.7, 8, 61, 138
Bradburn, Norman M., 80, 90
Bradbury, Ray, 10
Braddock, R., 61
Brain, hemispheres, 33
Brand, Alice G., 18 n.1, 19, 61, 189, 202, 211. *See also* BESW (Brand Emotions Scale for Writers)
Bransford, John D., 30
Britton, James, 3, 17, 20, 26, 104
Broadbent, Donald E., 55
Brodkey, Linda, 24
Brooks, Cleanth, 7
Brossell, Gordon, 103
Broun, Heywood, 10
Bruffee, Kenneth A., 3, 4, 37 n.6
Bruner, Jerome, 26, 31
Burgess, T., 3
Burke, Kenneth, 7
Burton, John K., 204
Butler, L., 48, 61
Byron, Lord, 12, 15, 173

Cannon, Walter B., 42, 43, 44; Cannon-Bard theory, 42
Carey, Linda, 21
Carkeet, David, 8
Carruth, Hayden, 12
Carver, Raymond, 16
Categorical and dimensional systems of the emotions, 52–54
Categorical systems of the emotions, 51
Cather, Willa, 12
Cattell, Raymond B., 75, 82, 91 n.1
Centralist theory of emotions, 42
Chain reaction of emotion, 47–48, 49
Cherry, Roger D., 61
Cheshire, Barbara W., 130, 197

Chester, Laura, 11
Ciardi, John, 195
Cicchetti, Dante, 36, 38 n.11
Clark, Margaret S., 28, 38 n.7
Cleaver, Eldridge, 14
Cluster scores, 63–66, 96–99, 101 n.2. *See also* Emotion clusters
Coffman, W.E., 61
Cognitive appraisal, 48, 49
Cognitive dissonance, 31; emotional aspects of, 16, 30, 125. *See also* Disequilibrium
Cognitive interpretation, 27, 28, 29, 36, 48, 49, 50, 58, 209. *See also* Interpretation
Cognitive interpretive system, 49–50
Cognitive memory, 28, 210, 211
Cognitive primacy, 54
Cognitive process model: of writing, 5, 19, 21–23, 32, 34, 35, 210; of revising, 23–24; limitations of, 24–25
Cognitive psychology, 1, 21, 31–32, 35–36, 46
Cognitive social psychology, 28, 48
Cognitive style, 25, 149, 150, 212
Cognitive theories of emotion, 46, 48–51, 58
Coleridge, Samuel T., 11, 173
College writers, 87, 93–101, 201
Comfort, 65
Comparison/Contrast essay, 105, 114, 120
Competence, 63
Composing style, 149–153, 158–165, 203–204, 207, 212
Composition theory. *See* Names of specific theories
Concept development, 26, 31, 54
Confusion, 11; and cluster scores, 97; and factor analysis, 80; state, 99, 105, 113, 114, 130–131, 165, 169, 178, 190, 194, 197, 200, 202, 203–204; trait, 110, 132
Connors, Robert J., 19, 61
Consciousness, 28, 32–33; emotional aspects of, 32–33, 50–51, 69–74; nonverbal, 33; verbal, 32–33
Conte, H., 76 n.6
Cook, John A., 62

Cooper, Charles R., 61, 62
Cooper, Marilyn, 24, 25
Council on Basic Education, 19. *See also* Basic education movement
Cowley, Malcolm, 8
Crane, Hart, 173
Crawshaw, M., 61
Critical thinking, 26, 31
Crowhurst, Marion, 103
Csikszentmihalyi, Mihaly, 60, 76 n.5, 201, 202

Daly, John A., 2, 62, 100
Dartmouth Seminar, 20, 204
Darwin, Charles, 42, 43, 44, 47, 60; *The Expression of the Emotions in Man and Animals*, 43; theory, 42
Davison, L.A., 61
Davitz, Joel R., 52, 57, 61, 68, 77 n.9, 80, 90, 96–98, 101 n.2; dimensions of emotional meaning, 53, 63–67, 96–98. *See also* Cluster scores
de Beauvoir, Simone, 12, 13
De Bono, Edward, 33
de Maupassant, Guy, 16
Demographic Data Sheet (DDS), 88, 89, 91 n.4, 94, 104, 126, 151, 174, 183, 198 n.1
Depression, 12, 76 n.3, 125, 196; and factor analysis, 80; state, 97, 178, 182, 200; trait, 141
Descartes, Rene, 25, 41
Descriptive essay, 104, 112, 123, 165, 204
Dickerson, Mary Jane, 23, 25, 37 n.4
Diesing, P., 46, 62
Differential Emotions Scale, 47, 63, 67–68, 75, 77 n.9, 82
Differential Emotions Theory, 51
Dimensional systems of the emotions, 42, 52
Discomfort, 65
Discursive modes of development, 19. *See also* Rhetorical modes of development
Disequilibrium, 15–16, 31, 200–201. *See also* Cognitive dissonance, emotional aspects of
Disgust, 67; and cluster scores, 65–66;

and factor analysis, 80; state, 109; trait, 110
DiTiberio, John K., 150, 207
Dittmer, A., 103
Dobrin, David N., 25
Dodson, John D. (Yerkes-Dodson law), 67, 208
Dollard, J., 44
Donohew, Lewis, 210
Doob, L.W., 44
Dougherty, F.E., 47
Drabble, Margaret, 11
Dreyfus, Hubert L., 25
Droppleman, Leo F., 52, 84
du Maurier, Daphne, 15
Dunaway, P., 11, 12, 13, 14, 15, 16
Dunham, Donald E., 103

Eastman, R.M., 131, 180, 205
Ebel, R.L., 61
Eckhardt, Caroline D., 26
Egocentric speech, 27
Eiseley, Loren, 11, 14
Ekman, Paul, 43
Elbow, Peter, 20, 38 n.9, 149
Eliot, George, 13
Emergency theory of emotions, 42
Emig, Janet, 2, 29, 61, 93, 122, 125
Emotional disturbance, 45, 173–174
Emotional expression and emotional experience, 36, 58, 91 n.2, 158, 181
Emotional intensity, 28, 42, 44, 46, 50, 58, 59–60, 67
Emotionality, 89, 124, 140–141, 180. *See also* Temperament
Emotion clusters, 63–66, 79–83. *See also* Names of specific clusters
Emotions: after writing, 210, 212; anticipatory, 205; "approach," 17, 98, 130, 200–201; before writing, 210, 212; complex, 44, 53, 54–55; definitions of, 57–60; during writing, 210, 212; methods of studying (*see* Research, methods for studying); mixed, 36, 44, 51–53, 67, 69, 196, 212; motivational, 45, 205, 210; outcome, 179; postwriting, 97, 98, 100, 101 n.1; prewriting, 97, 101 n.1; primary, 44, 46, 47, 51–53, 75, 77 n.9, 196; principal, 84, 91 n.2; "pure," 52, 66, 69, 196, 212. *See also* Names of specific emotion items
Emotion scales, 60–61, 76 n.3, 77 n.9. *See also* Names of specific scales
Emotions Profile Index, 53, 77 n.9
Emotions psychology, history of: contemporary theories, 45–54; early Western theories, 39–41; middle-level propositions, 46, 51–54; paradigmatic theories, 46–51; twentieth-century theories, 41–45. *See also* Names of specific theories
Engagement, emotional, 18, 204–205. *See also* Motivation
English and psychology students. *See* College writers
English education, 19–20, 142
English teachers, 87, 149–171, 200, 201, 203
Enhancement, 65
Enlightenment, the, 41
Epstein, Seymour, 61, 74, 76 n.3, 133 n.6
Ericsson, K. Anders, 1, 38 n.10, 45, 74, 75, 76 n.2
Erikson, Erik H., 31
Ethical orientation, 3, 31–32
Ethnography. *See* Social construction theory
Evolutionary theories of emotions, 42–43, 47–48
Excitement, 10–11, 66, 68, 96; and cluster scores, 97; and factor analysis, 80; state, 99, 114, 182, 199, 204–205; trait, 132
Exigencies, 22, 24, 34
Expository writing. *See* Traditional expository essays
Expressive writing, 3, 20. *See also* Affectively toned essays; Free writing; Personal experience essays; Personal writing
Eysenck, H.J., 61

Factor analysis, 79–83, 90, 91 n.1, 96–97, 98, 124 n.2, 130, 142, 200
Fagan, William T., 62
Faigley, Lester, 24, 61, 100, 207

Index 253

Fear, 44, 67; and cluster scores, 97–98; and factor analysis, 80; state, 98, 113, 114, 130, 165, 204; trait, 132
Felt sense, 55
Festinger, Leon, 31, 38 n.7
Field, Joanna, 9
Fish, Stanley, 4, 8
Fiske, Susan T., 28, 30, 38 n.7, 48, 54
Fitzgerald, Sally, 211
Flammer, August, 1, 30, 138
Flower, Linda, 2, 3, 21, 23, 24, 32, 34, 37 nn.2, 3, 4, 38 n.12, 61, 109, 149, 209
Folkman, Susan, 48
Ford Fund for the Advancement of Education, 19
Fox, Roy E., 62
Free associative thinking, 25, 150
Free write composing style, 149–150, 151–164, 189–191, 196–197, 203
Free writing, 20, 174, 178, 179, 184, 185, 186, 189–191, 197–198, 204. *See also* Affectively toned essays; Personal experience essays
Freud, Sigmund, 14, 16, 33, 43
Friesen, W., 43
Frisch, Max, 14
Frustration, 13, 43, 45, 65–66, 67; and cluster scores, 65–66, 98; and factor analysis, 80; state, 100, 109, 113, 130, 165, 175, 200; trait, 132
Frustration and aggression theory, 44
Fuentes, Carlos, 11, 15

Gass, William, 12
Gendlin, Eugene T., 55
Getzels, J.W., 38 n.9
Ghiselin, B., 38 n.9
Gilligan, Carol, 31
Gilligan, Stephen G., 27, 28, 29, 38 nn.7, 8
Giovanni, Nikki, 12
Glatthorn, Allan A., 25
Godshalk, F.L., 61
Godwin, Gail, 13
Goldberg, Marilyn, 26, 31
Goodenough, D.R., 149
Gordimer, Nadine, 13
Gorsuch, R.L., 83, 91 n.1

Gough, Harrison G., 76 n.3, 77 n.9, 82
Gregory, S., 9
Griffin, J.H., 9
Guba, Egon, 62
Gunther, John, 9, 15

Hairston, Maxine C., 25
Hall, Donald, 13, 15, 30
Hall, E., 30
Happiness, 9; and cluster scores, 97; and factor analysis, 80; state, 105, 128, 178, 182, 199; trait, 132
Harre, R., 28
Hastorf, Albert H., 28, 48
Hayes, John R., 2, 21, 23, 32, 34, 37 nn.2, 3, 4, 38 n.12, 61, 109, 209
Hedonic Tone, 63
Heilbrun, Alfred B., 76 n.3, 77 n.9, 82
Heller, S., 3
Hesse, P., 36, 38 n.11
Heuristic tension, 31. *See also* Cognitive dissonance; Disequilibrium
Hickey, Linda S., 103
Hidi, Suzanne, 30, 37, 38 n.13, 210
Hildyard, Angela, 30
Hillocks, George J., 26, 205
Hoffman, Eva, 12
Holladay, S.A., 62
Holland, Norman N., 8, 209
Holzman, Michael, 24, 25
Hopkins, Gerard Manley, 173
Hot cognition, 1
Hugo, Richard, 174
Hull, Glynda A., 103
Hunt, Morton, 29
Husband, W., 8
Husserl, Edmund, 56 n.1
Huyghe, P., 29, 189
Hyperactivation, 63, 65, 66
Hypoactivation, 63, 66

Images, 28
Imagination, 8
Imaging, 3
Inadequacy, 65
Incompetence/Dissatisfaction, 65
Information processing theory. *See* Cognitive psychology
Inhelder, Barbel, 3, 34

Inner speech, 27–28
Inspiration, 9, 13, 65, 67; and cluster scores, 97; and factor analysis, 80; state, 96, 99, 114, 130, 169, 175, 190, 194, 197, 199, 203, 204–205; trait, 110, 132
Instinctivism, 43, 44–45
Instincts, 44, 45
Instructor-rated writing skill, 89, 91 n.5, 99, 109, 114, 170–171, 178, 201. *See also* Skill writing
Interest, 10–11, 66, 67, 203, 210; and factor analysis, 80, 82; state, 105, 114, 128, 165, 178, 182, 199, 204–205; trait, 132
"Interestingness," 38 n.13
International Conference on the Teaching and Learning of English. *See* Dartmouth Seminar
Interpretation, 27–28, 29, 36. *See also* Cognitive interpretation
Interpretive communities, 3–4, 8
Intuition, 3, 8
Irmscher, William F., 207
Isen, Alice M., 28, 38 n.7, 48
Iser, Wolfgang, 27
Izard, Carroll E., 10, 46–47, 63, 67, 68, 76 n.3, 77 n.9, 82, 196. *See also* Differential Emotions Scale; Differential Emotions Theory

James, Henry, 12, 13
James, William, 36; James–Lange theory, 42
Jensen, George, 150, 207
Jensen, Julie M., 62
Johnson, Samuel, 17
John-Steiner, Vera, 11, 12, 13
Jolliffe, David A., 61
Jordan, June, 12
Journal writing, 20

Kafka, Franz, 11, 12, 15
Kagan, Jerome, 57
Kagle, Steven E., 189
Kanner, Allen D., 48
Kant, Immanuel, 41
Kantor, Kenneth J., 3

Kellerman, Henry, 53, 76 nn.3, 6, 77 n.9
Kelly, George, 29, 61
Kelly, Patricia P., 204
Kennedy, William, 9
Kiniry, Malcolm, 104
Kinneavy, James E., 3, 103
Kintsch, Walter, 1, 30, 138
Klatsky, Roberta, 38 n.10
Koestler, Arthur, 16
Kohlberg, Lawrence, 31
Kotsch, W.E., 47
Krathwohl, David R., 31
Kubie, L., 16

Lamb, R., 28
Land, Robert E., Jr., 103
Lange, Carl, 42
Langer, Judith, 61
Langer, Suzanne, 3, 26, 29, 37, 54
Larkin, Philip, 15
Larson, Reed, 45, 61, 76 n.5, 201, 202
Larson, Richard, 103
Lazarus, Richard S., 48–49, 54, 61
Learning style, 149. *See also* Composing style; Personality
Learning theory, 43–44, 45
Leeper, Robert W., 45
LeFevre, Karen B., 23, 25, 37 n.4
Leo, J., 173
Lewis, C. Day, 11
Lindemann, Erika, 61, 103
Linguistic thought, 44–49
Linville, Patricia W., 38 n.7
Literary criticism. *See* New criticism, the
Lloyd-Jones, Richard, 61, 103
Loneliness, 67; and factor analysis, 80, 82; state, 97, 182, 200; trait, 141
Long-term memory. *See* Memory
Lorr, Maurice, 52, 84
Lowell, Robert, 173
Lubin, Bernard, 76 n.3, 77 n.9, 84, 90
Ludlum, Robert, 10
Luria, A.R., 29

McCaffery, L., 9
McCarthy, Patricia, 201

McClelland, D.C., 32
McDougall, William, 43, 44, 47
McLeod, Susan, 182
McNair, Douglas M., 52, 76 nn.3, 6, 77 n.9, 84
Macrorie, Ken, 3, 103
Malamud, Bernard, 13
Mandel, Barrett J., 2, 3
Mandler, George, 30, 46, 48, 49–51, 209
Mansfield, Katherine, 11
Marquez, Gabriel Garcia, 11
Martin, Nancy, 3
Masia, Bertram B., 31
Matsuhashi, Ann, 61
Meaning analysis, 30, 50
Meckel, H.C., 61
Mehrabian, A., 80
Meichenbaum, Donald, 48, 61
Meier, Scott, 201
Meili, R., 61
Memory: 26–27, 28–30; affective, 28–30, 210, 211–212; cognitive, 28, 210, 211–212; long-term, 22, 27, 28–30; retrieval, 37 n.5; short-term, 4, 26; storage, 38 n.7. *See also* Schemas
Messick, Samuel, 149
Mew, Charlotte, 173
Meyer, Russell, 62
Middle-level theories of emotion. *See* Emotions psychology: middle-level propositions
Miller, George, A., 27
Miller, M.D., 2, 62
Miller, Neal E., 44
Miller, Susan, 2
Milosz, Czeslaw, 12
Milton, John, 17
Mind, faculties, 41
Mischel, Walter, 74
Mitford, Jessica, 10, 11, 12, 13, 15
Modernists, 9. *See also* New criticism, the
Moers, Ellen, 9, 11
Moffat, M.J., 9, 11, 13, 14
Moffett, James, 3, 26, 103
Moore, Michael T., 103
Moral orientation, 3, 31–32

Mordkoff, A.M., 61
Morgan, Robin, 12
Motivation, 22, 25, 34–35, 202, 204–205, 208, 211–212; and engagement, 18, 205, 208
Motivational emotions, 45, 205, 210
Motivational theories of emotion, 46–47
Moving against, away, toward, 63, 65, 66, 200
Mowrer, O.H., 44
Mullis, I.V.S., 61
Multiple Affect Adjective Check List (MAACL), 77 n.9, 84
Murdoch, Iris, 13
Murphy, Gardner, 43
Murray, Donald M., 4, 11, 16, 20, 125, 211

Nativism, 42, 44–45
Natural writing, 20. *See also* Expressive writing
Negative, Type 1 and Type 2 emotions, 63–66, 68
Negative Active emotions, 68, 84, 86, 90, 94, 97–98, 203; advanced expository writers, 105, 110, 112–114, 123–124; college writers, 94, 97–99, 100–101; English teachers, 156, 158–159, 165, 171; professional writers, 128, 130, 132, 134, 138, 140–141, 147, 147 n.1; student poets, 175, 180–184, 189–190, 196, 197–198
Negative emotions, 12–13, 52, 65, 68, 90–91, 125, 200–202, 204, 208; advanced expository writers, 112; college writers, 94, 99; English teachers, 153, 154, 158, 165; factor analysis, 79–84; preliminary studies, 85–86; professional writers, 125, 138, 140, 142, 143; student poets, 188, 197
Negative passive emotions, 68, 84, 86, 90, 94, 99–100, 199–200, 201, 202, 204; advanced expository writers, 105, 110, 112–114, 120, 123–124; college writers, 94, 97, 99–101; English teachers, 158–159, 165;

professional writers, 128, 130, 132, 134, 136, 140–142, 143, 147, 147 n.1; student poets, 175, 178, 182–183, 184, 189, 196
Neisser, Ulric, 25, 27, 29, 33, 34, 55, 213
Neruda, Pablo, 12
New criticism, the, 7–8
Newell, Allen, 22
Nin, Anais, 9, 11, 12, 14
Nisbett, Richard E., 69
Norton, Julia A., 84
Nowlis, Vincent, 75, 76 nn.3, 6
Nystrand, Martin, 213

O'Brien, Edna, 12
Ontario Institute for Studies in Education, 37 n.1
Opton, E.M., Jr., 48
Osgood, Charles E., 52, 80
Ottaway, M., 61

Painter, C., 9, 11, 13, 14
Paradigmatic theories of emotion. *See* Emotions psychology, history of
Performance anxiety, 22, 171
Peripheral theory of emotions, 42
Perry, William G., Jr., 31
Personal experience essays, 104–105, 112–114, 120–122, 165, 204–205. *See also* Affectively toned essays
Personal growth model of writing, 20
Personality, 25, 149–150; traits, 207. *See also* Temperament; Trait emotions
Personality theory, 43
Personal writing, 19, 91, 104, 189
Petrosky, Anthony, R., 24
Phenomenological psychology, 43, 45, 56 n.1
Piaget, Jean, 3, 27, 29, 31, 33, 34, 36, 38 nn.11, 13, 14
Piche, Gene L., 103
Pike, Kenneth E., 26, 103
Plath, Sylvia, 14, 173
Plato, 40
Plimpton, George, 8, 9, 11, 12, 13, 14, 15

Plutchik, Robert, 44, 46, 47, 49, 52–53, 57, 68, 76 nn.3, 6, 77 n.9, 196. *See also* Emotions Profile Index; Psychoevolutionary theory of emotion
Poe, Edgar Allan, 173
Poets, students, 173–198. *See also* Professional writers: poets
Polanyi, Michael, 3, 31, 55
Polivy, Janet, 80
Ponsonby, A., 13, 15
Positive emotions, 9–12, 45, 52, 63–65, 68, 125, 199, 200–202, 204, 208; advanced expository writers, 105–109, 110, 112, 113, 120, 122–124; college writers, 94–97, 98, 99, 100–101; English teachers, 153–154, 158–159, 165–169; factor analysis, 79–84; preliminary studies, 85–86; professional writers, 125, 128–130, 132, 134, 136, 140–142, 143, 147, 147 n.1; student poets, 175–178, 179, 180, 182, 183–184, 188–189, 196, 198
Posner, M.I., 33
Pound, Ezra, 173
Powers, William G., 62
Preliminary studies, 84–86, 90–91
Prewriting, 20, 164
Process models of writing, 20–21, 210. *See also* Names of specific models
Product vs. process (writing), 20–21
Professional writers, 7–18, 66, 87, 89, 125–147, 173–174, 200, 202–203, 206–207; definition of, 93–94, 125–126; poets, 134–140, 173–174; prose writers, 134–140
Profile of Mood States (POMS), 77 n.9, 84
Progressive Education movement, 19, 20
Project English, 19
Protocols, think-aloud, 21, 24, 32, 211; analysis of, 38 n.12, 62, 211; transcripts, 37 n.4
Psychoanalytic theory of emotion, 34, 43, 45
Psychodynamic theory of literature, 8

Psychoevolutionary theory of emotion, 44, 47–48, 52–53
Purves, Alan C., 8, 63, 76 n.4, 209
Purves, William C., 63

Rafoth, Bennett A., 3
Raimes, Ann, 103
Rank orders of emotions: state, 94–96, 105–109, 113–114, 128–130, 147, 165–169, 175, 189–190, 196–197; trait, 110, 132, 147, 175
Ransom, John C., 7
Reader-response, 3, 8; theory, 76 n.4, 209–210
Reading/Writing relationships, 209–210
"Real" assignment, 104–105, 112, 115–120
Recoding, 27, 37 n.5
Recursion, 21, 210
Reed, W. Michael, 204
Reform movement of 1960s, 19–20
Relatedness, 63–65
Relief, 14–15; and cluster scores, 97; and factor analysis, 80; state, 96, 99, 101, 105, 109, 113–114, 125, 128, 175, 180, 190, 193, 197, 199, 200, 204–205, 210; trait, 110, 132, 165
Required writing, 84–86, 88, 94, 100, 141, 197–198, 202, 204; compared to self-sponsored writing, 127–128; definition of, 93–94
Research, methods for studying: emotion, 60–61; emotion and writing, 62–63; the writing process, 61, 211; written products, 61
Research program, details, 86–89
Research writing, 19, 104–105, 109, 112–114, 116, 117, 120, 123, 124 nn.3, 4, 201, 204–205
Resetting emotions, 51, 66
Revising, 20, 21, 113. *See also* Cognitive process model: of revising
Rhetorical modes of development, 19, 104, 112–114, 123
Rico, Gabriele L., 20, 149
Rinderer, Regina, 201
Rocklin, Thomas, 209
Roethke, Theodore, 173

Rohman, D. Gordon, 20
Rose, Mike, 2, 61, 62, 204
Rosen, Harold, 3
Rosenblatt, Louise M., 8, 209
Rossetti, Dante Gabriel, 173
Roth, Lillian, 14
Rothenberg, Albert, 38 n.9, 201
Rubin, Donald L., 3
Rukeyser, Muriel, 14
Ruskin, John, 173
Ruzich, Constance W., 103

Sanchez, Sonia, 12
Sand, George, 12
Sarton, May, 11, 14
Sartre, Jean Paul, 13
Satisfaction, 142, 203; and cluster scores, 97; and factor analysis, 80, 82–83, 97, 142; state, 96, 99, 105, 109, 113, 114, 123, 128, 165, 169, 175, 179–180, 190, 193–194, 197, 199, 200, 203, 204–205, 210; trait, 110, 132. *See also* Satisfaction with writing
Satisfaction with writing, 89, 109, 123, 128, 142–147, 199
Scales measuring emotion. *See* Names of specific scales
Scardamalia, Marlene, 37 n.1
Schachter, Stanley, 46, 48, 52, 61, 203
Schemas, 27, 28, 30, 38 n.7
Schiff, P.M., 150
Schlosberg, Harold, 46, 52
Schoer, L., 61
Schriver, Karen A., 21
Schwartz, Delmore, 173
Scott-Maxwell, Florida, 14
Searle, John, 25, 59
Sears, R.R., 44
Self-rated writing skill, 89, 99–100, 109, 114, 170–171, 178, 181, 201. *See also* Skill, writing
Self-report, 61, 62–63, 76 n.2; limitations of, 69–74. *See also* BESW
Self-sponsored writing, 84–86, 87–89, 91–92 n.6, 197–198, 206, 207; and adolescence, 182–189, 198 n.1; definition of, 93–94, 125;

experience, 91–92 n.6, 122–123, 125, 141, 147, 170–171, 202. *See also* Sponsorship of writing
Selzer, Jack, 25, 207
Semantic differential, 52, 80
Setting, 159; effects of, 188, 193–198, 202, 203
Sexton, Anne, 14, 173
Shame, 76 n.5; and cluster scores, 97; and factor analysis, 80, 82; state, 165, 178, 190, 200, 202
Shange, Ntozake, 12
Shelley, Percy Bysshe, 173
Sherwin, Stephen, 61
Short-term memory. *See* Memory
Shrodes, Caroline, 8
Shyness, 67; and cluster scores, 97; and factor analysis, 80; state, 113, 114, 169, 182, 190, 200; trait, 141
Sign, 28, 58, 63. *See also* Valence
Simon, Herbert A., 1, 22, 38 n.10, 45, 74, 75, 76 n.2
Singer, Jerome E., 46, 48, 52, 61, 203
Singular, S., 14
Skill writing, 23, 25, 26, 87, 89, 91 n.5, 199–201, 206, 209, 212; advanced expository writers, 109, 110, 114–120, 122, 201; college writers, 99–101, 201; English teachers, 170–171, 201; professional writers, 89, 128, 131, 141–142, 147, 200–201; student poets, 178–182, 191, 201
Skinner, Anna M., 61
Smith, Louise Z., 104
Smith, Michael W., 2, 62
Smith, William L., 103
Snyder, C.R., 33
Social construction theory, 3, 37 n.6, 48
Social speech, 27
Sommers, Nancy, 201
Spender, Stephen, 12
Spielberger, Charles D., 59, 76 n.3, 207
Spiesman, J.C., 61
Sponsorship of writing, 87–89, 91, 92 n.6, 203, 206–207; advanced expository writers, 122–123; college writers, 100–101; definition of, 93–94; English teachers, 155, 159, 170–171; preliminary studies, 85–86;

professional writers, 125, 127, 141, 147, 203, 206–207; student poets, 182–189, 195, 197, 198 n.1, 202–203
Stage models of writing, 20–21, 210
Stallard, C., 61
State emotions, 36, 38 n.8, 67–76, 79–83, 88, 94–99, 105–109, 128–132, 138, 147, 158–169, 175, 199–203, 206, 210; definition of, 59
State emotion scales, 76 n.3, 77 n.9. *See also* Names of specific scales
State form of BESW (S form), 67–69, 75, 76 n.7, 79–80, 82–84, 88–89, 90, 91 n.2, 104–105, 124 n.2, 126–128, 150–151, 174
Steinnman, Martin, Jr., 213
Sternberg, Robert J., 29
Stewart, A.J., 32
Stewart, David H., 26
Stowe, Harriet Beecher, 11
Stratman, James, 21
Strenski, Ellen, 104
Strouse, Jean, 12
Structured exercises, 174, 189–190, 191, 196–197, 204
Structured/Planning composing style, 149–150, 151–165, 203–204
Student poets, 87, 173–198, 200, 203–204
Subjective criticism, 8
Suci, G.J., 52, 80
Surprise, 66, 67; and factor analysis, 80; state, 130, 169, 190, 194, 196, 197, 203, 204; trait, 110, 132
Swineford, F., 61

Tannenbaum, P.H., 52, 80
Tate, Alan, 7
Taylor, I.A., 38 n.9
Tchudi, Stephen N., 103
Temperament, 59, 66, 87, 89, 150, 180, 207. *See also* Personality; Trait emotions
Therapy, 14–15, 18 n.1, 170
Thomas, Dylan, 173
Thompson, Joan M., 209
Thompson, Merle, 170
Thoreau, Henry David, 17
Todd, J., 11, 12

Tolstoy, Sophie, 13, 15
Tomkins, Silvan S., 10, 46–47, 51, 52, 56 n.2, 66, 77 n.9
Traditional expository essays, 19, 20, 103–104, 112–114, 123, 204–205, 210. *See also* Names of specific assignments
Trait emotions, 66, 67–75, 79–83, 88, 110, 131, 132–134, 138, 149, 157, 158–169, 175, 203, 206–207, 210; definition of, 59
Trait emotion scales, 76 n.3. *See also* Names of specific instruments
Trait-When-Writing form of BESW (TWW form), 67–69, 79–80, 82–84, 88, 104–105, 126, 127, 128, 151, 174, 175
Transactional theory of reading, 8
Turner, Alberta, 8, 11, 125
Twentieth-century psychologies of emotion, 41–45
Type of writing assignment. *See* Specific assignment type

Unconscious, the, 32–33, 43, 50–51
Unskilled writers, 23, 25, 91 n.5, 99, 100–101, 109, 110, 170–171, 199–201, 209, 212. *See also* Skill, writing
Updike, John, 9

Valence, 28, 50, 63, 175, 184, 209
Van Gundy, J., 8
Variables (personal, rhetorical, situational), 87, 89
Verbal report. *See* Self-report
Very Moment (VM) page of BESW, 88, 89, 91 n.3, 104, 174
Vygotsky, Lev, 27

Warnock, John, 35
Warren, Robert Penn, 7
Wason, P.C., 24
Watson, James B., 43–44
West, Michael, 17
White, Edward M., 103
Wilkinson scales, 31
Williams, J.D., 208
Williams, Tennessee, 14

Williams, William Carlos, 10, 11, 14
Wilson, Angus, 9, 14, 15
Wilson, Deborah A., 62
Wilson, Timothy D., 69
Wilson, William R., 49, 55
Wimsatt, W.K., 7
Winter, D.G., 32
Witkin, Herman A., 149
Witte, Stephen P., 2, 24, 100
Wlecke, A.O., 20
Woodson, Linda, 103
Woolf, Virginia, 12, 14
Wordsworth, William, 10
Writers. *See* Names of specific groups
Writer's block, 2, 13, 17, 62, 101, 130; scales measuring, 62
Writing anxiety, 13, 62, 84, 99, 100–101, 171, 182, 200–201, 206, 209; and factor analysis, 80, 82–83, 98, 200–201; state, 98, 100, 109, 113, 114, 130, 165, 169, 190, 194, 196–197, 200–201, 202, 203, 204; trait, 110, 132, 140, 143, 147. *See also* Anxiety; Writer's block; Writing apprehension
Writing apprehension, 2, 62, 100, 101; reducing, 62; scales measuring, 62
Writing assignments: design of, 103–105; sequence of, 100, 103–104, 112, 123, 175, 195; types of, 105, 109, 112–124, 204–205. *See also* Names of specific assignment types
Writing process, 22, 210; frustration with, 13, 17, 100
Writing style. *See* Composing style
Wundt, Wilhelm, 42, 43, 47, 52, 56 n.1

Yarrow, Leon J., 61
Yerkes, Robert M. (Yerkes-Dodson law), 67, 208
Young, Paul T., 43, 45
Young, Richard W., 26, 103

Zajonc, Robert B., 1, 30, 37 n.6, 48, 54–55
Zoellner, Robert, 63
Zuckerman, Marvin, 76 n.3, 77 n.9, 84, 90

About the Author

ALICE GLARDEN BRAND is Director of Writing and Associate Professor of English at Clarion University of Pennsylvania. She is a rhetoric and composition specialist with particular interest in personality and writing, composing styles, and cognitive models of writing. She is also a practicing and published poet.